OTTAWA

The History of Canadian Cities

OTTAWA

An Illustrated History

John H. Taylor

James Lorimer & Company, Publishers
and
Canadian Museum of Civilization,
National Museums of Canada
Toronto 1986

Cover design: Don Fernley
Cartography: Christine Earl

Canadian Cataloguing in Publication Data:

Taylor, John H.
Ottawa, an illustrated history

(The History of Canadian cities)
Co-published by the Canadian Museum of Civilization.
Bibliography: p. 225
Includes index.
ISBN 0-88862-981-8

1. Ottawa (Ont.) — History.   I. Canadian Museum of Civilization.   II. Title.   III. Series.

FC3096.4.T39 1986   971.3'84   C86-094526-X
F1059.5.09T39 1986

This book has been published with the help of a grant from the Social Science Federation of Canada, using funds provided by the Social Sciences and Humanities Research Council of Canada and from the Research and Publication Fund of the Dean of Arts, Carleton University.

James Lorimer & Company, Publishers
Egerton Ryerson Memorial Building
35 Britain Street
Toronto, Ontario M5A 1R7

Printed and bound in Canada
5 4 3 2   88 89 90

Illustration Credits

Archives of Ontario: 22, 26 top, 33 top and bottom, 121 bottom; *Government of Ontario Art Collection:* 29 top, 53 upper right; *McCord Museum, Notman Photographic Archives:* 57, 75, 143 left, 144; *National Capital Commission:* 46, 76, 78, 123, 143 right, 147, 149, 177, 179 bottom, 189, 197 left, back cover lower left, back cover lower right; *National Film Board of Canada:* 184; *National Museum of Civilization:* 208; *Ottawa Municipal Archives Municipales:* 41, 52, 53 upper left, 54, 58, 59, 71, 82, 83, 87, 89, 91 left), 103 top, 103 bottom, 109, 113, 125, 127, 129, 130, 131, 132, 155 top, 159, 161 left, 167 top, 167 bottom, 170, 172 bottom, 176, 182, 185 top, 185 bottom, 191, 192, 193, 205 left, 205 right; inside back cover; *Public Archives of Canada:* front cover (*Old Dufferin and Sapper's Bridges,* 1877, by Walter Chesterton; C-605); 2 (Scene in By Ward Market, Ottawa, 1921, by Franklin Brownell; C-10533), 10 (C-608), 13 top (C-73702), 13 bottom (C-226), 16 left (C-5958), 16 right (PA-125208), 18 (C-2735), 19 (C-10872), 24 (C-1072), 26 bottom (C-116463), 28 (C-28020), 29 top (C-75264), 37 top (PA-120582), 37 bottom (C-2163), 43 top (C-600), 43 bottom (C-601), 44 (C-2813), 48 (PA-120580), 51 (C-2619), 53 lower left (PA-139587), 55 (PA-120161), 60 top (C-742), 60 bottom (C-1288), 62 top (C-1185), 62 bottom (C-6095), 65 top (C-11507), 65 bottom (C-618), 66 (C-11384), 67 top (C-17499), 67 bottom (C-3832), 72 (PA-25365), 80 (C-12195), 85 (PA-33947), 88 (C-43281), 91 right (PA-27437), 92 (C-4023), 93 (PA-139607), 95 top (PA-8541), 95 bottom (PA-34076), 96 right (PA-8487), 98 (PA-139588), 99 top (C-2185), 99 bottom (C-25781), 100 (PA-12222), 101 (C-1585), 102 (PA-137932), 105 (C-13323), 107 (C-20624), 111 (PA-139589), 116 (C-15971), 118 (C-46583), 121 top (PA-42494), 134 (PA-139610), 135 top left (C-37824), 135 top right (C-26679), 135 lower left (C-51835), 135 lower right (PA-12295), 137 top (C-72877), 137 bottom (C-5168), 138 (PA-139606), 139 (PA-139605), 141 top (C-2147), 141 bottom (C-2148), 145 (PA-112252), 152 left (PA-6898), 152 right (PA-8941), 153 (PA-136139), 157 (PA-9184), 158 (C-5418), 161 right (PA-139590), 163 (PA-93568), 172 top (PA-145800; photo by Malak), 173 (PA-115255), 179 top (PA-123537), 187 top (NMC-88268), 187 bottom (PA-145870), 195 top (PA-145783), 195 bottom (PA-145782), back cover upper left (Entrance to Rideau Canal, 1839, watercolour by Hency Francis Ainslie; C-518), back cover upper right (*Parliament Hill 1932,* by Adam Sheriff Scott; C-12065); *John H. Taylor:* 96 left, 122, 197 right; *University of Ottawa:* 155 bottom.

Table of Contents

List of Maps

Appendix
Statistical Tables

For my parents, who pioneered on a different frontier.

Foreword
The History of Canadian Cities Series

The History of Canadian Cities Series is a project of the History Division, National Museum of Civilization (National Museums of Canada). The project was begun in 1977 to respond to a growing demand for more popular publications to complement the already well-established scholarly publications programs of the Museum. The purpose of this series is to offer the general public a stimulating insight into Canada's urban past. In addition to the volumes already published in the series, the Museum — in co-operation with James Lorimer & Company — plans to publish books that deal with such varied communities as Montreal, Halifax, Quebec City, Regina, and Sherbrooke.

It is the hope of the National Museum of Civilization that the publication of these books will provide the public with information on Canadian cities in a visually attractive and highly readable form. At the same time, the plan of the series is to have authors follow a similar format. The result, it is anticipated, will be a systematic, interpretative and comprehensive account of the urban experience in many Canadian communities. Eventually, as new volumes are completed, *The History of Canadian Cities Series* will be a major step along the path to a general and comparative study of Canada's urban development.

The form for this series — the individual urban biography — is based on a desire to examine all aspects of community development and to relate the parts to a larger context. The series is also based on the belief that, while each city has a distinct personality that deserves to be discovered, the volumes must also provide analysis that will lift the narrative of a city's experience to the level where it will elucidate questions that are of concern to Canadians generally. These questions include such issues as ethnic relationships, regionalism, provincial-municipal interaction, social mobility, labour-management relationships, urban planning, and general economic development.

In this volume John H. Taylor vividly chronicles the 160-year history of Ottawa: a story that explains how a raw, frontier lumber town, with few amenities, became the attractive capital of the nation. The history of Ottawa is, in many senses, the history of a company town on a major scale. As Professor Taylor writes, the City of Ottawa has undergone several transformations "but much remains as it was. Fragmentation, marginality, and a corporate oversight are still central." Perhaps most interesting, however, is the clear sense that emerges from this study that Ottawa has always had a community life that reflected these realities. Known as Bytown between 1827 and 1855, Ottawa began its days as the main construction camp in the building of the Rideau Canal, but it quickly developed into a mercantile centre. In 1859, the city was designated as provincial capital and a government-based "industry" began. By 1867, when Ottawa became the capital of the new Dominion of Canada, its fate was tied to that of the new nation.

The author of this volume is a well-known urban historian. A long time member of the history department at Carleton University, Professor Taylor — and his students — have been responsible for a good deal of writing and publication about Canada's capital city. Prof. Taylor has also written several important articles on Canadian urban development generally and is a founding editor of Canada's major urban journal, the *Urban History Review/Revue d'histoire urbaine*.

Professor Taylor's text is enhanced by a wide variety of photographs and specially prepared maps. This illustrative material is not only visually enjoyable, it plays a critical role in re-creating the past in all its dimensions. While photographs and maps do not by themselves replace the written word, they do have a role to play as primary source materials in any historical analysis. The fine collection of illustrations in this volume capture images of a wide variety of situations in Ottawa, allowing our generation to better understand the forms, structures, fashions, and group interactions of earlier periods of our history.

Alan F.J. Artibise
General Editor

Acknowledgements

First debts are to pioneers. Gratitude is owed those women and men who cared enough about their community both to preserve its heritage and to communicate it. They have been a small band, including organizations like the Historical Society of Ottawa, and writers like Lucien Brault and Courtney Bond. For the book, itself, a debt is owed professors Alan Artibise and Del Muise, who conceived, nurtured and at times defended the series in which it appears. Acting with the National Museum of Man, they built the structure that we have come to inhabit. A special debt is owed Prof. Artibise who shepherded volume after volume, including this one, to completion.

Any book such as this owes much to the keepers of records. To mention all is impossible, but some can scarcely be omitted. At the City Archives, I owe much to Louise Roy and her staff, particularly Serge Barbe, who were as accommodating as they were encourgaging. People in nearly every division of the Public Archives of Canada provided help: manuscripts, federal records, library, photography, maps and pictures and prints. Of special help at critical times were Pat Kennedy, Joy Houston, and Jean L'Esperance. Librarians at Carleton and Ottawa universities, the National Library, the Ottawa Public Library, and the *Citizen* made salient contributions. Departments at City Hall and many people in the National Capital Commission, Michael Newton foremost among them, opened their doors to me.

Colleagues across the country made their contribution as well. Of central importance were those in the "urban group", with whom I talked, debated and learned, not only about this volume, but about the theory and practice of urban history. They were my sounding board and problem solvers. Some were especially important: Alan Artibise, Gilbert Stelter, Susan Buggey, Paul-André Linteau, Don Davis and Jim Lemon. It is probably not too much to say that without the intellectual framework created by this group over the past fifteen years, this book would have been impossible.

At Carleton University, many are owed thanks, first in my own department. But geographers, linguists, sociologists, economists, and political scientists were called on from time to time for their expertise. A list so long implies a general anonymity, except for historian and Dean of Arts, Naomi Griffiths, whose encouragement, moral and material, was critical. Many people have read all or parts of the material presented here, or the studies from which it is drawn, and in questioning judgements or pointing to solecisms have saved embarrassment. Details can cripple design, of manuscript as much as buildings. Ted Mumford, Pamela Fry, Robert Stacey, David Hogan, and others at the publishers knocked off more rough corners on the way to the printer. Word-processing of the penultimate product was done with cheer and accuracy by Debbi Badali, Bob Couch was a committed associate during photo research, and Ruth Kirk a pillar of support throughout the final stages.

I learned much from students at Carleton, many with roots in the valley, who over the years used Ottawa as resource and laboratory, and did much to illuminate the city's historical, geographical, and political record. Their names, given in the footnotes of this volume, are a testimony to their efforts and the reliance I placed on them. Many friends, as well, pointed to sources and records, but from them the special contribution was moral support, and, in the trying times of research and writing, discrete inquiry and often silence. For their tolerance toward an often absent and irritable father, my apologies to Sabrina and Alex.

Much is not in this volume. It was conceived of as an urban history of Ottawa. The life and times of Hull and other communities in the penumbra of the capital are mentioned only incidentally. Equally, the large institutions that made such an impress on the city have not been fully opened to inspection. Many of Ottawa's great enterprises, institutions and communities still await their historians, not the least of these the federal government, the Roman Catholic church, the world of women, and many of the woods-based industries. Such omissions, I hope, will not reflect too unfavourably on the story told here. They are, nonetheless, the author's burden alone, as are the errors and the thrust of interpretation.

John H. Taylor
August, 1986

Mill and tavern of Philemon Wright on the north side of Chaudière Falls, 1823. Wright's settlement, begun in 1800, anticipated the establishment of Bytown by a generation, but his exclusive control of the town and its enterprises constrained development.

Introduction

The Valley and the Founding of Bytown

A river and valley frontier preceded the settlement of Bytown. In 1826, the town was thrust into an economy and society already a generation old, and moving to the rhythms of rudimentary timber, agricultural, and commercial activity. Population was thin, but mixed, comprising the gentility of March township, the roistering, itinerant raftsmen of the embryonic timber trade, a few farmers, and the stern "Yankee squatters" of Wrightsville. Social hierarchies were taking shape, and political alliances being established. A valley community, half-formed and unfocused, anticipated the city.

The river was central to all early activity. It was pioneered as a transportation route by the aboriginal peoples of the continent and in the seventeenth century adopted by explorer, fur trader, and missionary. For 200 years, as the "Grand" or "Ottawa" river,[1] it provided the shortest, the easiest and therefore the chief link between the European settlements of the St. Lawrence and the interior of the North American continent. It was the corridor of what later generations would call "Central Canada", the great route via Lake Huron through the shield, to the Mississippi Valley, and to the plains of the North West and the Arctic and Pacific Oceans. It remained unrivalled by either the St. Lawrence-Lower Lakes System to the south, or the Hudson system to the north.

The chief drawbacks of the Ottawa route were its limited unimproved carrying capacity, the vigorous climate, poor soil on the upper reaches, and the lack of settlement. The route, with its thirty-five-odd portages between Montréal and Michilimakinac, tolerated nothing larger than the canoe, and the canoe with no oasis of settlement, was only sufficient to provision its paddlers as far as Fort William. By 1790 the position of the route had become clear:

> the route most generally used... is that of the Ottawa, or Great River ...yet such is the poverty of the country, that unless provisions can be procured from Detroit, the North West Trade would cease to be carried on, because of the insupportable expense that would accrue if transported in canoes by the Great River.[2]

As for the site of the future city, it was, until 1800, virtually untouched, although few travellers, traders or missionaries failed to remark on the spectacular beauty of its surroundings. It was flanked by the Rideau Falls and the Gatineau River, and as a centrepiece, featured Chaudière Falls, or in English "chauldron", first described in 1613 by Champlain:

> A league thence we passed a rapid which is half a league wide and has a descent of six or seven fathoms. Here are many small islands which are nothing more than rough, steep rocks, covered with poor, scrubby wood. At one place the water falls with such force upon a rock that with the lapse of time it has hollowed out a wide, deep basin. Herein the water whirls around to such an extent, and in the middle sends up such big swirls, that the Indians call it Asticou, which means 'boiler'. This waterfall makes such a noise in this basin that it can be heard for more than two leagues away.[3]

Though a site for certain aboriginal ceremonies, Chaudière Falls, for all its splendour, was in essence a magnificent obstacle, one to be portaged.

Settlement began to creep into the Ottawa Valley at the end of the eighteenth century, most of it confined to the five Ottawa River seigneuries near the junction with the St. Lawrence. The significant exception was the initiative of the New Englander, Philemon Wright. After some preliminary investigations, he and his family, five other families, and twenty-five hired men, established in 1800 a settlement on the north bank of the Ottawa at Chaudière Falls, on the site of present-day Hull, Québec.[4] Wright clearly intended to create an agricultural settlement of utopian aspect, but in fact, pioneered most of the essential elements of the nineteenth-century valley economy, including transportation, commerce, and rudimentary industry. He also, reluctantly, pioneered the timber trade. Wright's reluctance was perhaps justified, for this trade soon permeated all aspects of valley life, and in time, overwhelmed even Wrightstown, and Wright's agricultural utopia.

Prior to the War of 1812 most farmer-settlers, who often doubled as casual lumberers, were on the north bank of the river and represented satellites to Wright's initial settlement. Altogether, fewer than 1,000 people were established. Only three families maintained watch over the south shore of the Ottawa until the end of the war of 1812-1815, when military and humanitarian considerations blended to provide the first considerable impulse of settlement. Even before the war was ended, a policy was emerging to provide greater military security for the Canadas. It centered on "...the importance which has long been attached, by every military man, to the formation of a communication between the provinces of Upper and Lower Canada, by the line of the Ottawa."[5] Complementary to — and in fact preceding a line of communication — were the "...exertions to form a loyal and war-like population on the banks of the Rideau and Ottawa...,"[6] to protect Upper Canada from the predatory Americans.

Officers and men of three British regiments in Canada, scheduled for demobilization, were given the option of remaining in Canada as assisted settlers, an offer also extended to a number of Highland Scotch, who were victims of over-population in the old land. Three settlements were formed after 1818. One of them, the Richmond settlement — drawn from the 100th regiment — was reached via the Ottawa River, the men cutting a road from Bellows' Landing, at the foot of Chaudière Falls, through the bush twenty miles southward to their new home on the Jock River. It was a road the independent and pre-eminent March township settler — Hamnett Kirkes Pinhey — would later describe as "...the road to Ruin." It would become the future city's first road into its hinterland, or more aptly, the road by which many of the Richmond settlers would find their way back into the town established in 1826 near Chaudière, where they became central to the formation of the Tory and Protestant "gentility."[7]

Settlement was only the first product of the War of 1812. Hostilities also dramatically pointed up the deficiencies of the St. Lawrence and Lower Lakes corridor, the major line of communication from Montréal to the upper Canadian frontier. It was, first of all, vulnerable to military attack from the republican state to the south, especially across the throat of the St. Lawrence, between Montréal, the commercial *entrepôt*, and Kingston, the chief naval base at the head of Lake Ontario. Its strategic weaknesses were further compromised by its economic ones. As a little-improved waterway, the St. Lawrence was slow, requiring a twelve-day passage upbound from Montréal to Kingston, and it was expensive, at about £4 a ton for freight. Moreover, within a few years of the war's end, its commercial viability was threatened by the commencement of the Champlain and the Erie Canals, both of which were designed to draw the trade of the St. Lawrence and Great Lakes basin southward through New York to the Atlantic.

Contending interests in the Canadas adopted strategies at some variance to counter the weaknesses of the St. Lawrence. Commercial groups in Québec City and Montréal, with interests in both the St. Lawrence and Ottawa Valleys, favoured improvements in both places, particularly development of the Lachine Canal, canalization of the Upper St. Lawrence, and improvements in the Lower Ottawa. They were not much concerned with a Rideau waterway from Chaudière to Kingston, a duplication, for commercial purposes, of any St. Lawrence improvements. In Upper Canada, the focus was almost exclusively on improvements to the upper St. Lawrence, coupled with construction of the Welland Canal around Niagara, to join Lakes Ontario and Erie. A Rideau Waterway was of secondary import. Virtually unorganized, and population-poor, the embryonic Ottawa Valley community could exert little influence on the government of either province. Governors and governments, especially Imperial ones, held more promise for the men of the Ottawa.

For British military strategists and colonial governors, more concerned with security than with commerce, the Ottawa-Rideau communication was an improvement of essential importance. It was most generally conceived to be a waterway, though at one point in 1818, the deputy quarter-master general at Québec City advised that "for the present" a road joining Richmond, Perth and Kingston would be "more advantageous."[8] Whether road or canal, what was wanted by the British, charged with defending the Canadas, was a back door or alternate route between Montréal and Lake Ontario in the event of American invasion. A communication was also essential to the survival and growth of the "loyal and warlike population" already planted along the line of the Ottawa and Rideau.

C.W. Jefferys' depiction of the first raft of squared timber, named "Colombo," on the Ottawa, 1806. Philemon Wright, shown here directing operations, pioneered the venture, which delivered the lumber of the Ottawa Valley to Quebec City and thence to the British market.

Beginning in 1809. a small clutch of stores and a tavern were built at Richmond Landing, near Chaudière Falls on the south side of the Ottawa River, to service passing voyageurs and raftsmen. This 1830 sketch, attributed to Lt.-Col. John By, features Isaac Firth's tavern, established in 1819.

British authorities initially had hoped the cost of such a waterway might be shared by the Imperial and the two colonial authorities of Upper and Lower Canada. It was an optimistic sentiment, and, by 1825, Imperial authorities had abandoned any hope of Upper Canadian assistance. A British Commission reported in 1825 that "...there does not appear to be the slightest chance of any pecuniary aid from the Upper Province." "The important advantages of such a communication in the rear of the frontier, are not likely to be appreciated by the bulk of the inhabitants of the Province...."[9] Though some aid was expected from Lower Canada, it was clear that the canal, if it was to be built at all, would in the main have to be built by the British. As for help from the valley, it was not even considered.

A new and scattered valley community was not the stuff canals are made of. On its north shore was Wright's settlement, numbering, by the 1820's, about 1,000, with its various satellites numbering about 1,000 more. On the south shore, some 2,000 independent farmers and gentry dotted the line inland from the March settlement, through Richmond and Perth. Commercial activity moved mainly along the Ottawa between Montréal and Wright's settlement, though by 1810 Firth's Tavern complemented Bellows' store on the south side of Chaudière Falls. Commercial intercourse was enhanced in 1819 by the operation of a sail-and-oar packet between Chaudière Falls and Grenville. It was begun by Wright, in association with some valley entrepreneurs and Québec City merchants. By 1823, a steamboat replaced the original packet, and Montréal merchants had replaced those of Québec City. By 1824, the steamboat was arriving every second day at Wright's Landing. Finally, as early as 1818, Wright constructed a road — to replace the old Chaudière portage — from his settlement to Lac Deschenes, the beginning of navigation for the upper river.

Such commerce could not underwrite canal construction. Nor could the growing timber trade. Even though by the 1820's thousands of "sticks" of timber each year came down the Ottawa and its tributaries, most of the benefits were extracted in Québec City and in England. Moreover, there was no suitable place in the valley to mobilize the wealth of commerce, timber or agriculture on behalf of canal or any other improvement. Wrightstown was a family monopoly and loyal to the Wrights, not the conglomerate valley society. The valley had no central place.

The canal was thus left to the British. But as they were paying the whole bill, they were obligated to no-one. They could build the canal — and its attendant settlements — much as they wished. In the autumn of 1826 they established a construction camp at Sleigh or Rafting Bay, on the south side of the Ottawa River, across from Wrightstown. The man in charge was Lt.-Col. John By, of the Royal Engineers, who at forty-seven had been anticipating retirement on half-pay when assigned by British Ordnance to the Rideau waterway.

The camp was located in the middle of some 400 acres of land, purchased in 1823 by the Governor-in-Chief, Lord Dalhousie, in anticipation of canal construction. He paid £750 for the site, which ran along the high bluffs fronting the Ottawa River. Dalhousie had anticipated a "... considerable village or town ..." as well as a work, but a town focused on the canal, that is, a town "... for the lodging of Artificers, and other necessary assistants in so great a work." And to this end, he instructed By to survey a townsite, which was laid off in rather large lots to be leased from the Crown. The governor further instructed By that "... it will be highly desirable to encourage the half-pay officers and respectable people, should they offer to build on these lots." And, to check speculation, a condition of any lease was to be a house at least thirty feet square.[10]

But neither the workings of the town plan nor the *clientèle* that would descend upon the town were anticipated. Dalhousie had not recognized the valley's need for a place that would provide it with both some focus, and some identity: a place for gentility and lumbermen alike. A valley society imploded on a construction camp. Nor did he foresee that the centre of a great public work — ultimately to cost nearly one million pounds — would attract a myriad of contractors and subcontractors, merchants, fortune-hunters, and the flotsam of itinerant labour adrift on the North American frontier.

Neither had Dalhousie realized that land speculation would prove such an irresistable attraction, up to, and including, By himself.[11]

By the end of 1826, hundreds of people had been drawn to the canal site. By and his chief advisors spent at least part of the winter in the relative comfort of Philemon Wright's settlement, with its two hotels and pleasant society, before moving in the Spring of 1827 to their comparatively luxurious homes, constructed by the Sappers and Miners near the lip of Entrance Valley. That Spring, according to one local tradition, the "town" was named after By, in the course of a banquet at Kingston, 9 March 1827. For all those condemned to a winter at Bytown, however, there was only the small comfort of

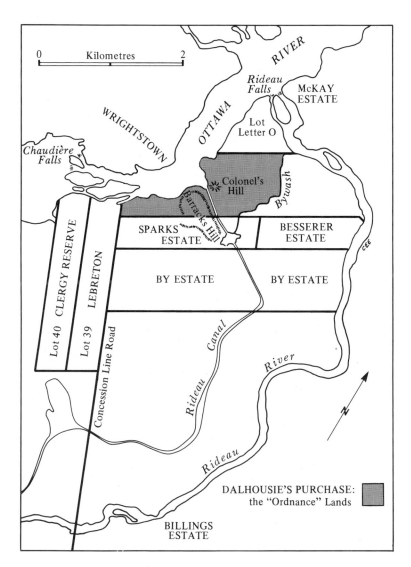

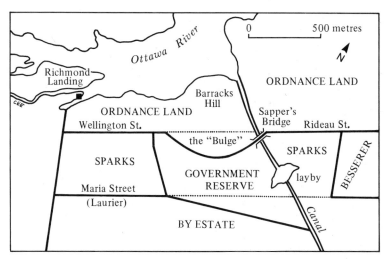

1 Bytown: early land ownership: A divided town emerged from early land ownership. Ordnance controlled some 400 acres of its own land and had rights over Lot Letter "O". Sparks also gave Ordnance about 20 acres for the canal right-of-way. In addition, Ordnance appropriated some 84 acres of Sparks' land as a military reserve. It forced roads to go around a portion of this reserve, thereby closing Wellington Street and creating the "Bulge". The reserve land was returned to Sparks in the 1840s and made development of the central part of the town possible. Extensive development of Lots 39 and 40 awaited arrival of the sawn lumber industry in the 1850s, and that of the Besserer and By estates the arrival of government in the 1860s.

Lord Dalhousie, Governor-in-Chief of British North America from 1820 to 1828. It was he who made the critical land purchase that determined the site of the canal headlocks and the city. Engraving by John Lupton after a painting by John Watson Gordon.

Thomas McKay (1792-1855) won the masonry contract for the headlocks of the Rideau Canal. This contract launched his long career as the founder of the milling establishment at Rideau Falls and the town of New Edinburgh. He also exercised a controlling influence in the politics of the region.

the civilian barracks in the Lower Town. And for those with means and some pretension to respectability, like the contractor Thomas McKay and his Scotch masons, the society of the barracks was for the most part that of men who spent the winter ". . . in drunken misery and half starved poverty . . . ."[12]

> Respectable tradesmen were dragged by falacious hopes and futile expectations to a spot where they had to be crammed into a habitation of three small apartments serving a set of drunken and dissipated beings to the number of nearly 200 or adopt the dreadful alternative of lying under the canopy of an unsheltered Canadian sky at the risk of being frozen to death.[13]

As for the town, military and engineering considerations had priority in planning. Terrain was a second consideration. People — and only favoured ones — third.

Land was obviously needed for a canal right-of-way, from Rafting Bay through Entrance Valley to the height of land and in a 200-foot swath to the southward. The effect on the prospective townsite was to bisect it from the outset. The effect became even more pronounced when reserves, for "defensive purposes", were made on the heights flanking Entrance Valley: Barrack's Hill to the west; Colonel's (later Major's) Hill and Nepean Point to the east. Immediately to the south of Barrack's Hill, some eighty-four acres — the Barrack's Hill bulge — was appropriated from the 200-acre lot of Nicholas Sparks. Sparks' property, along with the 200 acres belonging to Louis Besserer, were the only private holdings incorporated into the original townsite. In all, more than 300 acres of land in the heart of the prospective town was put beyond the reach of immediate development.[14]

In the valley itself, By constructed, on opposite sides of the canal, an engineering office and a commissariat, both of quite handsome stone rubble construction. At the foot of the canal, a wharf was put in place (and alienated to By's master carpenter). At the head of the canal and on its east side, a site for a works yard was located, and there the group of "civilian barracks" was constructed.

With the military and canal establishment taken care of, By turned to the matter of a townsite. Much of the land to the east of the military reserves, what became "Lower Town", was an almost impenetrable cedar swamp. It was nonetheless surveyed into town lots in 1826, but few were taken up, due to the condition of the ground. The only plot of land both owned by the government and also susceptible to development without much improvement was a rather small patch, more than half a mile west of the canal on the rocky heights overlooking the Ottawa River. It stood directly across from the best of Sparks' land, where, indeed, he resided. Given the scarcity of usable land, By set out the lots in the "Upper Town" on a rather smaller scale than Dalhousie had suggested. But he did offer them for lease, in perpetuity, at an annual quit rent of 2s 6p. By also encouraged their acquisition by the better class of people. Most were immediately taken up, many by speculators whose leases he subsequently cancelled. But in the long term, these lots became home to many of the gentility, who moved in from the military settlements, such as Richmond, and with the development of Sparks' land to the south, the area became the focus of the Anglo-Protestant community. But while they were fine sites for residences, they were, given the location of the canal, poor commercial sites. Nor were they satisfactory for the housing of the poor; they were too exclusive or, on Sparks' land, too expensive. Despite the efforts of Sparks, and his donation of market and church sites to encourage business and other activity, there was a clear need for other commercial locations, as well as residential ones.

The opportunity came in the spring of 1827 when By began to develop his works yard and ". . . it became absolutely necessary . . ." to drain the Lower Town swamp and run a connecting road — Sussex Street — to the wharf at the foot of the canal. The situation was "so improved" that the Lower Town lots became very attractive, precipitating a shift of some of the Upper Town lessees. As in Upper Town, the Lower Town lots were not given out indiscriminately. The first leases, and those with the most valuable locations along Sussex, and also closest to By's and Pooley's estate on Colonel's Hill, were given to the men of his civilian establishment: Fitzgibbon, master carpenter, Tormey, master smith, Burrows, overseer of works, McGillivray, clerk of stores, Clegg, clerk of cheque, ". . . and some others, not connected with the department . . . ."[15] They were also granted the leases in perpetuity at a quit rent of 2s 6p. That is, according to Dalhousie's orders, the better class of people were given the more attractive lots. They were also in many cases given the lots on better terms.

In order to curb the speculative impulse that had revealed itself in Upper Town, By adopted, beginning in 1827, the practice of leasing the remaining, and bulk of the town lots, not in perpetuity, but for thirty years, and at "different rents, agreeable to the supposed value of the situations . . . ."[16] In most cases, these rents were from £1 to £5

Headlocks of the Rideau Canal, 1830. The "Commissariat," to the right of the canal, still stands. At upper right is Barracks Hill, home to the Royal Sappers and Miners, and now Parliament Hill. During this period, the traveller's first view of the town would have been from the water.

One of the first public works undertaken by Lt.-Col. By was a series of bridges over Chaudière Falls to join "Bytown," "Wright's Town," and the portage road to the Upper Ottawa. Finished in 1827, they were washed out in the spring floods of 1835 and not replaced until 1844. R.S.M. Bouchette's drawing was made from the bluffs near "Parliament Hill."

a year. But many of the Upper Town and more valuable Lower Town lots retained the perpetual and more valuable terms.

The needs of canal and defence, combined with the social philosphy of Dalhousie and By, produced from the outset a town of curious proportion. Indeed, they produced two towns, separated by nearly a mile of rough trail, They contained at least three or four classes of people who could be recognized, among other ways, in terms of their identification with the land, and with the two active landlords in Bytown: Sparks and British Ordnance. Besserer, the third major landowner, did not immediately subdivide. The most favoured held their property in freehold from Sparks or, what was almost as good, held leases in perpetuity from Ordnance. Next was the group, in some cases multiple lot owners, who held thirty-year Ordnance leases or rented from Sparks, Besserer, or subsequently from By, who in 1832 purchased a 600-acre estate, immediately south of the townsite, for £1200. These lessees, in turn, often sublet land or rented dwelling and commercial space at sometimes inflated prices to the landless. This group included the squatters: canal labourers, many of them Irish, whom By permitted to raise turf or log shanties along the canal embankment, known as Corktown. They also penetrated to edges of the Lower Town swamp, or to the banks of the Rideau River, and built crude dwellings there without sanction. British Ordnance, at the outset, thus assumed a position of extraordinary importance, one it would maintain for a generation. Ordnance not only planned the town, but built and maintained the canal, the first improvements, the first institutions, and was virtually the town's first "society". Not only was Ordnance the dominant landlord, but, for all practical purposes, the Town's local government and police.

By and his successors could assume this function because the British alone paid for the canal. There was also the manner in which the Ordnance land — Dalhousie's purchase — was acquired and was managed. Dalhousie purchased the land in his own name, but in the right of the Crown, from monies available to him as governor, though whether from the military chest (as Ordnance would subsequently claim), or casual revenue, is debatable. He turned the land over to By personally, as Robert Baldwin Sullivan would later note, "in inadvertent non-compliance with the law",[17] along with a set of instructions as to its disposition and, By claimed (no document was ever found), for disposition of the rental monies. These latter, according to By, were to be spent on local improvements, and in the first few years a bridge at Chaudière, a timber channel, and some road improvements were made from these funds. This procedure gave By almost unlimited personal scope to strike the rudimentary outlines of a town. And since he was the only one with access to both funds and authority, however dubious, he was the only one able to carry such plans through. He also, by virtue of the control of the soliders on Barracks Hill, had practical policing powers; and through the military hospital and military surgeons, control of a major frontier institution. He was a reasonable approximation of an eighteenth-century British squire. There was little in the way of a civilian counterpoint. The juridical centre of the region was at Perth, miles away, over nearly impassable forest tracks. And, in the early years, the nearest justice of the peace was Captain Willson, residing in bucolic splendor at "Ossian Hall" five miles away in Hog's Back Falls.

Effective powers of control proved difficult for Ordnance to give up. As a result, the early Bytown community began, from at least 1829, a generation-long agitation to shake itself free of Ordnance (and other) control of its lands and institutions, whatever benefits that control might have brought in the first place. That theme of corporate dependence was a counterpoint to the two other major issues concerning that first generation. The first was the effort to focus and integrate the valley economy and society, both of which had pre-dated the present town. The second was to assert an independence from the larger, more powerful societies already established in the St. Lawrence valley and Lower Great Lakes, and as well, to break the timber trade's economic bondage to Britain.

CONTINUITY AND THEMES

Fragmentation, marginality, and corporate oversight emerged from the outset as the three themes that would resonate through Ottawa's history from those early days until the present. New communities would, in due course, be added to the original ones, compounding the primordial cleavages and introducing further complexity and new and different quarrels. Montréal, Toronto, Québec City — even Brockville and Kingston — would continue to assert economic and political power in the valley at varying times, in varying degrees and in varying ways. And huge corporate entities — chiefly the sawn-lumber industry and the federal government — would succeed Ordnance in asserting a preponderant oversight in the city. It was a resonance never resolved, for as much as Ottawans found discomfort in their situation, they also found much benefit.

Fragmentation was at the same time crippling and protective. The four or five self-contained communities that came to comprise the urban complex could rarely agree on an agenda or a strategy on any subject, from economic growth to a fire-chief. As a result, the city, divided within itself, persistently found it difficult to counter influences from outside, corporate oversight from the inside, or to assert a metropolitan influence of its own. There was, moreover, no wide acceptance of its image on the part of its own citizens. Rather there were a series of images, each emerging out of the particular communities that made up its total substance. Ottawa was at the same time French and English, Catholic and Protestant, lumberer and retailer, tradesman and bureaucrat, Tory and Reformer. But, unlike many places, no combination came to dominate: the balances were so even, and so deeply entrenched, there remained a continuing stand-off.

As a result, many of the themes that inform urban development elsewhere in Canada appear in Ottawa only within its limited communities, and not as a phenomenon of the whole. A literary consciousness, as much as a class consciousness, or a social consciousness, emerged in its communities much as they might have in a small town, and, it seems, with similar limitations, and configuration.

More characteristic, was the interplay, competition, and even violent confrontation of the city's distinctive communities, each of them rooted in a specific territory, each with a quite distinctive economic role, each with a peculiar religious and racial mix. Politics was thus the politics of Balkanization, and more likely to turn on religious or cultural questions than on economic or class ones. Consensus was rare, and when it occurred, fragile. It is also hard to say that "pluralism" in Ottawa was stimulating, for much of the time interaction was minimal. Each community was a bastion, bent in the first instance on its own survival and hypersentitive to the designs of its neighbours. But whatever its disadvantage, such urban particularism did permit survival, and did give the city a curious character.

If the city could claim to have an image, it was that imposed by the large, corporate-like entities that over-arched the fragmented society. Ottawa was successively a canal town, a timber town, a lumber town, and a federal capital. But these dominating elements — and the image they carried with them — were more artificially "stuck on" the community than the product of its own activity.

In this case, Ottawa can be seen as a series of "company towns" with all the problems and limitations that are common to such phenomena. For as much as its citizens recognized that prosperity and growth owed much to the "companies," there was also great resentment at their peremptory and often high-handed decision-making that ignored or over-rode the wishes of the community. As often as not, the city wasn't consulted at all. Persistent ambivalence was characteristic: the city chafed, but prospered.

Marginality, too, had its dark and bright side, though the former more often prevailed. Ottawa, and its sister city, Hull, are the only major communities on a provincial boundary. And both, as a result, are distant from the political capitals of their respective provinces, from their chief concentrations of population, and from their major economic centres. That is, the weight of politics, population, economy, and its influence, tends to be in favour of places other than those of the Ottawa Valley. It remains very much the frontier it was in 1800, with many frontier characteristics, and many frontier problems. Only, once in a major way, did Ottawa's marginal position prove decisive: in its choice as the capital of the Canadas. It was sufficiently remote that it did not compromise, too badly, any of the powerful, quarreling communities of the St. Lawrence and lower Great Lakes.

Complexities still remain in abundance in its history. And that, too, is important, for the persisting complexity of Ottawa in some ways provides the most enduring theme of them all.

Thomas Burrowes' 1845 sketch of the north entrance of the Rideau Canal looks out on the Ottawa River at Rafting Bay. Rafts of squared timber were often reassembled here after their component cribs passed the Chaudière Falls. The steamboat wharf is seen on the right. The steep trail near it rises to Major's Hill, where the chief British Ordnance officers made their home.

Chapter One

The Era of the Timber Trade, 1825–1849

Bytown was born a brat of the British army, was nurtured by the canal the army built in the years 1826-1832, and drew profit from its operation for years afterward. But the exigencies of timber proved more powerful and more lasting, and did most to confirm Bytown's place as a valley metropolis. It also brought the town under different and less mannered influences than the British military: the river barons of Montréal and of Kingston; the great lumberers of the valley; and the chain of creditors and suppliers that stretched through Québec City to Liverpool, Edinburgh, and London. The brat of the army was raised as a lumberjack.

Bytown's social ambience was as volatile and as ambivalent as its economy. It was a brawling, unstable settlement in its first generation. "No place," noted one observer, "is better calculated to exhibit the savages of civilized countries than Bytown. All that the art of unprincipled men can devise comes under my observation every day, and a mealtime seldom passes without witnessing the determination of an important case by 'wager of battle;' that is a few civil blows."[1] But if part brawling, it was also part sedate, a legacy of the gentility of the valley, secure behind the bastions of the Anglican and Presbyterian churches of Upper Town. And there emerged, in the first generation, a series of fragmented, self-conscious communities within Bytown, each with its own cultural institutions, social dimension, and political and economic ambitions, and each corresponding somewhat to those existing in the valley before 1826. Factionalism was rife; unanimity rare.

ECONOMIC AND METROPOLITAN GROWTH

On May 24, 1832, the steamer *Pumper,* renamed for the occasion *The Rideau*, left Kingston for Ottawa to inaugurate the canal and to provide a brief moment of glory for Lt.-Col. By, soon to leave for England to face charges of overexpenditure, which, while never proven, threw the remaining years of his career into a half-light. He left behind a raw frontier community and the first trunk waterway of the Canadas. The canal had indisputable local importance. For example, an Ordnance decision in 1842 to quadruple the canal tolls created "a mighty stir." "If the Ordnance had dropped a bomb shell amongst the merchants they could not have affronted them more." If they had "... blown up half the Locks of the Canal, they could not have more effectively injured the work or the trade of the country."[2]

But the Rideau never matched in importance the St. Lawrence waterway (even in its unimproved form), and the Montréal merchant, Simon McGillivray, more accurately predicted the canal's future as early as 1828:

> The Rideau Canal, I should think, will never bring down much produce, it is an important improvement in the country with a view to its military defence, but whilst the St. Lawrence is open, and whilst considerable craft can come down the St. Lawrence without impediment, I should think that many of them will never come down through the Rideau Canal. Boats may go up the Rideau Canal, but I should think the waters of the St. Lawrence will always be the channel in coming down.[3]

The Rideau Canal was both slow and expensive, mainly the result of its numerous, tedious, and expensive lockages.

The canal also failed to satisfy the large purposes of the valley and the town. For one thing, the established businessmen of Montréal and Kingston took control of the transportation business on the canal from the outset: legal control and manufacturing spin-offs resided elsewhere. For another, the ambitions of Bytown and the valley looked to an indigenous system, one independent of that of the "speculative gentlemen in the southern part of our province."

The Steamer Pilot *on the Rideau Canal, 3 August, 1844. The canal became an important route for commercial steamer traffic, for timber and sawn lumber, and for local travel. The steamer tows its barge and several canoes, leaving a gaggle of others in its wake. The juxtaposition of wilderness and modern technology was an enduring theme in the Ottawa country, and not simply a passion of the artists.*

The Ottawa River, not the Rideau, was the logical focus. What was needed, in short, was the Ottawa-Lake Huron Waterway. This waterway was in the very fibre of the valley. It was a reiteration of the old fur-trade route up the Ottawa and into the interior of the continent. Like the St. Lawrence entrepreneurs, the target was the wealth of the American mid-west and, by the 1860s, the "British" North West. The waterway was the "Central Canadian" way. And Bytown/Ottawa was the projected capital of "Central Canada".

From the outset, the Lake Huron waterway was vigorously pursued by the eminent men of the town as the great strategic requirement. It not only conformed to the need for an independent and indigenous transportation route, it was also perceived as repairing the two great flaws of the valley. The first of these was a lack of agriculture. From the 1830s to the 1850s, agricultural development was seen as the key to prosperity. Timber was in a sense temporary, its chief function to open land to the settler. The second great flaw was the related one of people, or the lack of them. That, too, would be repaired by the Lake Huron Waterway in its westward thrust. The transportation corridor would open the wild lands between the river and Georgian Bay and attract farmers and townspeople. As well, the waterway was a device to break the metropolitan control of the St. Lawrence, and to provide an integrating mechanism for the valley proper.

From at least 1829 until well into the twentieth century, the waterway project was pressed on governments, both Imperial and local. Its failure, in many respects, represented the failure of the valley to shake free of the dominion of the St. Lawrence. Its failure also represented certain political and geographical realities of Ottawa and the valley.

The Imperial authorities, after the Rideau Canal experience, could never provide more than verbal support for another canal; and Canadian governments were dominated by the capitalists of the St. Lawrence. The valley could never support a second waterway itself. The dream of agricultural settlement was mostly myth, too. Up river, both climate and geology worked against the farmer. At Ottawa the transition is mostly complete from the rich soils of the deciduous zone to the thin, acid ones of the Boreal forest.

The reality of the Boreal zone was the timber trade, economically and in nearly every other sense. As inveterate Bytown booster, Dr. Alexander Christie, said:

I have witnessed the birth, growth and prosperity, of Bytown from first to last and have been no inattentive observer of the causes on which they depend. Bytown owes its commencement to the Rideau Canal, its rapid and early growth to the money expended in building[?] that splendid work. It has since been indebted as well as the surrounding country for its prosperity to the lumber trade...and I confess I am unable to see by what great boon it could be compensated.[4]

It was the impact of the trade that was valuable to Bytown. The major role for the town was not the actual shaping or even handling of timber, for that job was taken care of almost entirely by the shantymen and raftsmen, who extracted the wood from the forest and stayed with it — or more properly on it, for timber was its own transportation — to the ocean port of Québec City. The timber rafts, however, were necessarily dismantled at Chaudière Falls to permit their passage, and the presence of the crews produced "a bustle of trade in their seasonal passages."[5]

Bytowners not only did little in the way of handling the wood that passed over Chaudière, they did virtually no processing of it. In 1841 the town had only one sawmill, by 1846 it had two, plus a shingle mill.[6] All were of small size, and all, it appears, serviced only local needs. Likewise, there was little other manufacturing or processing carried on in the town, whether related to timber or to other products, like those of the nearby farms. A grist mill had apparently opened at Chaudière Falls before 1827, but by 1843, none is noted in the town itself, though both McKay and Wright had operations nearby. A distillery, a tannery, three breweries, and two foundries rounded out the major industrial establishment of the 1840s. Only one of these — a foundry owned by T.M. Blasdell — can clearly be established as lumber-related. Blasdell produced the famous "Blasdell axe", that was used widely in the valley in the middle of the nineteenth century. Otherwise, there was only the usual complement of small traders: bootmakers, bakers, harness-makers, and the like, plus a small professional group of doctors and lawyers.

What, then, did Bytown do? Basically it was a provisioner, retailer and servicer to the timber trade. As early as 1841, with a population of about 3,000, there were thirty-eight merchants' shops. By 1845, that number had increased to fifty-one. Store-houses numbered seven.[7] The stores gathered and distributed the goods that came from outside, whether the manufactured goods of the St. Lawrence valley and Britain, or the agricultural goods of the surrounding countryside, or the Cincinnati pork and Genesee flour that were the staples of the timber trade. They flowed into Bytown on the Ottawa

Thomas Burrowes' sketch of Thomas McKay's mills and distillery, and part of New Edinburgh at Rideau Falls, 1845.

McKay's Mills, Rideau River. In the latter part of the 1840s, McKay expanded his mills, and from them in 1848 sent the first sawn lumber to the American market. They are seen here in 1851, in a wash-drawing by Major General Charles Erskine Ford.

River steamboats and the Rideau Canal barges in the summer, and by sled train along the ice of the Ottawa in the winter.

The products of the outside world were mixed in Lower Town with the agricultural products of the local farming community. Each fall the distribution began to the shanties, the bulk of them in the Upper Ottawa. The journey started with the twelve-mile portage of goods upward to the head of navigation at Aylmer: this portage was "another source of wealth and employment to the settlers . . . ." in Bytown and area.[8] Amounts were considerable. An 1850 estimate claimed the trade consumed annually some 29,000 barrels of flour, nearly as many of pork, besides fodder for the horses and oxen, and other articles.[9]

It was in Lower Town that the men, like the goods of the trade, passed, whether in their migrations outward in the spring or into the camps in the autumn. There they stayed, whether to amuse themselves in the numerous taverns, gaming houses, and brothels, or to wait for jobs, or spend time with their families, who had taken up residence in the row houses and shanties of the Lower Town.

The most numerous businessmen were landlords and tavern-keepers, carters and, especially, merchants. By 1849 some fifty-four boarding-houses were licenced by the town council and these were in addition to the lumberers' hotels and casual rentors.[10] The town had also licenced some seventy-two carts, twenty-one caléches, nine bakers' carts, two milk carts, four "waggons for loading," two stage-wagons, and an omnibus.[11] But most important were the merchants:

> As the supplies for the Lumber Camps up and down the Ottawa River were mostly purchased in Bytown the Merchants as a rule did a business which was not commensurate with the size of the Village. The business men of Bytown were always to the forefront, in all matters relating to the community and its welfare.[12]

A group of businessmen, with the merchants and some of the professional men in the van, became known in time as the "fixed commercial community" in distinction to the "itinerant" lumberers engaged in the timber trade itself.

This "fixed" group was in and of the town. It was sedentary, and its fortune largely identified with the fortunes of the place. There was, with the merchants, the crucial nexus of town and social group, the organic interdependence of economics and place, that gave rise to the nineteenth-century city booster, promoting, through his city,

his own fortunes. Specialization was not typical. Rather one found in these men a combination of merchant, land speculator, rentiér, and, often, casual lumberer. They were also men who were often deeply engaged in the politics of the town.

William Stewart was one of these. He was a Scotch Presbyterian who made his way to Bytown in 1827 from Longueuil. He established a business "principally confined to retail"[13] in the Lower Town, but at various points was engaged in the wholesale trade to various timberers. From time to time he engaged in the timber trade in his own right. He was a land speculator on a small scale, and a merchant tory who represented nearby Russell.

Stewart ran an essentially cashless business, relying on lines of credit, bills of exchange, plain barter, and the uncertain prospects of cheap supplies of food in the autumn and a good market in Québec City and Liverpool the following summer. A change in the weather or a change in the economy often left him skirting commercial disaster.

Dependency was hard to avoid, for not only did the valley derive credit from the outside community, but that outside community also set the terms of trade: Montréal (so far as Bytown was concerned) dictated commodity prices, especially for pork, as well as transportation costs both below and above Chaudière Falls, by virtue of its control over the steamboats and barges. The British market set the price for timber. It also demanded squared timber or the large, three-inch-thick planks, known as deals, all cut from the largest and finest pine to be found in the forest. Most sawing and other processing was thus confined to the mills and labour of Britain. As an industrial basin, the Ottawa Valley remained underdeveloped.[14]

Other demands were exacted at Québec City, chiefly for "culling" and storage in the timber coves of that city. The cullers established the quality of timber to be sold and therefore its value. But the cullers, until the end of the 1840s, were paid by the Québec buyers. Storage of the Ottawa rafts in the coves of Québec City likewise entailed costs dictated in that city, and the cost of storage — or its refusal — provided additional bargaining levers for the buyers and shippers. In the valley itself, government exacted a royalty from all "Crown" timber passing down the river, and, with some private operators, charged the lumberers for the use of slides and other facilities.

William Stewart, MPP for Prescott and Russell, epitomized the Bytown businessman of the 1830s and 1840s. He was at once a merchant, lumberer, land speculator, politician, and pillar of the Presbyterian church.

Much of the political activity of men like Stewart was, then, directed to ameliorating or changing the terms of trade. They sought agricultural development in the valley, and alternative forms of transportation to better control their costs of inbound goods, as well as applying directly to government for reduced lockage charges. They sought banks and bank branches as a handier source of credit. They agitated with the various provincial governments for more equitable and cheaper access to the Crown's timber, and for more of the royalties from timber to be plowed back into improvements in the valley. Above all, of course, they sought to maintain their advantage in the protected British market.

In the meantime, the merchants like Stewart were protected essentially by their caution and their intelligence networks. Stewart was an astute observer of the weather, and snow and ice conditions; a recorder of market conditions in Québec City and Britain; sensitive to commodity prices, credit, and the general political situation. He was also continuously corresponding with business and political associates to learn what he might, calculating high costs of supplies against the potential of a good market the following year; or bailing out of business in anticipation of a glut, "a Contagion", as Stewart termed it, "called the 'Lumber Fever'".[15]

There is little doubt that timber could make men rich, but they were few and most were probably outside the valley. More often, the timber business was a precarious existence, balanced finely on the edge of bankruptcy. Many men in the valley could probably say, along with Stewart, (who was relatively successful): "My white pine will ruin me."[16]

The value of the trade to the town is extremely difficult to gauge, but a conservative estimate of the cost of providing provisions and supplies for the trade of the Upper Ottawa in the 1840s would be in the order of £300,000 per season. How much of that stuck to the hands of Bytown's business community has proved impossible to determine.

But alarm and instant organization of all elements in town were the response to any outside threat. As Christie pointed out, in 1841, it was all very well for Montréal and Québec merchants to advocate the delay of the imposition of new Imperial duties, "in order to allow the withdrawal of capital invested in the Timber Trade...," but for those who "have resided in the heart of the Provinces, such an alteration will be a death blow to the country come when it will ....What other article...have we got for exportation?"[17] Christie

Building a Squared Pine Timber Raft, 1881, *by Archibald Barnes, after a photograph by W.J. Topley of the cookery on J.R. Booth's raft, c. 1880. Squared timber provided its own transportation from the forests of the Ottawa Valley to the coves of Quebec City. The rafts were comprised of cribs small enough to pass down the timber slides built alongside the "chutes" of the Ottawa River. Rafts were broken up and reassembled at each passage. The men ate and slept on the rafts, often for periods of several months.*

A timber shanty and shantymen at Booth Lumber Camp, Aylen Lake, c. 1895. Each fall itinerant lumbermen and supplies were assembled, often in Bytown, for the trip upriver into the "limits" for the winter's cutting operations. In the spring, the lumber would be transported to the mills of the Valley or to Quebec City.

was probably not exaggerating. A moderate drop in prices and production in 1842-1843 created lamentable conditions in the valley:

> the distress among the Farmers is really awful; — the depreciation of agricultural produce would not have pressed heavily on them had they been free of debts contracted under more encouraging prospects — they are torn to pieces by them —....[18]

The decade of the 1840s marked both peak and disaster in the timber trade. Despite the "alternate periods of prosperity and depression" that had marked the trade from its inception, nothing quite matched the peak year of 1845 or the ruinous slide that followed. The year 1845 was "the most prosperous to which my knowledge of the trade extends," according to Ruggles Wright. A record cut in that year, some 27,702,344 cubic feet reaching the Québec market, was nearly all exported at high prices, the result, it seems, of the demands of railway construction in Britain. With little stock on hand and the expectation of a good market in 1846, lumberers expanded production, and in typical valley fashion, large numbers of small and casual operators moved into the woods to reap an expected bounty. More than thirty-seven million cubic feet of timber was delivered to the Québec market and "several millions more" left lying between Québec and Bytown. But the export in 1846 was almost identical to that of 1845, and the oversupply depressed prices to the end of the decade.

For Bytown the situation was singularly depressing, and was reflected in a sharp drop in population between 1845-1846 and 1848, estimated as high as 2,000 or more than one-quarter of the total. Municipal government at the end of the decade was near bankruptcy. Feelings were expressed most strongly before select parliamentary committees, and in riot.

DEMOGRAPHIC GROWTH AND SOCIAL RELATIONS

Bytown's first generation was one of unsteady population growth. (See Table I). The canal works seem to have drawn about 1,000 people, a base that appears to have remained fairly stable in size (if not composition) over the period 1826-1832, while the canal was abuilding. Canal workers created a preponderance of males. Population growth was probably slow in the five or six years after the canal was completed as labourers moved elsewhere, or to other jobs, especially in the woods.

The shuffle of people that followed completion of the canal was followed by a depression that began in the winter of 1836-1837. Its effect on population was exacerbated by the rebellions of 1837 and 1838, and by bad winter weather for lumbering; that is, thaws and low water. Immigration virtually stopped. Food shortages in the winter of 1836-1837, and correspondingly high prices — nearly triple the usual — paralyzed growth of any kind. "Such a season as we have had I never experienced," wrote one Bytown merchant. "Many are determined to break up their shantys and Haul out what is made...."[19] By March of 1837 "...teams were daily arriving from the woods that are broke down from the scarcity and bad quality of oats." By April, there was "...not 6 days supply of Flour in Bytown for Bread & none to be purchased at any Price."[20] "Derangement in the monetary affairs" of Britain and the United States all but destroyed the fragile system of credit that fuelled the timber business, and despite a reduction in cut, markets were so bad that through 1837 and 1838 there was a surplus of timber at Québec City. "Business was completely at a stand..." by the winter of 1837-1838.

> As to lumbering there is hardly such a thing as a Shanty spoken of & the less the better. In fact, every person's attention Seems to be engrossed by the troubles of the times.[21]

It was a time when "...there was nothing only fair promises and disappointments without number."[22] In the circumstances, few people came.

Only in the winter of 1838-1839 did business improve sufficiently to prompt an increase in activity in the woods and in the town, though unusually heavy snows made provisioning difficult and expensive. By January, 1839, distant shantys were reported as "near starving." But the cut was fine and by mid-summer of 1839 good prices, good crops, and a country at peace gave rise to a more optimistic spirit, and, as usual, "a perfect mania for lumber."[23] About five years of prosperity and population growth followed for Bytown. The early 'forties' were good times.

In 1840, the population of Bytown was reported as 2,171. It had somewhat more than doubled in ten years, though little confidence can be placed in any of the early population figures. Growth could hardly be considered spectacular. The good times of the 1840s changed that. By 1841 population was reported at 3,122, and in 1845-1846 as 7,000, the high for the decade. People arrived at Bytown primarily, it seems, because of the flourishing timber trade in the early forties, coupled with the peak of use of the Rideau Canal before the St. Lawrence system supplanted it. Population growth then trembled and declined with the mid-decade collapse of the trade, the dismantling of the Imperial System, and the nearly full operation of the St. Lawrence canals. It was reported as low as 5,000 in 1847, and, possibly because of an influx of famine Irish, was just over 6,000 in 1848.

Bytown, in its demographic configuration, did not conform to the pattern of the surrounding countryside, which in the 1840s was growing more rapidly than the town. This was a factor that played heavily in its social conflicts and politics. While, in a general sense, the rural areas were British and Protestant, Bytown was preponderantly Irish, French, and Roman Catholic, particularly in the Lower Town.[24]

There were, as well, the occupational differences between town and country. Biases were toward lumbering in the town and agriculture in the country. It was a source of tension that penetrated the Bytown community itself. Even though the timber trade provided the "most commanding" agricultural market in the province, its importance could not dissolve more fundamental antagonisms between the two pursuits. The farmers saw lumbering as a transient business, and essentially a preliminary to the superior vocation of agriculture. The timberers saw farmers as an essentially disruptive element: they were often casual lumberers, who flooded the woods in times of good prospective markets and thereby contributed to gluts; they poached; they posed the threat of fire; they advocated protection against the cheaper American foodstuffs that fuelled the trade; and they persisted in attempting to farm land the lumberers felt was fit only for growing trees. Both farmer and timberer competed for labour and capital, both in short supply on the frontier.

Ethnic and religious differences between the country and the town reinforced the occupational conflicts. Bytown was dominated numerically by its Roman Catholic population (some 58 per cent), and the surrounding district by a Church of England population (some 38 per cent) and a Presbyterian one (some 21 per cent). Bytown also contained the bulk of French Canadians in the region, and probably those of Irish origin, particularly if Catholic.[25]

The significance of the differences lay chiefly, however, in their distribution within the town. In Bytown itself the Protestant population especially the "Scotch" were concentrated in the "West Ward" or Upper Town; the Roman Catholic, both French and Irish, in the Centre and East Wards, or Lower Town.[26] That is, the social characteristics of Upper Town, with its genteel society, tended to conform to those of the rural district surrounding Bytown. And in practice, the Upper Town found its numerical support and its political allies among the Protestant farmers of the county and district. The alliance was important in the early days, for the growing numbers of the rural areas supported the Upper Town's pretensions to social and political leadership, as against the Lower Town, where two-thirds of the people of Bytown actually lived.

The Upper Town and the rural areas surrounding, with religion and race in common, had a common antipathy to French, Irish, and Roman Catholics, an antipathy expressed through one of the most prominent Orange Orders of Upper Canada. They also had a similar dream of an agricultural utopia in the valley (headed by an urban gentility), and a fairly deep-rooted suspicion of lumbering, whatever its importance. They also resented the merchants of Lower Town, who battened on the canal and lumber business, and were clearly dominant. A genteel, liberal professional, Protestant Upper Town, with rural and agricultural allies, was set against a noisy, pushing commercial, and Roman Catholic Lower Town, that lived or died on timber.

One other social element — which had set the contending forces apart and tended to keep them there — was the town's biggest landlord, British Ordnance. It was the first *élite* and it was tiny, but, in the first generation, it had an influence that might even be considered preponderant.

Ordnance was theoretically neutral in the town's social relations, but inevitably, through the powers it wielded and status it claimed, it not only became embroiled in the conflicts of the town, but in some measure contributed to the making of them. Ordnance, as landlord, drew down on it the anger of all elements. Its leasing policies were, almost from the outset, the target of complaint, especially from the Lower Town. Petitions from leaseholders rained down on By and his successors for the better part of two decades. At bottom, they asked for conversion to freehold. Only through action of the legislature in the 1840s was provision eventually made to permit conversion to freehold, but even then leasing was permitted, and continued to exist in the Lower Town until near the end of the century.[27]

The Upper Town was less concerned with the leasing arrangements, since it had more generous terms. It had a rather different complaint. By, in 1827, took more than eighty acres of Nicholas Sparks' land — the Barrack's Hill Bulge — without compensation, and for rather dubious purposes, including docks larger than those in London, England, along a harbour that would have required water to run up hill.[28] Ordnance thus pre-empted the best commercial area in Sparks' freehold. It was land that was central to the commercial ambitions, not only of Sparks, but of the entire Upper Town. As a result, angry battles erupted between Ordnance, and Sparks and his Upper Town allies. They were fought over a period of twenty years in the courts, in the legislatures, and on the land. Sparks doubtless perceived his case as just. But to one Ordnance officer, he was a man "...of a very violent disposition, and weak enough, to be led by insidious people...."[29] In one incident, Sparks was thwarted only by the "opportune, but chance arrival of some Troops" on the way to Montréal.

> He has asserted his intention to take forceful possession of what he calls his property whenever he gets an opportunity, and yesterday while committing the outrage [the occupation of a lock house], sent for raftsmen with directions to give them plenty of Brandy! the conduct of this class of men is too notorious as "Shiners" to need any comment from us.[30]

The officer applied to two Upper Town magistrates, but they "declined to act" and he ultimately had to turn to the sheriff and the troops. The bulge, as a result of legislative action, was ultimately returned to Sparks in the latter part of the 1840s.

The various *élites* — Ordnance, the "gentility" and the "fixed" commercial community — were, of course, small. Most numerous were the tradesmen, carters, shantymen, raftsmen, and labourers. In an era of the property franchise, they had little practical political influence. They were also, for the most part, French and Irish Roman Catholics.

Prior to 1826, the French were the proletariat of the woods and the rafts, and perhaps in this sense the logical successors to their forefathers, who had paddled the canoes of the fur brigades along the "Grand River". When the canal construction commenced at Bytown, a number brought their special skills, as woodsmen and boatmen, to the construction camps. But the canal works also attracted their Irish co-religionists, who arrived in most cases almost directly from Ireland, and, without skills and without roots, were hired on for the most part as labourers. They were at the bottom of

the social scale and, in a characterization that would never have been applied to the French Canadian, the Irish were looked upon by some as a sort of sub-human species. As canal labourers they worked — and died — in great numbers.[31] Hazards were great, especially, it seems, for the Irish. Most deaths were from one, or several species of fever, often described under the omnibus heading of "swamp fever", and possibly caused "...by the disregard they pay to their health, by living as they do, and drinking *swamp waters,* if there be none nearer their habitations...."[32] With the primitive working conditions, and the inexperience of the Irish, death by accident was also common.

> On the public works I was often extremely mortified to observe the poor, ignorant, and careless creatures, running themselves into places where they either lost their lives, or got themselves so hurt as to become useless ever after. Some of these, for instance, would take jobs of quarrying from contractors, because they thought there were good wages for this work, never thinking that they did not understand the business. Of course, many of them were blasted to pieces by their own shots, others killed by stones falling on them. I have seen heads, arms, and legs, blown about in all directions; and it is vain for overseers to warn them of their danger, for they will pay no attention.[33]

One of the major concentrations of canal labour, including Irish, was at Bytown itself, where extensive works used a large labour force.

The Irish in Bytown were at the outset almost wholly concentrated, once again courtesy of Lt.-Col. By, along the canal embankment of the eastern edge of the Upper Town. The area of shanties and caves became known as Corktown. Conditions were primitive. A contemporary description, if prejudiced as to the Irish predeliction for dissipation and dirt, conveys some sense of the conditions.

> At By-town, on the Ottawa, they burrow into the sand-hills: smoke is seen to issue out of holes which are opened to answer the purpose of chimneys. Here families contrive to pig together worse even than in Ireland; and when any rows or such like things are going on, the women are seen to pop their carroty polls out of the humble doors, so dirty, sotty, smoke-dried, and ugly, that really one cannot but be disgusted; and do what we will for their benefit, we can obtain no alteration-...they will smoke, drink, eat murphies, brawl, box, and set the house on fire about their ears, even though you had a sentinel standing over with fixed gun and bayonet to prevent them.[34]

When the canal was completed, the Irish in Corktown were dis-

Upper Town from the west end of Wellington Street looking toward Barracks Hill. It was here that the Anglo-Protestant gentry established their community. Thomas Burrowes' sketch of 1845 indicates the many substantial homes built in the the Upper Town, especially on the freehold land of Nicholas Sparks, to the right of the road.

Lower Bytown looking north from the east bank of the Rideau Canal. In 1845, when Thomas Burrowes made this sketch, Bytown's population and most of its commercial activity were concentrated in the Lower Town. The latter's location adjacent to the canal and its "Lay By" or turning basin (centre left) were important reasons for its commercial pre-eminence. Barracks Hill, on the horizon to the left, divided the Upper and Lower towns.

placed from the canal embankment. While numbers of them appeared to have departed Bytown, others moved their residences to the Lower Town, where French Canadians, many associated with the lumber trade, had already established themselves. The Irish also sought alternative employment. It could, in the main, be found in the woods and on the rafts where the French were well-entrenched. The brawling, and what has been characterized as "recreational violence", endemic in Bytown from its inception, was given a new economic dimension on completion of the canal, and what might be described as a proletarian war, disorganized and episodic at first, began to emerge. It assumed a more organized form from 1835 upon finding a leader: Peter Aylen, "run-away sailor, timber king, ambitious schemer."[35] He gave the Irish both organization and purpose: "...to drive the French Canadians off the river and thus guarantee jobs and high wages in the timber camps to the Irish."[36] The episodes of violence, mutilation, revenge, jail-breaking and outright assassination came to be called the "Shiners' War", Shiner being a colloquial name of uncertain origin for the shanty Irish roughs.[37]

The "war" was given much point during the depression of those years. Initially, the French Canadians were the premier target of the Shiners, who had a good deal of permanent success in displacing them on the rafts of the Ottawa. But the outrages spread. Lumberers had their operations disrupted by the assaults of the Irish, the commercial businesses in the Lower Town were the scene of much disorder, and the gentility in Upper Town fell victim to Aylen and the Irish, who assaulted their institutions, such as the Bathurst Agricultural Association, as well as their persons. G.W. Baker, a Bytown magistrate, in a plea to the authorities to the south, wrote:

> I cannot Sir describe to you the situation of the town. If I could, you would deem it incredible and it is becoming daily, worse....No person whatever can move by day without insult, or at night without risk of life — thus whole families of unoffending people are obliged to abandon the Town, and nothing, except a Military Patrol will succeed in arresting the evil, and dissipating the general alarm....I have not moved without Arms since the 14th May....[38]

By the winter of 1837-1838, the respectable element of Bytown organized, and with some assistance from the military, succeeded in bringing the Shiners under control. The Shiners' leader, Peter Aylen, perhaps seeing the inevitable, decamped Bytown for Aylmer, a few miles up the Ottawa on the Lower Canadian side. There he flourished as a lumberer and one of the leading citizens. His followers subsided.

There were clearly many reasons for the Shiners' War, but probably at bottom were economic imperatives. The Irish, with the end of canal work, needed jobs. As the group at the lowest end of the social order, they had nothing to lose in the brawling offensive that was part of their received tradition. They certainly had little vested interest in maintaining the contours of respectable behaviour. Equally, the nature of the frontier, with its legacy of violence, confirmed the pattern of the "War". Merchants were often tolerant of riotous raftsmen. And certainly the role of Peter Aylen was critical. But perhaps what opened the door was the fragmented and competitive nature of the town itself. The *élites,* already warring among themselves, were incapable of dealing with any organized force within it.

The Shiners were defeated, but the animosities remained, among the *élites* and among the lower classes. They were to be mitigated by the prosperity of the early 'forties, but burst out again the latter part of the decade. The legacy of bitterness remained and the social cleavage became permanent. Bytown's member of the provincial assembly, Stewart Derbishire, though a man of the Tory Upper Town, warned of the consequences as early as 1841:

> I do not desire to see the Irish if put upon a fair equality strive for an ascendancy; but I doubt not it will be attempted & most likely obtained if the Scotch do not speedily come to terms and abandon their nationality & dislike & sometimes persecution of the Irish. Throughout the country the Irish have behaved well in the elections & they want much more for them, & are entitled to it. The sort of opposition offered at Bytown by the Scotch cannot be expected to procure any exaggerated favor to them.[39]

The Scotch, as well as many other groups, remained intransigent. The town remained differentiated. Its "mixed population", there from the beginning, crystallized.

THE URBAN LANDSCAPE

Physical division in first-generation Bytown paralleled the social. It was marked most prominently by the canal right-of-way and the "Barracks Hill Bulge". The other remarkable characteristic of the first generation were the tawdry buildings on the urban landscape. Only those built by Ordnance and some in Upper Town were of any permanent quality, and of these only the Ordnance commissariat remains. Division and impermanence are not atypical of an urban frontier, but in Bytown, the power of the landlords — and one in particular — did much to create both.

There were, as previously mentioned, only three landowners on the original 800-acre townsite: Nicholas Sparks in the southwest part of the townsite; Louis T. Besserer in the southeast; and British Ordnance over the entire northern half.[40] Around the townsite was a girdle of monopoly landlords: Thomas McKay in New Edinburgh to the east; the By Estate to the south; the LeBreton/Sherwood holding to the west; and the Wright family across the river to the north. Both the Wrights and McKay were able to develop small family towns, based on agriculture and on hydraulic milling, and both were early centres of competition for Bytown. Besserer's land, the By Estate, and the LeBreton/Sherwood properties remained largely undeveloped in the first generation. The landscape of the early town was chiefly to be moulded by British Ordnance and Sparks.

Development in Bytown did not spread out or radiate from a centre of activity, but rather as a sort of tug-of-war between two highly polarized communities. The town developed in spite of its grid plan, not in comformity with it. In a curious way it flowed around the square corners of the streets and spread out like some sort of distorted magnetic force. One of the poles of development was Upper Town, embracing an isolated corner of the Ordnance lands, and the western holdings of Nicholas Sparks; the other was Lower Town, owned entirely by Ordnance.

Sparks was an Irish *emigré* of uncommonly good luck, but one who knew how to cultivate fortune's favour. In 1821, while working as a labourer for the Wrights, Sparks had the opportunity to buy some 200 acres across the river, and, in local legend, did so for £95, sight unseen. He is reputed to have wept when he actually saw the property: isolated, rocky, and covered with hemlock forest and beaver ponds. All the same, he occupied the small house of the former owner and set about making a hard-scrabble frontier living, until, of course, Dalhousie and By determined that the Rideau Canal would run through the eastern end of Sparks' land, and a townsite for "half-pay officers and the better class of people"[41] would abut the western section.

Sparks proved, from the outset, to be an enthusiastic developer, and exerted every effort to make his part of Bytown its commercial, residential, and market-centre. He provided, from the beginning, a canal right-of-way and part of the Wellington Street road allowance. He presented sites in the western part of his lands to both the Anglican and Presbyterian churches. He provided a market site there, as an inducement to both commercial and residential activity. In the eastern part of his lands, he provided not only a second market location — which he ultimately turned over as a city hall site — but a site for the jail and courthouse. And he busily subdivided and cut roads.

Sparks profited not only from the land sales, but from an elevation in status. He was, by his death in 1862, accepted as one of the Ottawa gentry, and known as a man who had endowed his community with land for its important institutions, and who had held a number of distinguished local offices, including that of alderman. Sparks' hopes for his land, despite his energy as a developer, were only partially realized. He was unable, in his lifetime, to make his Upper Town lands the centre of commercial development. In part, this was due to the more advantageous position of Lower Town for commercial purposes.

In Bytown's first generation, the most powerful pole of development was in Lower Town, by virtue of its location at the intersection of canal, river, and land commerce. In an indirect and convoluted fashion, its main streets, Rideau and Sussex, tied it into the major portage roads, waterways, and tracks to the farming communities. They were thus able to focus much of the commercial activity of the area on Lower Town. Bytown did not so much have a crossroads, as it had a corner, where Rideau joined Sussex, and the canal.

By's plan for Lower Town — based on the sixty-six foot "surveyor's chain" — supported the area's commercial orientation. The design was clearly functional, and intended for marketing and other commercial services. It was the nineteenth-century version of a shopping mall: the stores faced outward to the wide, abutting streets that provided "parking"; restricted access for supplies and the like was provided from the laneway to the rear. The Colonel reinforced this commercial intent by establishing the first market-square in the area. It was made permanent in 1847, after the town acquired a site nearby.

But if the plan encouraged commercial activity, Ordnance leasing practices discouraged construction. Few permanent buildings went

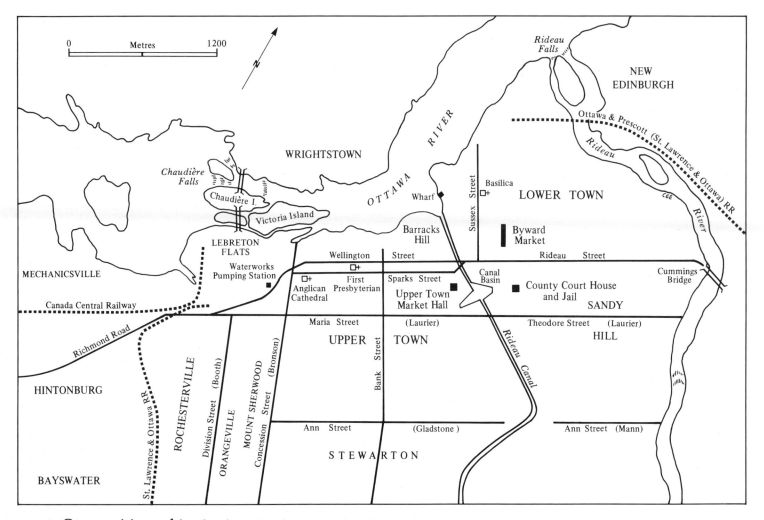

2 Communities and institutions: By the 1870s, four communities had emerged in the city: Lower Town, Upper Town, Sandy Hill, and LeBreton Flats. Each had a distinctive economic role, and a distinctive racial, religious, and political character. Two other communities that remained distinct and separate were Wrightstown (Hull) and Thomas McKay's New Edinburgh.

The degree to which Upper Town was isolated from the centre of the city is indicated in this 1857 photograph, taken from Barracks Hill, looking west up the Ottawa. Even more distant was the industrial community then developing around Chaudière Falls beyond the bluffs.

Looking east down the Ottawa from Barracks Hill was Lower Town, with the Rideau Canal at the bottom of this P.J. Bainbrigge sketch. The large house in the centre is likely that built on Major's Hill for the chief Ordnance officer. Again the separation created by the Ordnance reserves is evident.

up in Bytown during the first generation of growth, and those that did were either constructed by Ordnance or built on the freehold land of Nicholas Sparks. The short or insecure nature of Ordnance leasing militated against the building of substantial and permanent structures. The result was perhaps inevitable. The more substantial members of the commercial community, who identified with the town, and could afford to erect permanent buildings, did not do so. Those of a speculative bent built mostly wooden rental housing, meant only to last the term of the lease. And those who could afford no more — mainly the tradesmen of Lower Town — built their wooden, frontier-vernacular cottages on the periphery of the market area. It is the few of these, plus some speculative row-housing, that remain as the chief legacy of the first generation. The commercial structures of stone and brick all date from the 1840s, when conversion to freehold became possible.

Some sort of "radical solution" to the land mess was even recognized as necessary by Ordnance by the 1840s. But it was not an easy problem to solve. Ordnance, for one thing, was reluctant to lose the control it had exerted for a generation, and resisted even giving up the streets to the incorporated town. It, after all, "owned" them. There were also mechanical problems. What was to be done with the sublet land? What was to be done with the 140 Lower Town lots occupied by squatters? What were the terms of conversion to be? How were back rents to be collected? How much land was to be converted? "The city that is *to be* ought to be built upon a plan, & Gov't should not let all its ground out of hand until this point of where the Capital is to be is settled."[42] The other details were equally intractable. The Ordnance lands questions involved ". . . the prerogatives of the Crown, the anomalous rights of the Ordnance Department, and some personal rights even of deceased individuals being mixed up in most assured [?] confusion . . ." . . ."A seven year's sturdy grievance is not to be removed in a day."[43] Moreover, the individuals and organizations involved were testy, self-righteous, and often with much at stake.

Though its opponents characterized Ordnance as a ". . . a difficult Department to deal with, belonging to the military branch of the Government, and obdurate as all military bodies are,"[44] Ordnance did have responsibilities at Bytown for operation of the canal and for the defense of Canada. It also had built and operated the town for a generation. The control was not easy to relinquish, especially to the rising, aggressive motley of merchants from Lower Town and their roistering gangs of lumberers, or even to the abrasive Nicholas Sparks and his Upper Town allies. Ordnance was facing ambitious townsfolk, determined to establish their own control over the community.

The effect of Ordnance and private development was to offset the town permanently along two axes. Along the Rideau-Wellington axis, the sixty-six foot Ordnance grid met the sixty-foot grid of the private owners, and the streets of the one did not necessarily join the streets of the other. Along the canal, any functional union was blocked by the canal and other public usages near the headlocks. The canal right-of-way, owned by senior not local authorities, also restricted bridging activities and, by the end of the nineteenth century, the city of Ottawa had not built, nor did it own or control any of the Rideau Canal bridges. The town, taken as a whole, had a rather hour-glass shape, the bulge in the Lower Town narrowing down to the thin neck of Sapper's Bridge, over the canal, then swelling again on the Upper Town side, with the whole thing at a diagonal to the grid system. All the axial roads were compromised at both ends; they ended on water or made awkward unions with other rights-of-way. These features complicated any systematic expansion of the town. The urban landscape was of two natures, as was the urban community.

THE URBAN COMMUNITY

Much of Bytown's first generation was spent in establishing a political side to the urban community and of gaining a necessary practical autonomy. Bytown, when it first emerged in 1826, was simply a part of Nepean Township, which, in turn, was tucked away in a corner of Bathurst District (created in 1822), with Perth (from 1823) the district capital. It was therefore not only under the sway of Ordnance, but also Perth, as well as two different districts, two kinds of counties, magistrates of its own and others' communities, and a township government. It did not have its own provincial member until 1841, and as a kind of irony, the first Bytown representative, Stewart Derbishire, was a total stranger, allegedly having neither property nor residence in the town.

However, as early as 1828, the townsfolk had appointed a council "to conduct the Municipal business" and petitioned the provincial authority to legitimize it.[45] The province responded only to the extent of appointing magistrates from the town. Further demands for a separate status emerged in the Shiners' War, with the formation of the "Bytown Association for the Preservation of Public Peace." In addition to Ordnance, an early form of township government fulfilled basic local needs for such things as fence viewing and statute labour for roads.[46] Bytown, as part of Nepean Township, appears to have been first involved in 1835 or 1836, when a township meeting appointed a number of commissioners for Bytown. Regardless, it seems that the town was not too comfortable in the arrangement. It argued successfully in 1837, that only its representatives, and not those of the township, had the authority to demand statute labour from its citizens. In any event, Bytown continued to be represented among the township officers until it was incorporated in 1847, and began running its own affairs.

In addition to disentangling itself from the township was the more serious concern of getting free of Perth. The control exercised by Perth was not only aggravating, it was also inconvenient. Any legal business meant a harrowing sixty- or seventy-mile trip up the canal, or over the crude strips that passed for roads. Often, it was easier to let a debt or grievance pass than go through the arduous physical exercise of taking the matter to Perth. It also encouraged short-cuts to redress, such as main force: a few blows to make good a claim was easier. Still, the jail at Perth often contained a preponderance of Bytowners. Violence was perhaps common in early Bytown, not simply because it was a lumber frontier, but because it lacked even the most primitive means of mediating civil disputes.

From at least 1828, the citizenry of Bytown agitated for what they called a "division of the district", which occurred in statute in 1837-1838, as a more general revision of local government, and in practice in 1842. Under this legislation, parts of three older districts were carved off to create Dalhousie District, with Bytown as district capital, and the centre of a new district government. After 1850, when districts were dropped as a form of government, the name Carleton County was adopted. This was the administrative and juridical Carleton County. There was also an electoral Carleton County that had a somewhat different history and covered a somewhat different territory.

Dalhousie District brought Bytown some local government as well as the courthouse and jail. But the chief officers of the district were appointed, and many came from the surrounding rural townships. Though the preponderance of taxes came from the town, it found it difficult to get the rural representatives to provide money for the sort of improvements that an ambitious community wanted. The district council also tended to be dominated by the Anglo-Protestants from both Upper Town and the rural districts, and the Lower Town, which was the centre of mercantile activity and population growth, felt particularly left out. Incorporation was the widely accepted solution.

Efforts to incorporate were, however, repeatedly frustrated. Some objections were made by Ordnance. For one thing, Ordnance wanted the memory of Lt.-Col. By preserved in the name of the town. Residents were not that enamoured of either By or Ordnance, and some thought the name Bytown rather trivial for a place that by the 1840s was aspiring to be the capital of Canada.[47] But more serious for Ordnance was the matter of taxes and land. Ordnance wanted all its considerable property to be tax exempt. Bytowners were prepared to exempt certain parts of Ordnance property in use for the common weal, like Barracks Hill. But they distinguished between what "in reality" was "Her Majesty's Property" and "Real Estate held by the Ordnance for speculation,"[48] like the lots of Lower Town. Ordnance countered that "...it cannot be supposed that Her Majesty's Government holds landed property for purposes of speculation — the presumption being, on the contrary, that all property belonging to the Crown is held for the interest of the community at large, and it ought therefore to be wholly exempt from taxation."[49] In practical effect, half the town would be put beyond the reach of the tax collector.

The other sore point was the streets. Most of the streets in Bytown had been laid out by Ordnance and were on Ordnance land. Ordnance insisted the town council be permitted to change or alter them only with the agreement of the governor in council, the commander of the armed forces, or the Ordnance officers. Such a practice would deprive the Town "of the entire use and control of the Streets." Ordnance also wished to prohibit guaranteed access to Sappers' Bridge, the only bridge in town.

After several failures, the town in 1847 successfully pushed an incorporation bill through the provincial legislature. Ordnance was not prepared to concede. It struck back by using its influence in London, and in the autumn of 1849 the Bytown incorporation bill was disallowed. Part of the intransigence and delay may well have been spite, for as the *Packet* argued, it was to some extent a matter of manners: "...the Ordnance Officers here were not treated with due respect by the municipal authorities of this Town."[50] The incorporation legislation was nullified, as were the local elections, bylaws, and taxes. The town, in effect, ceased to be, and it went into a state of drift until the Baldwin Municipal Act was introduced and became operational in 1850. Then the entire process of building a local government was begun again.

Practical problems underlay much of the demand for local government. The town had been "labouring under countless evils in consequence of not being incorporated."[51] Chief of these were the absence of regulation, lack of protection, and inadequacy of community services. The town was "swarmed with a great number of unnecessary taverns."[52] Many were unlicensed. There was no regulation of the price and quality of market commodities, such as bread and beef. Citizens were under constant threat of fire, not only from the "decrepit condition" of the fire apparatus (run by private voluntary companies), but from "... the careless practice of running stovepipes through the roofs of houses, often not more than three or four inches from the dry shingles ...,"[53] and, as well, were threatened by "... the disorderly conduct of individuals who have disturbed the peace of the town...."[54] Community improvements in the dusty (or muddy), treeless town, were almost non-existent.

> ...the streets are blocked up with piles of wood and heaps of stone, without taking into account the heaps of obnoxious dirt thrown here and there in many public places throughout the town.[55]

There was no proper market-place and, almost every day, sleighs and wagons blocked up the Lower Town streets that served as a market. Adequate water for drinking and fire protection was at a premium, and the few wells were of questionable virtue from lack of adequate maintenance and protection. Among other things, dead dogs were dropped into them; and horses were washed beside them. Sidewalks were non-existent, and the potholes and obstacles were a menace to the limb, if not life, of a walking population. Order, too, was a serious concern.

There were few institutional devices before the 1840s to check or channel grievances, since, until 1842, both courts and jail were in Perth. Escape from authority was easy: if not across the river into Lower Canada, then into the woods. Perhaps most important, what "good" society condemned was exactly what the society of the camps and rafts encouraged. The lumberers were probably pretty much what their peers expected them to be. In their eyes, "spend-

thrift habits, and villainous and vagabond principles",[56] were marks of approbation and requisites for acceptance.

A tradition of law-breaking, or protecting lawbreakers from arrest, or even of rescuing prisoners, persisted into the 1840s.

> ...frequent breaches of the peace are committed not even at night but also in broad day, prisoners are rescued before they can be brought to Jail and fire arms discharged in the streets, this state of things are mainly to be attributed to the large number of unemployed raftsmen who have remained here in an idle state since their return from Quebec the past season and are now prowling about the Streets in groups ready for any mischief they can devise and rescuing of prisoners from the lawful authorities is to them a chief amusement and from the Sympathy of a part of the community towards those delinquents and the fear of the peaceably disposed part of the inhabitants to incur their revenge the Constabulary force are not supported and the result is that the violators of the public peace go at large unpunished.[57]

The condition of the new jail did not help. Jail windows peering from the half-basement of the Courthouse were accessible from the street, and "... the public have free access all round it to communicate with the prisoners at their cell windows and hand them liquor or implements to break jail and effect their own escape."[58]

Riots, discontent and fear in 1846 once again led to a series of petitions to the provincial government for an armed, voluntary police, to be provided at provincial expense. The executive council, though concerned with the "disgraceful outrages", the origin of which they found in "... the unhappy party difference which exists among certain classes of the Community", refused.[59] They argued that Bytown should soon be incorporated, and would then have resources of its own to deal with law and order.

At a practical level, then, the first council of 1847 could agree on much. The first order of business was order. A clerk and constables were appointed immediately. The second bylaw approved by the council was to regulate nuisances. Roads, streets, rivers, canals, and vacant and occupied lots were, for example, to be cleared of "... any Timber, Firewood, loose stones, heaps of Dirt or Gravel, dead Animals, putrid Meat or Fish, or any other Nuisance or obstruction...."[60] Violence by insult also fell under proscription: in law, at any rate, "Indecent words, figures or pictures" and the "profane oath, or other scandalous actions" were to be gone from the public places of Bytown.[61]

Local government proved capable of solving a number of practical problems, but it failed to transcend the divisions in town, or to integrate the elements of the urban community. Rather, it became their servant. Basically, politics became identified with the punctual socio-economic groups in the town. The Catholic community and many of the merchants in Lower Town became, by the 1840s, identified with Reform, perhaps due to the antipathy toward the rigid Toryism of the Upper Town, there from the outset. But Ottawa "Reform" did not turn *bleu* as did that of Canada East. Nor did it subscribe to the Canada West "Grittism" of George Brown. If anything, it was like the eastern Ontario reformism of Sandfield Macdonald. Ottawa Tories, however, seemed to align themselves more successfully with the "conservative" part of John A. Macdonald's Liberal-Conservative party.

Since each of the punctual communities of Bytown was identified with a particular territory, the struggle over ward boundaries was critical. In 1847, Tory representatives introduced the Bytown incorporation bill into a Tory legislature and, in effect, a Tory gerrymander was "foisted" on the Lower Town by the "Tory" MPP, William Stewart. In the gerrymander, the Lower Town was "...betrayed and robbed of a fair proportional representation...."[62] Upper Town was raised into a solid, undivided political block — West Ward — with three representatives for some 234 assessed householders; Lower Town was divided into two wards — North and South — with two representatives each. The total of four represented some 645 householders. The property franchise probably created some additional distortion. There was a 300-pound property qualification for office, which ruled out all but the richest as candidates: and the thirty-pound freehold and six-pound leasehold probably left many of the rentor community — most of them on Lower Town Ordnance land — without a vote. Of additional significance was the division of Lower Town into "North" Ward and "South" Ward. Catholics, Irish and French, would contend for representation in North Ward. The commercial community would be represented mostly in South Ward, possibly by a Catholic candidate, but certainly not a French one. Tory Upper Town, meanwhile, was coherent in its society and politics. Reform Lower Town was split, and pitted against itself.

"Reform" Lower Town was probably not too unhappy to see Ordnance kill the original incorporation, for in the 1850 reincorporation, Lower Town had the ear of the new "reform" govern-

Daniel O'Connor, merchant, county treasurer, and justice of the peace: one of the early residents of Bytown, whose daughter was the first child born in the town. He was an Irish Catholic who operated a store on Wellington St. in Upper Town, and only with great difficulty managed to walk a tight-rope in the divided community.

ment of Baldwin and LaFontaine. Three new wards of equal representation were established along the north-south axis. One covered Upper Town, now with only two representatives: the West Ward. A second, Centre Ward, embraced the commercial community of Lower Town, and part of the Catholic community. A third, East Ward, also in Lower Town, took in a mostly solid Catholic bloc. Qualification and franchise were reduced. And most important, those of Reform bent, largely in Lower Town, achieved preponderance in local government.

Bytown's first municipal election in 1847 was unpredicitably quiet and the Reform *Packet* preened itself on "The quietude and good order which prevailed, and which... gives the lie direct to the thousand-and-one assertions with regard to the mischievous disposition of the inhabitants."[63] But if the quietude was unpredictable, the result wasn't. Lower Town voted as a bloc and four Reformers were on council, and "...it is generally supposed, from the construction of the Council, that Mr. John Scott will be made choice of as mayor."[64] An Upper Town candidate, John B. Lewis, was first proposed, and defeated on a straight Upper and Lower Town split. Scott was then proposed, and accepted.[65] Despite the gerrymander, Reform was in control, but just barely. A Reform mayor presided over a council divided three-three. During the two years that followed, the Tories would prevail.

Any threat to the structures in the town produced political discord and even violence. The typhus-afflicted Irish of the 1847 famine migration was one such threat. More than 3,000 passed through Bytown, some staying. Apart from closing the town down in the summer of 1847, the migration locked the community in an institutional duel. The Tories, through control of the magistracy and the District Council, controlled the machinery of relief and the limited relief funds, as expressed through an *ad hoc* health board. The board, alas, had no health facilities at its disposal. These had only just been developed by the Catholic Sisters of Charity, whose small hospital and rudimentary nursing skills were the only aid for the town's small corps of doctors, who volunteered with alacrity to attend the sick. One died. Much of the actual management — including construction of a fever hospital — was handled by the Emigration Agent, George Burke, an officer of the Province of Canada. Functional responsibilities were thus fragmented along socio-economic lines, and were manifested in a series of clashes between the health board, charged with administration and funding, and other ele-

ments of the town actively engaged in prophylaxis.

The board resisted any payment to the Sisters of Charity on the grounds that their hospital was not a truly "general" and public hospital. The board quarrelled with attending doctors, implying that some had shown favouritism to certain classes of patients. And it accused the ministering priests and nuns of proselytizing among the sick Protestants. The upshot was that the board spent much of its energy generating a movement for a "Protestant" General Hospital.[66]

It was, however, the depression, two years later, that triggered the greatest of the early confrontations: the Stony Monday Riots of 1849.[67] The Riots bared the social, economic and political lineaments of the town. They were also — as an event — both the most dramatic of their kind and the last. In many ways, the Riots signalled the end of the frontier stage.

The immediate occasion of the Riots was simple enough. Lower Town Reformers and a number of moderate Tories wanted to show the town to the new Governor General, Lord Elgin, as a prospective site for a new capital for the Canadas. The Upper Town Tories did not want to indulge an obviously liberal governor general, who represented eclipse to Tory Bytown, just as he symbolized ascendency to Bytown Reform. It was Elgin, after all, who had presided over the granting of "responsible" government, and thereby removed power from the hands of the Tories and placed it in the hands of the Baldwin-LaFontaine reformers. Worse still, he was serious about it. In 1849, he took the advice of his Reform government and signed into law the Rebellion Losses Bill, which, in Tory eyes served only to compensate the French and Catholic rebels of 1837-1838 for damages incurred in rebelling. That action had triggered a riot in Montréal, one led by its Anglo-commercial community, in which Elgin was stoned and the buildings of the provincial legislature burned to the ground.

In the hungry days of 1849, with the timber trade still severely depressed, there were many sparks in the volatile Bytown community. The town was on edge. Twice the Tories, through Tory mayor Robert Hervey (a beneficiary of the Tory gerrymander of the 1847 town charter), refused to call a meeting to tender an invitation to Elgin. But two Lower Town councillors, Charles Sparrow and J.B. Turgeon, as justices of the peace, called one of their own for Monday, September 17, 1849, in the Lower Town market square. Mayor Hervey countered by calling a similar meeting, but for opposite

Lower Town looking east from Barracks Hill, about 1855. The buildings of the Roman Catholic church are in a cluster to the left, while the warehouses and stores of commercial Ottawa are seen near the canal locks to the right. Lithograph after drawing by E. Whitefield.

Upper Town looking west from Barracks Hill, about 1855. The Presbyterian (at the left) and Anglican (centre) churches are evident symbols of this Anglo-Protestant enclave. To the right, the new lumber mills of Victoria Island are seen just above the raft of squared timber at the foot of one of Chaudière's timber slides. The new suspension bridge can be seen (far right). Lithograph after drawing by E. Whitefield.

A bird's-eye view of Ottawa in the 1850s before the construction of the Parliament Buildings. Divisions made by planners and nature are clear. Lower Town is at far left, Barracks Hill at centre left, Upper Town at upper right, the new Chaudière community at lower right, and Wright's Town at lower left.
Lithograph by Sarony and Major.

purposes, for September 19, 1849, in Upper Town. High tension flowed through the crowd of 1,100 at the Monday meeting. Reform forces, mostly from Lower Town, had gathered in strength. They apprehended, quite correctly, that they would have to face the counter-demonstration from the Tories and their allies from the farms and towns of the rural county. Efforts to name the new Reform MP and former mayor, John Scott, as chairman of the meeting, were countered by attempts to substitute the incumbent mayor, John Hervey. A bellicose crowd began shoving and shouting. The endeavours of Turgeon, Scott, and others to calm the mob collapsed, along with the closely-packed platform from which the meeting was being staged. A stone flew through the air. Within moments, the two opposing camps were in full conflict.

> At once it appeared every Orangeman had a bludgeon, although concealed to then and being about one to three of the others, you may suppose they had the best of it, although some hard Bricks were given on both sides. As soon as the parties got separated a little the Stones began to fly in all directions in a perfect hurricane. Then commenced the discharge of firearms, and in a few minutes more it was a regular pitched battle the parties standing at a distance and taking deliberate aim and firing at each other, which was kept up for ten or fifteen minutes....[68]

With the Upper Town and Orange forces in control of the terrain, the Tories assumed control of the meeting, called Dr. Hamnett Hill to the chair, and, far from inviting Lord Elgin to Ottawa, passed a resolution condemning the Reform government. Finally, Hervey called in a detachment of the Canadian Rifles from Barracks Hill. They were led into the fray by the mayor, who directed both the dispersal of the rioters and the arrests that followed. Everyone apprehended was a Reformer, including John Scott, MP. When it was over, one man was dead and thirty wounded.

Neither side wasted time preparing for the scheduled Wednesday rematch. Reinforcements were called in by both parties. The Reformers allegedly obtained three small cannon, sixty rifles (with bayonets), and 260 small-arms stored in the Wright armoury. Efforts to obtain more were thwarted by Ordnance troops. Some 1,000 Reformers gathered in Lower Town. Facing them, across the canal and up the hill were some 1,700 Tory supporters, allegedly with 1,000 small-arms and nine cannon. Between them, on Sappers' Bridge, stood fifty soldiers, supported by some artillery, sited on Barracks Hill, and trained on the crowds. In Lower Town there were

the Reformers, with more "...Muskets and Bayonets than all the soldiers, and fierce resolute devils they were and chafing like chained tigers to get at their enemies."[69] And in the Upper Town were the country residents who "...attempted at the beck of unscrupulous leaders in Town, who are in a minority in the Town, to walk upon their fellow-subjects — to stifle free discussion, and to commit crimes disgraceful to a free or Christian people."[70]

Level heads eventually prevailed, persuading Mayor Hervey to "disperse the meeting which he had called." The leaders of the two groups then quieted the crowds and sent them home. Special constables were appointed to patrol the uneasy town, and more arrests were made. Inquests, indictments, and trials followed, and though most of those brought to court were acquitted, a reservoir of bitterness remained. Bytown's potential as a capital was thrown even further into question. Elgin waited until 1854 to visit the town.

These harsh, early years had roughed out the contours of Ottawa, its social and political, as well as its physical shape. Some rough edges would be smoothed, but in the long term the town proved remarkably resistant to the impact, not only of new industry and government, but even to the great secular changes of nineteenth-century industrialization and twentieth-century corporate enterprise. Ideas of race, religion, and politics, deeply embedded in the community, would prove the master of economic opportunity, of change, and of municipal ambition. The original fragmentation would persist.

View of Ottawa before construction of the Parliament Buildings. The Lower Town and undeveloped Sandy Hill are seen looking southwest over Barracks Hill, still the site of military barracks.

Chapter Two

A City Emerges
(1850–1867)

INTRODUCTION

The 1850s and 1860s were the crucial decades in Ottawa's history. Economic foundations, resting on the sawn lumber industry and government, were established in the period, but metropolitan ones, resting on the Ottawa-Lake Huron canal and trunk railways, were shattered. Demographic and social contours were settled and began to harden; political autonomy was won and political cleavages established. Bytown was transformed into Ottawa in 1855, in metaphor as well as in fact.

The Union Act of 1841 had moved Bytown from the periphery of two provinces to the centre of one. In Union, the wild lumber town could claim centrality, and, when the time came in the 1850s to choose a capital for the Canadas, it was a powerful rationale. A claim of centrality could not always be made good, however, and was even delusive. Such was the case with Ottawa's metropolitan ambitions, as expressed in its railway ventures. The town's entrepreneurs — in a vision perhaps greater than reality would dictate — saw the city, as capital of "Central Canada", at the crossroads of a North American transportation system. This vision would be partially realized and then would dissolve. The argument of centrality, so powerful in the choice of the capital, proved vulnerable in the harsh world of economic self-interest.

The new economic forces brought with them much growth, much prosperity, and many new people. But they did little to alter the social and political contours, set, as if in stone, in the first generation. Lumber, railways, and government proved to have minimal corrosive powers, though the rough and casual violence of the first decades was articulated more through the political system or turned inward in a kind of cultural exclusiveness.

Like many Canadian cities in the period, Bytown also grappled with the opportunities and problems of local autonomy. It received its first, permanent charter in 1850, and in 1855 became a city called Ottawa. With city status, Ottawa at last shook itself free of the county, and the residue of the magistracy. It was master, for the first time, of its destiny.

ECONOMIC DEVELOPMENT AND METROPOLITAN GROWTH

A sawn timber industry began in 1848; the capital role was won in 1857. Their acquisition reignited ambitions to establish Ottawa as "...the center and regulator of the mighty reciprocal exchange between the West and the East."[1] Ottawa was "...destined by nature, and in the opinion of all competent judges, to be metropolitan."[2] The Ottawa-Huron ship canal was a centrepiece once again. And once again collapsed. But the same dream — of the same continental proportions — was again articulated through the medium of the steam railway.

Railways, as well as canals, Bytowners argued, would have to respond to the logic of the Ottawa. In 1851, Montrealers were told that they:

> ...must lay their main line through the valley of the Ottawa. That river forms the backbone of Canada, and must eventually be its great commercial thoroughfare. Before another generation has taken the place of the present one, the Ottawa country will number its population by the hundreds of thousands, — nor is the day far distant when a communication between it and the shores of Lake Huron will be effected that will relieve the St. Lawrence of the Western trade....[3]

Bytowners saw themselves as being at the crossroads of a great trunk rail system. One arm would link the Atlantic, via Montréal and Bytown, to Toronto and the communities of Lake Ontario and

Cribs of timber being assembled into rafts at the bottom of a Chaudière slide. Barracks Hill, Major's Hill, and the steamboat wharf can be seen in this rare 1857 photograph.

Lake Erie. The other arm would link Lake Huron (and beyond it, the Sault and the interior of the continent), via Ottawa, to the American transportation systems and markets to the south. Ottawa was to be the centre of both an "Imperial" and a "North American" rail system. The valley would contribute its own share from its timber resource; the city would dominate the forwarding and trans-shipment function; and the railway would open the valley's "valuable" agricultural lands.

Such railway ambitions were perhaps megalomaniacal for a town of 10,000, only incorporated as a city in 1855, and it is not surprising that,in time, each branch of the scheme was systematically sawed off by opposing factions. And, in the case of the only railway actually built, by the efforts and actions of Ottawans themselves.

Much of Ottawa's future as a rail junction — and its failure as a metropolis — was determined in Montréal, where by 1850 three schemes were emerging for a grand trunk system.[4] One, via the Montréal and Bytown Railway, included Bytown. This was the so-called "northern" route. But a Montréal scheme — employing the "southern" route — was the one finally realized. It struck directly up the St. Lawrence from Montréal, bypassing Ottawa altogether.

Despite this turn of events, there was still the second string to the Ottawa bow, a purely "North American" system, joining Lake Huron and the interior of the continent, via the Bytown and Pembroke, to the American market, via the Bytown and Prescott. The western branch of this scheme was broken by the pre-emptive march of Brockville, which made the first rail penetration into Ottawa's timber hinterland. Within a few years, all that was left of the glorious ambitions of the 1850s was the city's first railway, the Bytown and Prescott. It was possibly misconceived from the start, but the *coup de grace* was administered by the town itself.

The promoters of the Bytown and Prescott scheme recognized a potential relationship between railways and an emerging American market for the sawn timber of the valley. It was, in fact, the local men who first shipped boards to the American market who also promoted the first railway: Thomas McKay, of New Edinburgh, and his partner and son-in-law, John McKinnon. From the outset, it was predicated on a flow of lumber out to the American market, with a reciprocal return of American supplies. In effect, the future of the railway depended upon its capacity to compete with the river.

The prospect, given the initially high rates for water transportation, was perhaps not unrealistic.[5] For the town, itself, the prosecution of the railway seemed imperative, not only as a prospective part of a trunk scheme, but essential if it were to compete at all as a site for the capital of the Canadas.

Progress on the Bytown and Prescott was slow, but by the autumn of 1850, a provisional committee on the railway had been formed, headed by McKinnon, as chairman, and Robert Bell, as secretary. Bell was a surveyor, editor of the *Packet* — which became the railway's most ardent advocate — and the business associate of McKay. By 1851, Bell was also on city council as one of three representatives of East Ward, in the Lower Town, which conveniently embraced some of McKay and McKinnon's mill properties. Bell was also among the six "Reform" members, all from the two wards east of the canal. The railway was a creature not only of monopoly lumber millers, but also of the Reform political interests of the Lower Town against "...the pauper Punch and Judy Squireality that live by their wits and at other peoples' cost,"[6] in Upper Town.

It was the "Reform" council of 1850-1855, of which Bell was a central figure, that subscribed for £15,000 of Bytown and Prescott stock and in 1852-1853 guaranteed a £50,000 loan for the line.[7] It was also this council that approved a site for the railway terminal and used its good offices to obtain the necessary land. The recommended site was in the northeastern section of Lower Town, the line passing through McKay's extensive Gloucester township properties, his New Edinburgh townsite, and his millsites on both sides of the Rideau Falls. The railway would also pass through Lower Town, represented by the majority Reform interest on the town council. The first train, pulled by "The Oxford", reached New Edinburgh on Christmas Day, 1854. The following summer the Rideau River was bridged and the rail line brought into Ottawa. It was already in trouble.

By 1853 the rapidly developing sawmill industry at Chaudière had eclipsed the one at Rideau Falls. The Chaudière section of the town had become the logical terminus for a lumber railway. Most important, freight rates for large volumes of barged lumber had dropped from about $6 to $3 per 1,000 board feet. The railway could no longer compete with the river as a transportation route.[8] As well, by 1855 depression had begun in the wake of inflation and, in the same year, Tories took control of the council. By October of 1855 they were pressing the railway for the interest on the loan the town had guaranteed.[9]

For seven years, largely due to the efforts of Bell, the railway gamely hung on from crisis to crisis, including an attempt in 1863 by a group of Upper Town luminaries to take over the railway by main force.[10] The militia was called in to restore order. But as the railway slowly sunk into insolvency, so too did the city, the legacy of its 1850s optimism.[11] In 1864 an angry and virtually bankrupt city[12] refused to guarantee additional aid to the railway under the terms of a provincial relief bill. The action finished the railway as a local venture. Under somewhat mysterious circumstances, the Grand Trunk Railway (GTR) forced sale of the rolling stock at a sheriff's auction, and the Bytown and Prescott became a feeder of the GTR. Symbolically, the name was changed to the St. Lawrence and Ottawa. The last leg of an independent system was sawed off, and the railway was now firmly attached to Montréal.

Perhaps nothing could have saved the Bytown and Prescott, but the group that finally drove it into the waiting arms of the GTR was a most unlikely one: the dominant commercial and industrial interests in Ottawa itself.

Ottawa's precarious financial position in the early 1860s, only in part a result of its involvement with railways, gave rise in 1863 to the Municipal Reform Association of Ottawa. They claimed that whereas

> ...in consequence of gross mismanagement of the municipal affairs of this city, for some years past, a large outlay has unnecessarily and wastefully been made and large debt created, involving the necessity of imposing an amount of taxation found to be most burthensome to the ratepayers, prejudicial to trade, detrimental to the value of property and destructive to the general interests of the city.[13]

The membership of the MRAO coincided in large part with the three most powerful interests in the town: the Board of Trade, representing the "fixed" commercial community, the Ottawa Board of Lumber Manufacturers, representing the "itinerant" lumberers, and some newcomers, the Chaudière lumberers, in what was perhaps their first initiative with the other business *élites* of the city.[14] Their candidates, headed by Moss Kent Dickinson, a prominent Ottawa and Rideau River forwarder, as mayor, placed strongly in the local elections of January, 1864. It was this group, opposed mainly by Lower Town members of council, that refused to

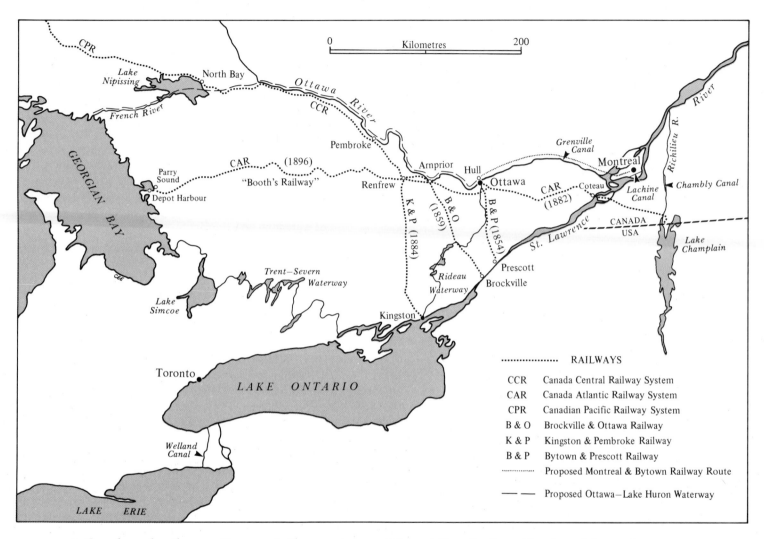

3 Canals and railways: Ottawans' efforts to create a "Central Canadian" corridor from Montreal to Georgian Bay were rooted in the east-west thrust of the geography. But the richer St. Lawrence corridor prevailed, either through control of valley schemes or by competition with them.

OTTAWA AND PRESCOTT

RAILWAY.

JOSEPH MOONEY, *Secretary & Treasurer.*

ROBERT BELL, *President.*   B. FRENCH, *Superintendent.*

TWO PASSENGER TRAINS DAILY EACH WAY,

Leaving Ottawa at 7 A.M. and 1.30 P.M., connecting at JUNCTION with the GRAND TRUNK RAILWAY Trains going East and West, and at PRESCOTT with the

Royal Mail and American Line of Steamers,

FOR ALL PORTS EAST AND WEST;

Also, with the N. O. R. R. and R. W. & O. R. Trains leaving Ogdensburgh

FOR

NEW YORK AND BOSTON.

RETURNING:

Will leave PRESCOTT at 6.45 A.M. and 1.30 P.M., on arrival of all connecting Lines, and arrive in OTTAWA at 10.15 A.M. and 4 P.M., connecting with Steamers for Ports on the Upper and Lower Ottawa River.

An 1864 city directory advertisment for the Ottawa and Prescott railway. The railway would soon fall into other hands, be renamed the St. Lawrence and Ottawa, and become part of the Grand Trunk system.

respond to the pleas of the Ottawa and Prescott, and it was Mayor Dickinson who negotiated the final deal with the GTR.

None of them had a clear vested interest in the railway. The lumberers and Mayor Dickinson were all river men and when they did use the railway, they found it inadequate, as did the Bronson company in 1860,

> ...having had trouble enough with the RR officials to satisfy us for life if no other way of Shipping Lumber will do we choose to be excused from shipping at all...the matter of shipping this small amount of lumber to you has been a whole winter long annoyance an incorrigable [ibid] set of heedless drones the whole pack....[15]

As well, the railway traversed no section of the country in which the lumberers were particularly interested. For the Chaudière lumberers, and the Upper Town Tories, the terminus was at the wrong end of the city.

While metropolitan dreams centering on transportation went afleeting, a hard reality, the sawn timber industry, began in the 1850s to develop as the lynch pin of the city's economy. This industry, created for an American market, seems to have been the brainchild of the ambitious and able Thomas McKay. Sawn lumber from his Rideau Falls mills was likely the first produced at Bytown for the American market. The chief motivation for dealing with the Americans,was, it appears, low prices on the British side. The immediate problem was transportation.

> ...the manufacturers of Deals in this neighborhood have determined on shipping their stuff for the New York market: the latter enterprise we must look upon as an experiment, as the expense attendant on transport by the present circuitous route must be very heavy — the hopelessness of obtaining remunerative prices in Quebec will alone account for the fact of parties hazarding the *adventure*.[16]

McKay and McKinnon, with a new mill of forty saws and a daily capacity of 40,000 feet, hazarded the adventure in 1848, a venture deemed so risky "...that none of our Forwarders would entertain the proposal for carrying lumber...until Mr. McKinnon...succeeded in opening up this new branch of the trade of Bytown by employing American vessels."[17]

The first season was a losing one. But in 1849 the New Edinburgh mills shipped 2.4 million feet, again by American vessels. Once it became clear that the American market was likely to be a profitable one, other mill sites were sought. One of the largest in the Ottawa

Robert Bell, politician, newspaper editor, and promoter of the Ottawa and Prescott railway. Photo by Topley, 1851.

Valley was, fortunately for Bytown, mostly within its town limits: Chaudière Falls.

Some efforts had been made from the earliest days to exploit Chaudière, most notably by the Wrights in Hull. But on the Ottawa side the efforts were small in scale and confined to the mainland. Most were apparently grist mills. The first major lumber operator at Chaudière was probably Captain Levi Young, originally from Maine, and a sometime operator of boats on the Lake Champlain-Ottawa waterway. In 1851, he built a sawmill on the mainland at Chaudière, and there began making lumber for the American mills on Lake Champlain. Shortly afterwards, O.H. Ingram and A.H. Baldwin established mills close by. But the greatest potential sites of hydraulic power were offshore, on islands adjacent to the crashing falls. They were in the hands of the Crown and stood unused.

The reasons are not clear, but possibly there were no entrepreneurs capable of meeting the technological, and capital demands of such a massive source of power. There was also, for such large-scale production, no assurance of a market, and, perhaps even more critical, no certainty of an assured and regular supply of logs. The first of the entrepreneurs to investigate the potential of the islands arrived in Bytown in 1852. He was Capt. J.J. Harris, a principal of a firm operating in Lake George, a southward extension of Lake Champlain. The mayor of the day, R.W. Scott, recounted in his memoirs that a public dinner was tendered for Harris and he was given "...assurances of good will if he and his friends decided to make the venture."[18]

Subsequent events are somewhat murky. Scott, Horace Merrill, the provincial officer "in charge of improvements at Chaudière", and some others, appear to have importuned the Commissioner of Crown Lands to sell the hydraulic and building lots on the islands, and to lease the water power of the channels flowing by them. The chief agent in this matter seems to have been lumber magnate, John Egan. The beneficiaries of the lots were certainly grateful to Egan for something. In October, 1853, a "splendid carriage" was presented to Egan "...by several American gentlemen, who are engaged in erecting large sawmills at the Chaudière."[19]

At any rate, the basic improvements to the hydraulic sites were built by the Province of Canada as "...it would not be practical to have them properly constructed by the joint instrumentality of the several parties purchasing lots."[20] Costs would be recouped through the sales of lots and lease of power. A pattern of joint provincial and

John Egan of Aylmer, top left, a power in the squared timber trade and the politics of the Valley, was instrumental in organizing the Ottawa Valley Lumber Association in 1836.

(Sir) Richard W. Scott, top right. As mayor, MPP, and senator, Scott was prominent as the Ottawa representative of both Roman Catholics and the timber barons. Best known for his temperance legislation (the "Scott Act"), he wooed and married the daughter of touring entertainers in a celebrated romance. Portrait by G. T. Berthon, c. 1872, after a photograph.

Henry F. Bronson, bottom left, a partner in the firm of Harris and Bronson, was one of the first to saw lumber from mills on the Chaudière Islands. H. Ball & Sons photo dated c. 1879.

Ezra Butler Eddy, of Burlington, Vermont, arrived in 1854 at the Chaudière where he manufactured matches, wooden pails, clothespins, and bowls. He later became one of the major figures in sawn lumber and pulping. Photo dated c. 1905.

private sector collaboration at Chaudière was thus asserted. Government and private interests would be interlocked at Chaudière, but the great identification could be with the Canadian government, which regulated as well as improved the hydraulic sites. The city, from the start, was a bystander to the lumber industry situated within its boundaries. On September 1, 1852, the auction for the lots of Victoria and Amelia Islands was held at Bytown. Scott, as good as his word, and despite newspaper advertising as far as Boston, saw the hydraulic lots go at one shilling above the £50 upset price to Harris, Bronson and Co., and to Perley and Pattee, both lumber operators in the Lake Champlain/Lake George areas.[21] With Levi Young and the others on the mainland, the "American Colony" established itself at Chaudière.

Within months, the two firms had begun construction on Victoria Island. The mills of Harris and Bronson were reported to have a capacity of 100,000 logs annually. On the mainland, Blasdell, Currier and Co. had added a 40,000 log mill and attached foundry, to the existing establishments, and by 1853 Philip Thompson had a sawmill with a 40,000 log capacity under construction on Chaudière Island, with attached flour and oatmeal mills, a carding and cloth dressing mill, and woollen factory. By 1853 a great future for the town was predicted, as a result of their efforts: "So much improvement in a single summer is calculated to shew the pith there is in Bytown, and its fitness to become an important commercial and manufacturing city . . . ."[22]

Some rapid shifts in ownership occurred to make the location even more thoroughly "American". Blasdell gave up on milling and returned to his smithy and foundry works. His partner, Currier, in 1853 joined Moss Kent Dickinson, the "King of the Rideau", in renting and operating McKay's mills at Rideau Falls. The American entrepreneur, A.H. Baldwin, took over the Chaudière mills of Blasdell and Currier. Their timber limits on the Gatineau River went to the Gilmour interests. In 1854, E.B. Eddy launched a cottage industry in match-making at Chaudière, where he rented the upper floor of the old Wright smithy. He was to expand rapidly in sawmilling and wood-related manufacturing, and soon reached the first rank of the lumber manufacturers. Somewhat later, the man who would become the greatest of the Chaudière lumberers, J.R. Booth — a Canadian — arrived at Chaudière, where he rented a sawmill near the Thompson gristmill, and for a few years produced laths from sawmill scraps. Booth seems to have made a first big coup in 1857 when John Egan died, and he acquired the bulk of the Egan limits, among the largest in the Valley. Booth now had his supply. Two years later, in 1859, he secured the contract for much of the lumber for the Ottawa Parliament Buildings.

The Chaudière group, however, for many years was a fairly closed oligarchy that remained apart from both the town and the other lumberers who had preceded them to the valley. They cooperated among themselves for the transportation of supplies upriver and of the logs going down.[23] None were charter members of the Ottawa Board of Lumber Manufacturers. For two decades they belonged to little else either. They were not among the petitioners for any of the city's early railways,[24] its horse-car line, gas company, or telegraph company. None had a share in the Bank of Ottawa, the so-called lumbermen's bank,[25] nor any other Canadian bank for that matter.[26] They were not among the 1865 charter members of the Rideau Club, a veritable litmus test of Ottawa society, though many of the "itinerant" lumbermen were.[27] They did much of their business in the United States, often with companies in which they maintained an interest. They sold their lumber there, bought supplies there, and, in large measure, discounted their money there.[28] They seem to have used Montréal forwarders or their own fleets to ship lumber.[29] There seems to have been little sense in the early period that their commercial destiny was bound up with that of the city. The fact that Ottawa embraced the Chaudière hydraulic site was mere chance. Nevertheless, they were important to the town, and seemed to have had dealings with practically every member of the "fixed" commercial community. But it was extensive, not intensive, and all on a small scale.[30]

By the end of the decade, spurred by the Reciprocity Treaty, the Ottawa mills were producing more than twenty million board-feet of lumber. Output doubled by the early 1860s despite the American civil war, and in 1868 reached 100 million board-feet. By 1871, some 1,200 saws were cutting logs, and production had passed 200 million board-feet, with the production of the Rideau Falls and Hull mills included.

The lumber mills were for the most part at Ottawa, but, typical of the Ottawa disease, were not of it. The important relationship of Chaudière was with the provincial government before 1867, and both the provincial and federal authorities, depending on what was at stake, after 1867.[31] The city's role was mainly irrelevant. Distribution remained the central activity of the city, with few goods coming

John R. Booth (centre) was one of the later arrivals at Chaudière, but grew to be one of the giants. He was known as the "Chaudière Carnegie." Here he inspects one of the last loads of white pine from his Madawaska limits. His son, C. Jackson Booth, is at left.

from Ottawa itself. The technology of the mills was American, and perhaps that dictated a traditional source. But even such an obvious import substitution as saw-sharpening, was carried on outside the city, and even wagons were imported in 1857:"...we know of no place under Heaven where they need good wagons more than they do here."[32]

Whatever the reason, import substitution was limited in Ottawa, as was diversification. Apart from Eddy, and a few others, little happened in the way of a wood products industry. Rather, there seemed to be an intensification of specialization, limited largely to the production of rough-sawn boards for the American market. The grist and other mills started at Chaudière by men like Thompson were for the most part converted to the sawing of logs. Lumber seemed to militate against the development of the city as an *entrepôt*, and as a place of secondary manufactures.

By the time a "standard saw log" reached Chaudière it had cost about $1 to extract it. In 1861 some 200,000 logs went through the mills. By the time the log was out the other side, now a rough-sawn product, it had about doubled in value. Labour costs would account for about one-third of the value added. That would stay in the city. But capital gains seemingly did not. Here, too, was a critical area of non-development. Such capital accumulation as did occur as a result of the lumber manufacturing business, did not appear to accumulate in Ottawa.

While there is no question that the sawn lumber industry was of enormous benefit to the economy of Ottawa, it may well have imposed structural strains that in the long run were crippling. The Chaudière lumberers in some respects, especially in the early years, represented yet another of the competing fragments of which the city was composed. And the nature of their trade was such — or their personal propensities were such — that the sawing of logs into rough boards, without much effort at diversifying, was their more or less single-minded pursuit. The upshot was a rather one-dimensional industry.

Diversification of the Ottawa economy would depend, as it turned out, not on the lumber industry, but on political serendipity: the city, on the last day of 1857, was announced as the capital of the Province of Canada, an announcement confirmed by the assembly later in 1858.

A turn-of-the-century observer of Ottawa remarked that

... it is quite open to question whether, had it not been made the Seat of

Government, it would have ... been more than an important lumbering centre, and a distributing centre for the surrounding district, of the staple articles of retail commerce.[33]

He was probably right. But there seemed no question in the minds of Bytown boosters, at least as early as 1840, when the Union of the Canadas was clearly going to be effected, "... that Bytown, or Sydenham, might be the seat of the Legislature & *I really cannot see what is to prevent it someday* — it is so obviously the place for the choice, possessing every requisite."[34] It was a while coming.

The capital was first placed at Kingston, "half built up and half burned down", but ... the strong political opposition to the Gov't of the Orange & Compact-ridden inhabitants of this town has lost it every chance. The present Council will go into retirement for ever rather than *live* in Kingston."[35]

A shift was made in 1843 to Montréal "better for Bytown & the Ottawa than Kingston",[36] but still not the capital. Montréal, however, put itself out of contention as capital in 1849, with the rebellion losses riots. But the Assembly, in its widsom, determined on a capital that would perambulate between Québec City and Toronto. This system proved unsatisfactory, and in the early 1850s agitation began for a "fixed" site. That point of principle settled, the next question was where?

Initially, the provincial assembly attempted to arrive at a consensus, but only managed to achieve deadlock. It was a deadlock that threatened the precarious majority of the Macdonald-Cartier coalition. Macdonald prevailed upon the assembly to submit the choice of the capital to Queen Victoria. That did not mean, in any real sense, that the choice was the Queen's. The "Queen's Choice" meant in simple terms that the choice of capital would be made by the executive branch of government, not the legislative branch. Democracy had rarely favoured population-poor Ottawa; decisions of the executive branch had generally proven more favourable.

Ottawa was a central location, both in terms of the Union of the Canadas, and any fancied expansion to the North West. It was the capital, as it proclaimed, of "Central Canada". In 1854 it was also a small grubby, riot-ridden frontier town, with an unprepossessing name (Bytown), but it did have a magnificent site for government buildings (Barracks Hill) that was owned by the Crown, and by 1855 it had both water and rail transportation to the populated areas of the Province. It was thought to be defensible in the event of American invasion. In 1855 it had achieved city status and a more presenta-

Chaudière Falls, looking upstream, 1866. Some notion of the size of the falls is given in relation to mill buildings at upper left.

Loading barges at Chaudière Island, about 1872. Most would head downriver for the American market. Through the summer months the activity would be unceasing. The suspension bridge, 1844, designed by T.C. Keefer, is in the background.

Architects, superintendent and draughtsman of the first Parliament Buildings, about 1860. Photo taken at Temporary Office in the old Barracks.

A rather idealized depiction of the lumberers' regatta, 1860, which was part of the reception for the Prince of Wales. The Prince came to Ottawa to lay the cornerstone of the Centre Block of the new Parliament Buildings. Engraving after drawing by G. H. Andrews, for The Illustrated London News *(20 October 1860).*

View from Parliament Hill looking southwest during construction of the stone walls surrounding the Parliament Buildings, 1873. Wellington St., running toward the west, bisects the old Upper Town community.

ble calling card: Bytown became Ottawa. It even attempted to turn its mixed and warring population to good advantage in an early example of "symbolic nationalism". Ottawa was

> ...within the territory of Upper Canada, but connected with the lower province by the "Union" suspension bridge, with a population of French and British origin equally balanced, the political and social effect of its selection would be to forever set at rest any feelings of jealousy on the part of either section, and would tend more firmly to cement a union which has already been productive of the happiest results.[37]

But probably what was crucial was politics, despite Macdonald's disclaimer of non-interference. Macdonald and Cartier, if somewhat uneasily, were in control of the government as the leaders of an embryonic and still somewhat fragile Liberal-Conservative coalition, whose main support came from the commercial men and ridings of the central part of the province. The selection of any other place except Ottawa exposed Montréal, in particular, to commercial danger, and Macdonald and Cartier to political risk. In many ways, Ottawa was the surrogate of Montréal. Even Ottawans in those heady days saw themselves as the political metropolis and Montréal as the economic.

The capital was a mouthwatering economic plum that the city was able to take in two bites: construction of the government buildings; then the arrival of the government. Each stage had a quite different impact on the city.

The cost "for the whole of the work" was to be $627,310, with additional funds subsequently provided for heating and ventilating. A modern system of central heating was to be employed, but failed to work. The ducts were so large that cold air coming down overwhelmed warm air coming up. The effect was to provide air-conditioned buildings throughout the Ottawa winter. Stoves and fireplaces had to be employed everywhere in the complex, generating more construction activity.

Commencement of the works in late 1859 brought a flood of labour and business to the city. Ottawa's lumberers (especially J.R. Booth), its landlords, provisioners, and carters experienced a boom. But, typical of Ottawa, most capital, skill, and material were imported. The great exceptions were Booth's lumber, the Perth sandstone used on some of the buildings, and the cement manufactured near Hull.

The explosive and cyclonic nature of Ottawa's economy, so dependent on decisions made elsewhere, was once again in evidence

with the Parliament Buildings. On September 27, 1861, with the buildings only partly completed, Barrack's Hill in a tangle of stone and lumber, and the townsfolk prospering mightily, the work was suspended by the Commissioner of Public Works.[38] Cost over-runs, due in part to unanticipated engineering problems (especially with foundations), and in part due to oversight that was more self-interested than disinterested, had exhausted the appropriation. The immediate impact of the suspension

> ...was instantly to throw out of employment between sixteen and seventeen hundred mechanics and laborers; representing a population ...of between five and six thousand. That no riot or disturbance took place in consequence, testifies favorably to their good conduct and management of the works.[39]

After an internal inquiry and a Royal Commission, the works resumed in 1863. Suspension of the works, at the least, compounded the crisis of the early sixties that threatened the lumber industry and the city's railway, and led the municipality to the edge of bankruptcy.

In October, 1865, with the buildings still incomplete, the first apprehensive civil servants made the move from Québec City to Ottawa. The first, and only session of the Parliament of the *Province of Canada* opened 6 June 1866. The following year Ottawa became the home of the new *Dominion* of Canada. The impact of government on the city, unlike the construction, would be continuing.

While external rivals and internal rivalry thus vitiated much of the city's metropolitan thrust, the events of 1867 would have a final, telling effect. Once again political boundaries changed, and though Ottawa was the capital of the new Dominion, the city was once again thrust to the periphery of two provinces, whose centres of gravity were far distant, and whose ambitions were much different than those of the divided valley. Not much could be expected from the denizens of Queen's Park and Toronto who considered the Ottawa River a "mere creek".

DEMOGRAPHIC GROWTH AND SOCIAL PATTERNS

After the setbacks of the later 1840s, people once again by the 1850s were surging into and through Bytown. Like other nineteenth-century cities, it appears to have been subject to the transiency of the period, when a population three or four times the size of the place would pass through it in the course of a decade. But Bytown

Looking northwest toward Parliament Hill across a section of Sandy Hill, about 1866. With the arrival of government, this area of the city boomed.

Celebration in front of the Centre Block, 24 May 1867. The lawn of Parliament has traditionally been the site for national celebration and protest.

was also a lumber town, subject to the seasonal flows of the shanty-men, raftsmen and bargemen who were a permanent part of an industry always on the move. Much of the workforce of the town or the valley at a given time might be hundreds of miles from its usual place of residence. These were the "itinerant" Bytowners, and embraced rich and poor alike. Indeed, some of the most powerful members of the community were numbered among the "itinerant". The "itinerant" on a lumber frontier had a separate place alongside the permanent or "fixed" community, and the "transient".

The population grew rapidly, nearly doubling between 1851 and 1861. (See Table II) In the next decade, a respectable 47 per cent increase was registered. Among these numbers were the more permanent, like the parliamentarians, civil servants, and their families, as well as those of doubtful passage, like the construction workers for the Parliament Buildings.

The immigrant population of the original frontier community was becoming more thoroughly British North American, and probably much more Ottawan. In 1848, just over half the people in Bytown were born in the Canadas, while in 1871 some 75.6 per cent were Canadian-born. Births, the birth-rate, the numbers in school, all point to a young population, expanding more and more by natural increase, rather than migration. Native-born Ottawans, so rare in the 1840s, were becoming the norm by the 1860s. As for the migrants, the American colony jumped from about 100 to 400. The English-Anglican colony increased, too, and may have represented the most significant change, for it gave strength to the Upper Town community.

These alterations were paralleled in the Roman Catholic community. Growth in the number of Irish Catholics had been marked in the 1830s and 1840s, due to the arrival of the canal labourers in the first decade and famine Irish in the second. Sometime in the 1840s they appear to have passed their French co-religionists in size. By 1852 there were some 2,732 Irish Catholics, compared to 2,066 French Catholics. By the 1870s, probably due to in-migration of French from Canada East, numbers reversed: by 1871 of the 12,735 Roman Catholics in Ottawa, some 7,214 were of Canadian birthplace *and* French. The number represents about 56.5 per cent of Roman Catholics and about 33.5 per cent of the total population of Ottawa. One can assume, fairly reasonably, that most of the remaining 5,521 Roman Catholics were of Irish origin. It seems to have been a point of near equilibrium.

Distribution of the Catholic community in the city also seems to

have been at the beginning of a subtle, but significant shift. Most Catholics in the 1850s lived in Lower Town, but the proportion of Irish dropped in the 1860s, the start of a dispora of Catholic Irish from the Lower Town into all other parts of the city.

It was a healthy time to be born and to live, if statistics can be believed. A death rate of 18.7 per 1,000 for 1848 was abnormally high, due to the typhus epidemic, and the famine migration. More typical was the 11.6 rate of 1851, which remained about the same for 1861. Ottawa was reputed to be the healthiest place in British North America. The city seems to have been relatively free of epidemics, though there were cholera scares in the 1850s and 1860s, and a cholera hospital was built for the latter. Its only patient was a man with a broken neck who "was not cured."[40] Smallpox ran its course on a number of occasions, but the epidemics were not of sufficient scale to alarm council. The great killers seem to have been infant mortality and consumption.

In-migration in the period also had an occupational dimension of great importance. Construction workers, including large contingents of tradesmen, arrived to build the Chaudière mills in the 1850s and the Government Buildings in the 1850s and 1860s. Subsequently, mill owners and mill workers moved in to create the city's first large industrial work force; and in 1865 politicians and civil servants arrived to create the city's first large "white collar" group.

The impact of the construction workers is hard to ascertain. Most were probably birds of passage, but the tradesmen, many of British origin, gave rise to some of the earliest efforts of union militance in the country. Labour problems were frequent during construction of the Government Buildings: "There have been more strikes on this Parliament Building than on any other job on this continent..the most despotic slave-owner in the Carolinas might at least have listened to a humble request from his stable servant." It is probably no coincidence that Ontario's first labour MPP, Daniel O'Donoghue, was elected from Ottawa in 1871.

Numbers of industrial workers doubled between 1851 and 1861, and doubled again by 1871. (See Table IV). Given the activities at Chaudière and Rideau Falls, the increase is not surprising. But exhibiting even more dramatic increases were those in the commercial and professional classes, the former no doubt in place to service the two new centres of economic activity — lumber and government — and the latter almost wholly accounted for by government. (See Table IV)

Though the precise size and composition of the civil service migration is not clear, it seems to have been in the order of 350 employees, who with their families and servants numbered about 1,500 and with domestics, labourers, craftsmen, businessmen and others expected to accompany them, "upwards of 2,000",[42] or something in the order of 15 per cent of the existing population. Few were left behind in Québec City, apart from some in lowly jobs, and "Such as are inefficient or useless whether from illness or other causes . . . ."[43] By 1872, when more accurate figures became available, there were some 400 "headquarters" personnel, with an annual payroll of $421,880, about the value of Bronson's logs after milling. The Crown employees, while only something in the order of 5 per cent of the labour force for 1871, and only about one-eighth the size of the industrial establishment, made up for their size with their pay. It averaged about $1,000 per year per employee, compared to about $275 for those in the lumber industry. This higher pay, and the equally important fact that it was not seasonal, meant a greater capacity to purchase services. The commercial character of the town thus changed, for example in the construction of several "monster" hotels, ". . . built but unoccupied, patiently awaiting the flush of business,"[44] and in the growth of the legal profession and the "great many new stores".[45] In the fever of construction, the forest had been knocked down. Not a tree remained and not one was planted: ". . . they swelter . . . in the unshaded streets of their dusty capital . . . ."[46]

THE URBAN LANDSCAPE

The Chaudière islands and nearby LeBreton Flats, covered with bush in 1850, were by 1870 covered with mills, and lumber piles, the modest stone houses of the entrepreneurs, and the hundreds of rough-cast wooden dwellings of the new industrial labour force. One of the city's three major railway centers was emerging there. Thus was confirmed one image of the city — "the lumber village": mills and lumber piles, fed by the booms and rafts of the Upper Ottawa; a bustle of railways and barge traffic nosing into the docks and platforms heaped with pine boards.

The other city image was inspired by the Gothic temple that, by 1865, had emerged atop "Barracks Hill." For 100 years the Parliament Building and the two departmental buildings would dominate the Upper and Lower Town as the mills would dominate the falls. Nothing — except perhaps the railways — would, for three genera-

tions, challenge their presence in the urban landscape.

Between 1850 and 1870 was the golden age of Lower Town, where population concentrations and activities intensified, shops were refurbished, and the market took on new activities. Just the same, its character did not much change. Lower Town remained caught in time: the modest businesses of the shopocracy still flanked Rideau and Sussex. Behind the shops and market grew a modest town. The typical wooden homes of tradesmen now contrasted with the odd dwelling of brick or stone. The whole of the area was dominated by the towers of the Basilica, the other churches, and their institutional buildings. By 1870 a landscape of the faithful had assumed a central presence in Lower Town. By 1870, it had nearly assumed its terminal form.

While the industrial community of LeBreton Flats mushroomed between 1850 and 1870, and that of Lower Town boomed, the Upper Town showed little change in aspect. Its urban landscape was more symbolic of its ambitions than of their fulfillment. The community was anchored at its western end by the principal Anglican and Presbyterian churches (Christ Church and St. Andrew's), both were enlarged (1841 and 1854 respectively), at the start of the period, and both replaced by the present structures as it ended (1872 and 1873).[47] At the eastern extremity, Nicholas Sparks' failed market building was converted into a city hall, police station, jail, and general meeting hall, used by the Anglican Sunday School,[48] and "The Club of Amateurs" for theatrical purposes,[49] as well as Board of Trade and Orange Order. By the 1870s, the peculiar wooden structure, with the town's chief fire-bell in its tower, had itself turned into a fire-trap and pesthole. In the words of the Board of Works, it was ". . . in a very dilapidated state and unworthy of the Capital of the Dominion."[50] It was soon to be replaced. As for the rest of the Upper Town, few commercial buildings had been established along any of the major streets, though a clutch of fine homes had begun developing along the bluffs in the northwest corner of the area. Mostly, the land waited to see what the monument on Parliament Hill would bring. For the nonce a rearguard action was fought, against Lower Town and growing Chaudière.

Nor for the period did Besserer's land — in the southeast corner of the tiny city — known as Sandy Hill, show much sign of activity. There were few buildings of note, except perhaps for the home (1844) of Besserer himself. His land awaited the arrival of government, and then from the 1870s boomed.

The city continued to be frustrated in dealing with its thorough-

The lumberers' view of the government city, 1865.
Photo by Notman.

The commercial core of the city, Rideau and Sussex, is at centre left in this view from Parliament Hill to the southwest, about 1861. The piles of lumber and stone are evidence of continued construction, and the crude, treeless aspect of the city is apparent.

This is reputed to be Wellington Street in the late 1850s or 1860s, somewhere near Nicholas Sparks' Upper Town property. It was to be an important street of the capital.

fares by its lack of complete control over them. While the long conflict with Ordnance over the right to ownership was resolved by the 1850s—and Wellington Street was actually opened—Ordnance, the province, railways, and other jurisdictions maintained control over the bridges. City council was told in 1869 that there was no bridge in Ottawa that it actually owned. Bottlenecks persisted at Sappers' Bridge, over the Rideau Canal, and at Pooley's Bridge (between Upper Town and LeBreton Flats), and little improvement could be made on bridges over either the Rideau or Ottawa Rivers. Nor was it clear whether the city could build bridges of its own over the Ordnance-owned canal. It was a serious problem in an essentially linear town: "There is only one road," Ottawans complained, "to go from the Chaudiere, and Upper and Centre Towns, and Hull and Aylmer, to jail or to the railway station."[51]

Despite problems, efforts were made in the 1850s to deal with the roads, primarily to drain, grade and (for the major ones) macadamize them. Success was limited. In part, this was due to the squabbles between Upper and Lower Town, but also because what money was available was being devoted to railways above all else. Technical errors, stemming from parsimony, also crept in. Adequate drainage, even on the major roads, seems to have been neglected as a preliminary to improvements; and the little macadamization then done employed, not the somewhat expensive igneous granite (from Hull), but a broken, sedimentary stone available nearby. This was soon crushed to a powder by wagon-wheels, creating the typical description of Ottawa as a sea of mud when it rained and of dust when it didn't. That one early governor had himself rowed in a boat along the Ottawa River between Government House and Parliament Hill, rather than risk the roads, is no surprise. The roads were also a receptacle for household and animal waste in an era when garbage pick-up did not exist, personal sanitation was casual, and nuisance bylaws were enforced (usually minimally), by the works committee rather than the health committee.

Descriptions of the city in the 1860s were not flattering, though in 1864 a committee was established by the city to get the use of Major's Hill for a park. On 2 July, 1866 the province turned the site (if not ownership), over to the city corporation. Two years later the city established a committee on public parks to run this first venture in "Capital" beautification.[52]

Much of the Chaudière-LeBreton Flats area, where the lumbering community lived and worked, is seen here from the bluffs near Parliament Hill, looking westward.

Lt. Pooley's famous bridge, which joined the lumbering district and the Upper Town. Painting by Walter Chesterton (1845-1931), dated 1879.

POLITICS AND THE URBAN COMMUNITY

"From the beginning the contest was political . . . ," was how *the Packet* characterized the election of 1850,[53] the first for the newly re-chartered town. One was not expected ". . . to introduce party and political questions into matters of a local nature, tending as they must to injure the interests of the town . . . ."[54] But after the Stony Monday Riot of 1849 ". . . there had not been a single fight worth looking at,"[55] and where, if not in the political arena, were the strong differences in the town to be vented. Moreover, the incorporation of 1850 was itself, profoundly political. Reformers, in control of the Province, gerrymandered the Bytown wards to favour the Reform cause. Results of local elections were predictable: from 1850 to 1854, the two Lower Town wards (Centre and East) each elected three Reformers, while three Tories, or independents, were elected from the one Upper Town ward (West). The mayors, elected from among and by the aldermen, were all "Reformers".

But "reform", so clear an idea in 1850, had become very unclear with the passage of only three or four years, because of the splinter-ing of the provincial Reform party, where some Reformers had joined forces with moderate Tories, like John A. Macdonald, to create the "Liberal-Conservative" party. It was next to impossible for Ottawa Reformers — French, Catholic, and Lower Town — to effect a wholesale alliance with the "lousy pack of Scotch" from the Conservative Upper Town, though some did. The memories, the ambitions, and the territorial contest were all too close. The result was some splintering of the apparently solid Lower Town.

As early as 1851 in the East Ward ". . . strenuous efforts had been made . . . to divide the liberals on national grounds, attempting to put the French Canadians . . . against the others . . . ."[56] Roman Catholics, too, were pressed to follow "Old Reform" into the Liberal-Conservative coalition. James H. Burke was disgusted with it: ". . . its liberality began and ended in sustaining, by false pretenses, a crew of deceitful bigots through the community,"[57] His disgust gave birth to *The Tribune* in 1854, a new newspaper in "the Catholic interest." Reform became confused.

In 1855, when the town was transformed into the city of Ottawa, there was much less confusion on the part of the Tories. When the city bill went through the provincial house, the ". . . member for Carleton intrigued to cut and carve the municipality . . . ."[58] in such a way as to ensure, if not a preponderance of Tory influence, at least an end to the Lower Town stranglehold. The Lower Town was halved — on an east-west alignment — into two wards (By and Ottawa), north of George Street, and a new ward was created (St. George's), covering the Old Besserer Estate, or Sandy Hill, but also picking up much of the Rideau Street business community. Upper Town remained a single ward (Wellington), and a new ward was created (Victoria), embracing the mixed population of LeBreton Flats, but with a curious panhandle through a heavily populated and wealthy portion of Upper Town. This configuration, with additions to embrace annexed areas, was to remain more or less intact for 100 years. The intent, apparently, was that the three, population-poor, and predominantly Anglo-Protestant wards across the southern part of the city would dominate the population-rich Lower Town area, particularly so if it fractured. The council was large — two aldermen and two councillors from each ward — for a total of twenty. Until 1859, the mayor was elected annually by majority vote of the council, and thereafter to 1867 — directly by the voters. It would prove an unstable and clumsy political instrument for what would be trying times.

A Tory mayor, John B. Lewis, and a council with a bare, but sufficient Tory majority, began in 1855 with a house-cleaning. The city fathers "commenced their official career" by removing and replacing all officers of the city and "vigorously excluded all Cathol-ics from employments."[59] An unsuccessful effort was also made to refuse the customary £100 honorarium to outgoing Mayor Friel, a Catholic. After the house-cleaning, they moved house. With Nicho-las Sparks among the majority group, council voted to move from the By Ward Market Hall in Lower Town and to "meet henceforth" in the Wellington (late West) Ward Market Hall, Sparks's white elephant.[60] The measures, it appears, were premeditated by what the *Tribune* called "the cabal of an unreasoning clique of fanatics."[61] The impact was not in doubt: "It clearly shows that the Catholic portioa [sic] of the population is disfranchised by the present division of the wards . . . ."[62] The judgement was perhaps too harsh, for Catholics, both French and Irish, would, from time to time, be first magistrate, but more on sufferance, or in temporary alliance with the new boys on the street: those from the new, more "diversified" wards, St. George's and Victoria. The Upper Town could not always have its way.

Whatever group took power in 1855, however, faced unpleasant times. The shares the city held in the railway were, by the end of the decade, worthless, and loan guarantees and borrowings on behalf of

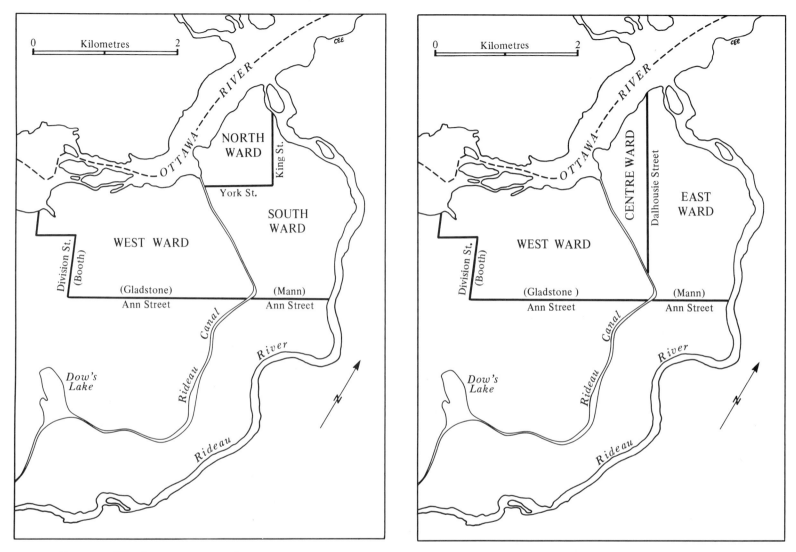

4 Bytown Wards, 1847-49 and 1850-55: A "Tory" gerrymander gave the West Ward or Upper Town political control from 1847 to 1849 (left). A "Reform" gerrymander shifted political control to Centre and East wards or Lower Town from 1850 to 1855 (right).

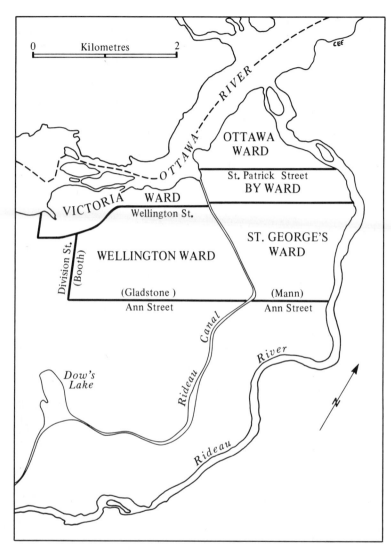

5 Ottawa Wards, 1855: This was intended as a "Tory" gerrymander to minimize the influence of Lower Town (By and Ottawa Wards), and for a time it worked. But both Sandy Hill (St. George's Ward) and LeBreton Flats (much of Victoria Ward) grew rapidly and proved resistant to the direction of Upper Town (represented largely by Wellington Ward).

the railway ate up most of the city's credit. A narrow and non-expanding tax base, coupled with mismanagement and corruption, soon had the city on the financial ropes. *The Gazette,* in a long article on the city debt, concluded the city was in desperate shape and noted that fire-engines were sold by the sheriff on executions against the Corporation.[63] It claimed that at one city council meeting "...one of the aldermen stated that the very chairs upon which they were then sitting were under seizure for debt."[64]

Some improvement in the economic picture occurred in the latter part of the decade as the Reciprocity Treaty of 1854 spurred sale of Ottawa lumber to the U.S. and as the great public work began in 1859 on Barracks Hill. But suspension of that work in 1861 and the American Civil War shattered the local economy again. Additional insult was added by the Province in 1859, when it imposed a five cent in the dollar levy on the city ratepayers, in the form of a "railway tax," to cover the city's £50,000 loan guarantee. The city council ordered the clerk not to collect it: the province insisted he do so. A lengthy legal battle commenced, won by the province. In the meantime city finances had become very confused. Some taxes had been collected with the railway tax, some without. Some ratepayers simply waited it all out, and did not pay at all.

By the end of 1862, the nadir had been reached. The finance committee was virtually compelled to recommend the following amounts (cents per dollar of assessment): Local rate 3 cents; school rate 2½; special rates of 4¼ and $2^1/_6$ for money bylaws; the 5 cent "railway tax"; a sheriff's rate of 3 and 5 cents against amounts borrowed from the municipal loan fund in 1859 and 1860; and 3½ to cover executions of the courts in favour of four individuals. The total rate was $27^5/_{12}$ cents in the dollar, of which only 3 cents was for the actual operation of the city, and 2½ for schools.[65] Rates totalling some 16½ cents had been imposed by the Province and the courts on the debt-ridden city.

But hard times and railways were not all the problem. As early as 1853, the practice of "ward improvements" had begun. Each alderman had available discretionary funds for his ward, which tended to create a "regular traffic of the individuals in the corporation to have contracts...."[66] The cheques passed through city council in bunches at year's end, and often monies were over-expended, since everyone was in on the game. Money was poorly allocated: improvements (often in the aldermen's immediate neighbourhood) were of limited or questionable civic value. And, as in most cities in the period, both assessment — the foundation of municipal finance — and tax collection, were ward-based. Assessment was not standardized, and tax collection was carried out with miniature tax farms: each collector in each ward retained, as a fee, a proportion of monies collected. Single entry book-keeping was the norm, and financial management was largely dependent on the skill and integrity of one or two corporate officers whose political appointments made them always subject to influence.

By the eve of Confederation, politics and social institutions had begun to intertwine as a superstructure of clubs and associations emerged from the social and economic patchwork of Ottawa. Their officers identified an *élite*, but it was not a strongly interlocking one, or even much of an overlapping one. Each group was a solar system unto itself, often with a territorial locus, but also with an ethnic, or religious one. Orbits sometimes paralleled, sometimes opposed, and on occasion intersected. Only caution and discretion prevented collision. Collaboration, too, was difficult, perhaps because interests so often were tangential. At its healthiest, there was friendly rivalry, for example among the various sporting clubs and the volunteer fire-brigades, but more often the religious and ethnic clubs and associations turned inward onto themselves, their backs turned to the backs of their fellow-townsmen. Such communities tended to be sufficient unto themselves, and a source of friendship, support, of reward or favour, and too often of prejudice. But to be outside was to be nothing. Only disaster, it seemed, could draw the community together. Fire or plague provided a common enemy for a common cause, but then only briefly and partially.

In many cities, the economic association provided a link to the social and political ones. Such was not the case in Ottawa. At least five layers were discernable in the Ottawa social strata in the 1850s and 1860s, and probably the most powerful of these was the "itinerant" lumberers, whose roots were in the older square-timbered trade, and who, by mid-century, had established some social precedence, though a somewhat declining influence by 1867. They were chiefly represented through the Ottawa Association of Lumber Manufacturers. As well, the Board of Trade assured the "itinerant" lumberers of places. There was, it is to be noted, no representation, guaranteed or otherwise, to the Chaudière group. The Board of Trade was to some degree a meeting ground for the old "mercantile" communities, both fixed and itinerant. Few French names were ever found on its executive or council, though there

Alexander Workman, mayor (1860 to '62) and hardware merchant. His store, at the corner of Rideau and Frieman, was for years a city institution.

The Hon. James Skead, about 1865. A leading conservative politician and senator, he was prominent, though not always successful, in lumbering enterprises in the Valley.

was a sprinkling of Irish, like Henry Friel. There was an obvious overlap of "English" names on the City Council and the council of the Board of Trade, but they were invariably from the "fixed" mercantile community.

The old gentility connection might be found in the sports clubs, but more often they were firmly entrenched in the sinecures of the city corporation — chiefly the result of the Tory revolution of 1855 — and in the civil and juridicial offices of the County, whose politics they controlled. They were, of course, prominent on the Boards of the Protestant Hospital and the Orange Lodge, where the leading members of the old "outside" (as opposed to "headquarters") provincial civil service could be found: Horace Merrill, superintendent of the Ottawa River Works, on whom the lumberers so depended; or Francis Clemow, immigration agent and official assignee for Ottawa and Carleton and Russell counties, merchant, and manager of the Ottawa Gas Co. (and later Ottawa Electric Co.).

A new intelligentsia had arisen in the Mechanics' Institute, the Natural History Society, the Literary Association, the Educational Institute of Central Canada, and in the less prestigious and generally new chapters of the various Masonic and Orange Lodges. It was in these associations that the middle ranks of the town were to meet the middle ranks of the newly arrived "inside" service. The peak of the pyramid was to be found in the Rideau Club, and even it was divided into ordinary and "privileged and parliamentary" memberships. But the civil service, too, formed its somewhat exclusive organizations, one of the earliest and most important being the Civil Service Building and Savings Society, dominated by the senior members of the "inside" establishment.

The Chaudière group, new and mostly American, seemed to keep to itself, and apart from church memberships, was not very evident in the Ottawa community at Confederation. Its political connections ran in a number of directions, through Currier, John Rochester, and James Skead, but most particularly, it seemed, through the MPP, R.W. Scott, a Catholic.

Lower Town was a world unto itself, but like the rest of the city fissures of religion and ethnicity ran through its organizations. The Lower Town was fundamentally divided between the Irish and the French. St. Joseph's Orphans Home had its counterpoint in the St. Patrick's Orphans Home; the Canadian Institute Hall in the St. Patrick's Hall; the St. Patrick's Literary Association in the French Canadian Institute (where the liberal professional élite and its political arm were found); the St. Jean Baptiste Society, and the Union de St. Joseph d'Ottawa (embracing the political arms of the mercantile and trades groups).

The divisions extended into the volunteer fire-brigades: Chaudière (Upper Town, Anglo-Protestant), Ottawa (Lower Town, Irish Catholic), Rideau (Lower Town, French Catholic), Queen (French and Irish Catholic), Central Hook and Ladder (Anglo-Protestant), Lower Town Hook and Ladder (French and Catholic).

The institutional arrangments were not surprising: they reflected the social and economic contours of the city and its divided ideologies. And, like the economic elements, the social and ideological ones were, by Confederation, beginning to assume, to a large extent, a closed or corporate form. Occupational and class organizations were almost non-existent before Confederation, except perhaps for the embryonic civil service associations, and a few of the building trades.

Looking west toward the city from Rideau Falls, across Lower Town, 1869. This was the area of earliest milling activity and it remained productive into the twentieth century. The terminus of the city's first railway, the Bytown and Prescott, was nearby.

Chapter Three

Victorian City and National Capital (1867-1900)

On July 1, 1867, Ottawa had formally become capital of the new Dominion. But, at the same time, it also became a provincial outpost. It was, to use a variation on an earlier theme, thrust from the centre of one province to the periphery of two. Such an ambivalent position within the new federation may have accounted for the mixed enthusiasm given "Dominion Day" by the city, now a rutted, gap-toothed community of some 18,000 souls, perched on the bluff overlooking the lumber piles of Chaudière. Though a majority of city council had proclaimed July 1 as a public holiday and struck a committee " . . . to arrange for the proper inauguration of the new dominion,"[1] a persistent minority of council sought to eliminate the celebration, and particularly the $500 appropriated for it, failing at times by only a single vote.

The arrival of government had, willy-nilly, grafted a second personality onto the city. It was very unclear in 1867 how this new personality would blend with the old, and who would assume its care and custody. A new, central theme was thus set up: could "Ottawa as City" be reconciled with "Ottawa as National Capital"?

The portents were not good. By 1867, Ottawa had had some eighteen months experience as capital of the Province of Canada, and strains were already evident. It seems to have been assumed that it would now provide roads, utilities, fire-protection and the like. It was an onerous burden for a small city with shaky finances. And many profited, perhaps excessively, from the arrival of the civil service, producing outraged cries of rent-gouging and profiteering. As well, "the hostility of the tradesmen, horse-racing on the streets, cold houses, lack of water facilities, lawlessness, and even the weather were items of complaint . . . ."[2] As for the locals, the civil servants " . . . .came to be regarded as favoured although inferior citizens in what was otherwise a working-man's town."[3] They were "a set of men who got high salaries for doing next to

nothing."[4] Regardless, the small, local *élite* were eager to emulate the new arrivals, which " . . .allowed the politicians — particularly the cabinet ministers — to assume Ottawa's social leadership without pain or opposition."[5] There was either a social decapitation or an absorption.

On the economic front, lumber and government had diverted attention from railways and industry. The city fathers sought, especially after 1867, to create a more solid economic base, in which Ottawa, as capital of "Central Canada" would become the national and continental hub of the projected "Pacific Railway". Rail activities, in turn, would underpin and generate industrial growth. The city also turned with enthusiasm, about 1890, to hydro-electric generation as the maker of its fortunes. This new technology was incorporated into a grand scheme to revivify the Ottawa-Lake-Huron waterway, but this time to industrialize the Ottawa Valley as well.

Lumber and government, however, underpinned steady population growth, which remained rooted in the old cultural solidarities. Even in the business community, cleavage rather than a common sense of purpose prevailed. The federal politicians and public service revolved in an orbit of their own. Labour was weak.

Ottawa was now seeking the appurtenances of a modern community. Associated regulations, bylaws, and resolutions emerged to ensure a more orderly and perhaps more certain civic life. Provision of this "infrastructure" preoccupied the city. Together with the concern over railways and industry, and the relationship with the senior government, it became one of the three major themes of the late nineteenth century. Politics and political alliances were in the main, conditioned by all three, and when mixed up with the city's traditional cultural divisions, formed the core of the political dynamic, and the driving force of community and social relations.

The raftsman's view of Parliament Hill and the capital of the dominion.

ECONOMIC GROWTH AND
METROPOLITAN DEVELOPMENT

Ottawa in 1867 was still smarting from the loss of its home-grown railway, the Ottawa and Prescott, but generally prospering from its substantial lumber industry, the older trade in squared timber, and also in its new role as capital of the Dominion of Canada. Lumber and government would remain the sheet-anchors of the city's economy in the nineteenth century, though both seemed to sustain, in chief, a service industry. In the sixties the forests of the valley produced the largest estimated cut in their history.[6] The prosperity was fragile, however, and masked major structural changes that would strike the industry like a one-two punch. Nearly every firm, however huge, was either a family operation or a partnership with two or three principals. Most, in fact, appear to have been heavily reliant on a single individual. None, until Eddy was forced to in the 1880s, turned to new forms of corporate organization. None seems to have made much provision for succession. It has been suggested that an "American" *mentalité* of personal free enterprise militated against change, but more likely, a series of adjustments in the 1860s and 1870s successfully derailed pressures for change in attitude or organization.[7] The unreformed industry, run by elderly lumber barons, proved incapable in the 1890s of making the major adjustment required by market, product, technology, and — especially — a declining and inferior supply of logs.

Two disasters — the depression of the early 1890s and the great fire of 1900 — seemed to shake things out for a final time. The depression finished most of the smaller companies. The fire, in 1900, wiped out most of the mills at Chaudière, and created a great deal of public antipathy toward the piling of lumber inside the boundaries of the expanding city.[8] The only companies to rebuild after the fire were Eddy, primarily for pulp and paper production, and mainly in Hull, and Booth's Ottawa mills. The Bronsons concentrated on hydro-electric generation. Lumber production, which had climbed to a peak in 1896, fell off sharply after the turn of the century and apart from a spasm upward in the First World War became a second-rank industry. By the 1920s most of the mills on the Hull side of the river were absorbed into the American conglomerate, International Paper. By the 1950s what remained of the Ottawa lumber industry was a number of derelict mills, and the vestiges of an industrial community in LeBreton Flats.

Despite the scale and erratic vitality of the sawn timber industry in the late nineteenth century, it sent out few manufacturing off-shoots. For the most part, there was a single-minded devotion to cutting trees down and sawing or grinding them up. Little effort was made to go beyond simple primary processing to more highly manufactured products. If the Chaudière lumberers wouldn't diversify, their monopoly of waste power at Chaudière (and Rideau) Falls meant others couldn't. A confidential report in 1882 argued that the original Chaudière monopoly militated against manufacturing since, "now when there is a demand for power in the city, it cannot be obtained." Worse, perhaps, the power at Chaudière was seriously under-utilized.

> There is a large amount of power constantly going to waste, the situation for mills has been sold and occupied principally by saw-mills, and as piling ground for lumber. These mills only work one-half the year, the other half of the power goes to waste. They employ little labor, in comparison with cotton or woollen mills. They are the only description of mill which manufactures its own fuel. Steam is to them as cheap a power as water; their monopoly of the power is a direct loss to the productive capacity of the community.[9]

As one city father put it in 1892, "if certain gentlemen had not grabbed up the water privileges at Chaudière we might have had manufactures here long ago."[10]

Industrial ambitions were, by default, linked to the "Pacific" railroad. Ottawa's strategy was again to control the rail link to the Great Lakes, along the traditional route of the fur trade. It could then become the hub of trunk lines forking eastward to Montréal and the Atlantic, and southward to the United States. All would be in the "National" interest, and all would trigger a great manufacturing industry around the repair and car shops of the railways. Promotional activities, including civic "bonusing" were thus largely directed to railway activities. The encouragement of other industrial activities, related to the lumber industry or government, for example, were largely neglected.

The efforts to control "Central" Canada via railway were originally rooted in an 1856 alliance with Québec City and Brockville, and embodied in an act to "provide for and encourage the construction of a Railway from Lake Huron to Québec,"[11] the Canada Central Railway. But control of the CCR, in circumstances that are not clear, fell into the hands of Montréal interests. Ottawans were initially enthusiastic. Ottawa would once again ". . . be assured of its

The great fire of 1900 began in Hull, swept through the mills and piling grounds of Chaudière, and destroyed much of the working-class community of Le Breton Flats. It led to demands that the lumber piles be removed from the central areas of the growing city, and marked a point of decline in the city's sawn lumber industry.

proper position in relation to the trade of the North West."[12]

> Briefly stated, the route from Montreal to Nipissing is assuming an importance which is destined to make it one of the great trunk lines of the Dominion, forming as it will a link of the great overland ocean-to-ocean Canadian Pacific Railway system; and that the commercial importance of the capital as well as its metropolitan character will be vastly increased by the completion of the Canadian Central is true beyond the slightest opportunity for controversy.[13]

The enthusiasm was short-lived. The Montrealers were more concerned about assuring a federal land grant, and Ottawa was patched into the Brockville and Ottawa system, and the trade of Ottawa and the valley continued to drain off through Brockville. City council and Ottawa ratepayers thus proved critical when the CCR in 1875 made a request for bonusing, and rejected a proposed bylaw.[14] By 1877, the *Citizen* was calling for a "thoroughly independent" line.

By the early 1880s, then, Ottawa's ambitions of a central role on a great Canadian Pacific transportation corridor had been usurped by Montréal. The loss inspired an alternative system, one that in the mind of its ultimate promoter, the Chaudière lumberman J.R. Booth, would turn the city into "a Second Minneapolis."[15] The new railway would join the North West, via Ottawa, to the Continental United States. It became known as the Canada Atlantic Railway (CAR) or more simply as "Booth's Railway." The scheme also intersected with two other ambitions of the city, especially those of the rapidly growing Upper Town community: the railway shops as foundation for manufacturing growth; and a station and yards in the central part of the city. The first CAR train pulled into the capital 13 September 1882, and a month later some 500 celebrants left Ottawa from the Stewarton Station, for the "preliminary opening" of the southern leg of the CAR. It soon became clear that if the CAR, were to rival the CPR, it needed a link to the west. A first element was the Ottawa, Arnprior and Renfrew Railway (chartered 1888), a line designed to link Booth's Ottawa mills with his valley timber limits. A second element was the Ottawa and Parry Sound (also chartered in 1888), which effectively connected Ottawa to Lake Huron, and, via its ships, to mid-America.

In 1892 Booth asked the city for a $100,000 bonus for his railway and an additional $50,000 bonus for a new Union Station, close to the heart of the city, one that would rationalize the growing railway "nuisance".[16] Booth again held out the carrot of shops, and the

development of manufacturing. The new railway venture would "bring back" to Ottawa's merchants and traders their role of supplying the valley, would establish the city as a grain distributing centre, and, with the application of water power to milling wheat, create a great flouring centre.

Booth's railway was a success. By 1903 some four million bushels of prairie wheat were moving to the east and the Atlantic, via Ottawa, in addition to the thousands of board-feet of lumber from the Ottawa mills of Booth and others. Flouring mills, driven by hydraulic power, did not emerge. The repair shops were built, but did not provide an industrial and manufacturing base. In the early twentieth century, Booth sought federal money for improvement and further expansion westward,[17] but ferocious opposition from inside Laurier's cabinet stopped him. His lines in the valley competed with Montréal's CPR. Booth's western link to Parry Sound stepped on Toronto toes. But the most strident opposition came from Maritime Liberals. Booth's railway was allegedly drawing off the traffic of the Intercolonial Railway (ICR) and taking it to American rather than Canadian ports on the Atlantic. Booth recognized it was the end of the game. He sold his interests to the Grand Trunk Railway.

Once again, the ambitions of the city were in conflict with the political and other priorities of the government corporation within it. Ottawa, the city, lost to the political requirements of Laurier and his need to appease vested economic interests in Montréal, Toronto, and the Maritimes. The national cry was used against the capital, as was democracy, which had never served the city very well. Industry linked to railways was likewise doomed.

In its efforts to promote its grand railway schemes — and create manufacturing as a by-product of them — large sums of civic money were periodically committed to a few, large railway projects. An unwilling city also bonused, indirectly, Government. The considerable government properties were tax exempt and the city received no grant-in-lieu of taxes to compensate. Government employees, under 1866 legislation of the *Province* of Canada, also successfully claimed exemption from municipal *income* taxes, which partially compensated for exempted government property. The flow of funds the city might have commanded for direct bonusing of industry was thus reduced, by both railway and government. Bonusing, successful elsewhere, was stillborn in Ottawa.

A final phase of the manufacturing or industrial strategy was

Canada Atlantic Railway engine no. I.

very "new-fashioned" and focused on electric power. Ottawa was especially blessed with numerous power sites. The city embraced the new energy source with enthusiasm: it would be the "Water-Power" as well as the "political" and "lumber" capital of the Dominion.

Once again, it would seem, the city's reach exceeded its grasp. Ottawa did not have a diverse manufacturing base to which it could apply the electricity that it could so easily generate. There was little market. There was, equally, no assurance of an electric industry — motor manufacturing and the like — that could compete with existing manufacturers. There was also an absence of strong financial institutions. Nearly all — apart from some building societies — were branches of the St. Lawrence/Great Lakes cities. In the late nineteenth century, only the Ottawa merchandiser C.T. Bate, appears to have had any standing in the Canadian financial community.[18]

Finally, the development of power assumed, in the 1890s, a form familiar since the time of Philemon Wright: monopolies of a personal kind. They did not often engage other groups within the city and they did not seek allies in other powerful centres, like Toronto and Montréal. They were independent, but also extremely brittle, as was the case with Booth's railway.

The grand hydro scheme, nonetheless, emerged, most clearly in the mind of Erskine Bronson, the capable and enterprising son of one of the original American colony at Chaudière. Bronson "... planned that one large hydraulic company would eventually control all the power sites in the Ottawa Valley and undertake their development into a new industrial heartland."[19] A new version of the Ottawa-Lake Huron Canal Project — an Ottawa River seaway — could run parallel to the hydro generating scheme. It was, in a nutshell, Laurier's "Pittsburgh" of the North.

Bronson allied his Standard Light Co. with the enterprises of Thomas Ahearn and Warren Soper, who controlled the Ottawa Electric Co., to create by the 1890s a near monopoly in hydro generation at Chaudière. In 1894, these men and a coterie of associates, including Francis Clemow and Robert Blackburn, of New Edinburgh, had also established a monopoly in traction, and another in gas generation and distribution.

> In effect Bronson, Ahearn and Soper had, in large part, established firm control over most of the utility services offered in Ottawa. Politically powerful and dominating the Liberal Party in the city, they held sway over the public and business affairs of the area. For them Ottawa had become a private city, the source of their wealth and power. They could if they disired [sic], control the pace and direction of its development.[20]

Bronson's scheme failed. In part he lost his influence with the provincial government when, for reasons of health, he had to resign as MPP. He also lost control at city hall where Tory anti-monopolists opted instead for public power and traction. As well, the hope that hydro-electricity would be the key to attracting an industrial base failed.

> Most companies turned down offers to locate in the region largely because they could not purchase power sites for themselves and did not trust the rival industrial interests as suppliers ... It was this competitive situation which finally defeated all attempts at further industrial diversification. Unable to attract new industry, Ottawa and Hull watched helplessly as their private economic sector shrank after 1900.[21]

The final scenario was probably written in large measure by provincial governments. Provincial forest policy was increasingly dictated by the lumberers in the western parts of the province. Ontario and Québec by the twentieth century had also divided up the Ottawa River for the purpose of hydro generation: the public Ontario Hydro, run from Toronto, managing Ontario's share; private, non-valley companies, the Québec portion. Only the federal authority might have preserved some measure of coherence in the valley by developing it as a deep-water shipping corridor.

In the early years of the new century the Laurier government invested about one million dollars in a comprehensive examination of the Ottawa-Lake Huron ship canal. It was hotly opposed within Laurier's government by a southern Ontario lobby that successfully sought funds for improvement of the Welland Canal.[22] The parochial issues and ambitions of the St. Lawrence valley once again defeated the Ottawa. It was the centre of government, but the periphery of nearly everything else.

DEMOGRAPHY AND SOCIAL RELATIONS (1867-1900)

Population more than doubled in the last three decades of the century, with the greatest growth in the late 1880s and 1890s. It was sufficiently strong to make up for a period of absolute decline in the depression of the 1870s, and of stagnation in the depression of the 1890s. Nor did the fact that Ottawans were increasingly

Ambroise Gagnon and family in front of their house at 106 Church (now Guiges) St. in Lower Town, in 1900. Gagnon was a carpenter with the Ottawa Car Co., which made the city's streetcars.

native Canadians cause them to slough off the habits or predispositions of their ancestors. The city appears to have remained divided — even more severely divided than in earlier years — into its entrenched sectors, despite the increasingly "Canadian" character of its people. The "ethnic" or "national" or "religious" origins of its people were little changed. The tiny numbers of "Others" in 1871 (304 souls), grew considerably by 1901 (2,663), to form some 4.6 per cent of the city's population and provide the beginnings for Ottawa's "ethnic" communities, chiefly Jewish, German, and Italian. Protestants and Roman Catholics remained divided at about half each.

If the gross contours of Ottawa society remained much unchanged, internal social patterns shifted dramatically and created new and severe tensions. Lower Town, still the commercial centre of the city in 1871 and home to half its people, grew slowly after Confederation. Of greater significance was the "Irish Diaspora". Lower Town at mid-century, a community shared by French and Irish Catholics, was at century's end, a largely French enclave[23] (See Table VI). Where the Irish had gone is to some degree speculation, but it seems their English language heritage was the vehicle to upward mobility, and a ticket to the more affluent areas of the city.[24]

Lower Town, though not growing, fought a vigorous and successful rearguard action in the nineteenth century to preserve its perquisites, political, social and economic, and only really succumbed in the twentieth. And especially with respect to the dispersed Irish community, it struggled for, and successfully gained a dominance in the city's Catholic community. After some bitter confrontations it was also able to control the University of Ottawa, and to protect the French language within the Roman Catholic Separate School Board.

The story was quite the opposite in the Upper Town. The mainly Anglo-Protestant enclave grew rapidly in population. By the end of the century, its size reflected its ambitions to be the dominating force in the community. It found, however, that the perquisites of power had still to be shared, not only with the stubbornly resisting Lower Town, but with the newer, growing areas of Sandy Hill and LeBreton Flats, the former with *élite* pretensions like Upper Town, the latter, the enclave of the Chaudière barons, and home to their mill hands.

Significant shifts in "class" contours paralleled those of "culture."

By Ward market in horse-and-buggy days, c. 1900. The view is to the north from George to Clarence. The "Annex," one of two market buildings, is at the right.

The French population, in particular, got stuck. Franco-Ottawans appear to have been displaced in some skilled and business occupations by Europeans, and otherwise only maintained what became a corporal's guard of lawyers and doctors, as these professions quadrupled in numbers during the last third of the century.[25] "In ethnic terms, it generally appeared that the less prestigious occupations such as those found in the semi-skilled category were well-represented by the French, while the prestigious occupations, such as those found in the professional category, were dominated by the non-French."[26] In the community of the Flats, adjacent to the Chaudière Mills, some 83 per cent of the unskilled workers were either Irish or French, and 71 per cent Catholic.[27]

The English came to dominate the occupations of high or growing prestige, such as law and medicine. By the turn of the century, most lawyers and doctors were entrenched in Upper Town, the lawyers near Sparks and Elgin, the doctors near Somerset and Metcalfe. Few lived near the court house or the city's hospitals, all east of the canal.[28]

Government and civil service, arriving in 1865, imposed its own, curious changes. A survey, based on 1871 data,[29] indicates that in the lower and middle income ranges, the civil service located according to cultural background: the Roman Catholics, French and Irish, largely in Lower Town, and the Protestants in Upper Town. Those in higher income brackets were to be mostly found in Sandy Hill, without much regard for race or religion. The overall result was a reinforcement of all the major cultural cleavages within the city, except at the top. Here, the government and civil service gave Sandy Hill (St. George's Ward) a new personality, making it an important and prestigious new player in the city's community life.

In the latter third of the century the working man began playing a more noticeable role. Organized labour was, however, somewhat weak in Ottawa, facing powerful cultural solidarities, and the corporate-like woods industries, and government. In the Ottawa mills, men were apparently engaged at a weekly salary ($7 to $9.50 per week in 1890). The usual work day was eleven-and-a-half hours, with forty-five minutes for lunch; the work week (1890) averaged close to sixty hours, with varying arrangements for full or half-days on Saturday.[30] But the work was seasonal. From the arrival of the first booms and barges, following the opening of navigation, the mills, drying yards, and loading docks operated virtually non-stop through the daylight hours of summer and autumn until ice closed navigation. Through the winter, the mills were largely quiescent, and the bulk of workers dismissed. The new season could begin, from management's point of view, with a virtually clean slate. The mill workers, however, unlike the woods workers, were sedentary, usually living in nearby LeBreton Flats or in Hull, and propinquity at least gave them the potential of organizing. This sense of community seems to have been an important element in the Chaudière Strike of September and October of 1891.

A severe winter delayed the start of milling operations in 1891, and this, coupled with economic depression, caused mill owners to reduce weekly wages by fifty cents, but with a promise of a ten-hour day.[31] As it turned out, however, wages were cut, but hours weren't.[32] On September 12, 1891, a small group of men at Perley and Pattee's mill demanded reinstatement of the fifty-cent wage reduction, and were refused. They called on fellow workers to strike. In short order, virtually all the wage earners in the Ottawa area mills were off the job, as well as some employees of the CPR and Booth's railway. Numbers approached 2,400.

The rapidity with which the strike developed, and its early success, indicate that while there may have been little or no formal labour organization, there was a fairly coherent working-class community associated with the mills, and one that had an accepted place in the life of Ottawa and Hull. By mid-October the strike had vanished rather than ended. The Chaudière lumberers convinced civic authorities to use police — and the militia as an aid to the civil power — to protect loading operations. Though a short-term failure, the strike prompted in 1892 organization by the Knights of Labour, and ultimately negotiation with the mill owners.[33] Greater labour activity in the political arena, especially local, is also more evident after 1891, though its relationship to the strike is unclear.

Apart from the mills, the other large employer in the city was government, and in the public service there was little evidence of class activity. Conditions of work — pay, hours, pensions, and the like — appear to have been negotiated between various civil service associations, generally dominated by senior civil servants, and the government ministers. Class action, reflected in a labour organization, was not spoken of, and likely not thought of as a plausible course.

There were few other centres of potential class or labour activity

Staff of the Geological Survey, 1892: like much of the Civil Service, a male bastion. It was as part of the Survey that Elkanah Billings, of the pioneer Billings family, gained fame as a paleontologist. The collection of the Survey was the basis of that of the Museum of Natural History.

in Ottawa, except for the trades. And it is among the trades organizations that practically all significant action, including the political, seems to have occurred. But it was limited, not only by the embryonic nature of labour organization in late-Victorian Canada, but by the relatively small numbers of tradesmen in a work force dominated by mill workers and civil servants.

Possibly the first formal labour organization in the city was that of the stonecutters, brought to Ottawa in large numbers for construction of the Parliament Buildings.[34] Another early labour force was the Ottawa Typographical Society, organized in 1866 by Daniel O'Donoghue, an Irish Catholic with some experience in the American labour movement. It would appear that in Ottawa, as other centres there was considerable latent pressure for trade union organization, first made legal in Canada with John A. Macdonald's Trade Unions Act of 1872. Upon passage of the Act, organization was swift.

> Between mid-March and mid-May, 1872, fifty journeyman painters and paper-hangers formed a union, bricklayers and stonemasons organized, as did cabinet makers, carpenters and joiners, and plasterers. They met in Lower Town, usually, in St. Patrick's Hall or Gowan's Hall, or Starmer's saloon, on the corner of George and William Streets, in the By Ward market area.[35]

Even day-labourers associated with the trades, while not organizing a union, pressed for increases in wages.[36] In appreciation of the Trade Unions Act, the skilled workers on 5 September 1872 gave Macdonald a torchlight procession. They also decided to continue meeting as the Ottawa Trades Council (OTC),[37] and entered politics.

On January 10, 1874, O'Donoghue, then president of the Ottawa Typographical Union, was chosen as "The Workingmen's Candidate" to contest a provincial by-election set for January 20. This was apparently for the "...purpose of feeling the way for a more determined effort at the general elections..." expected in 1875.[38] O'Donoghue won the election, in an unusual set of circumstances, that variously mixed up partisan, cultural, and labour politics in the city.

O'Donoghue, an Independent workingmen's candidate, was adopted by the lumberers and Conservatives. He was also, apparently, adopted by the Irish Catholics, as a surrogate of R.W. Scott, whose resignation as MPP prompted the by-election. Liberal-Conservative candidates were persuaded to stay out of the by-election in order to create a two-man race and, with the support of the Conservative press, including the anti-labour *Citizen*, it was won by O'Donoghue.

He was a winner again in 1875, but ultimately defeated in the provincial elections of 1879, coming in third. His defeat was symptomatic of the state of labour in both the city and the province. The depression of the late 1870s had devastated the labour movement, and at the time of the election, the Typographical Union was the only one left in the city.

The return of prosperity in the 1880s produced a resurgence of the labour movement in Ottawa. A host of local unions, most of them short-lived, were organized.[39] More enduring were trade unions with international charters. They rose from one in 1880 to an estimated seventeen in 1890, twenty in 1897, and thirty-seven or thirty-nine in 1902. But the great phenomenon of the 1880s was the growth in Ottawa, as elsewhere, of the Noble and Holy Order of the Knights of Labour (KOL), a secret society with somewhat Masonic rituals, first organized in the United States in 1869. The fact that they were one type of labour organization sanctioned by the Catholic Church may have made their reception in Ottawa a more palatable one. Their first appearance in Ottawa was probably in 1883, with the Telegraphers Local Assembly. By 1887, there were three Local Assemblies of the Knights in Ottawa, and in 1890 a peak of nine.[40] An Ottawa "Knight," interviewed in 1886, said that his local "assembly" was a mixed one, containing all kinds of tradesmen and a few professional and businessmen. It numbered about 700, and met once a month. "We had engaged a hall in Ottawa and are doing well." He described the Knights as "...a benevolent, educational and protective organization...."[41]

Despite the revival of labour in the city, Ottawa was slow to reorganize a local council to replace the defunct OLC. It was only on 20 February 1889 that the Ottawa Trades and Labour Council was formed. It was reorganized in the summer of 1897 as the Allied Trades and Labour Association, which lasted until absorbed into the present Ottawa and District Labour Council.

The other major "class" relationship was with the poor, and here Ottawa's relationship was fairly typical of Victorian cities. Their numbers in the Ottawa community are difficult to determine. Seasonal employment, due to lumbering and construction, was endemic. It was also the practice of employers to cut both people and wages in the winter. In times of depression the layoffs were prolonged, where work was available at all, and wage-cuts severe.

In front of Rowan's Hotel, 34 York Street, in the By Ward Market area. Such hotels were numerous in the Lower Town. The itinerant work-force of the timber and lumber trade formed a major part of their clientèle.

D.J. O'Donoghue, Vice-President, Canadian Labour Union, 1873-74, MPP, and first Dominion Fair Wage Officer, 1900-07.

Lumberers, for example, responded to the depression of the 1870s by a common agreement to cut production by 10 per cent. They subsequently halved it. The federal government terminated a number of projects, and the city itself decided to postpone a subsidiary drainage plan. By 1875 Bronsons and Weston were employing half the men they had used in the previous year, and were paying an average of $11 a month, as opposed to $17.[42] Labourers' wages, paid by the Dominion or local government, dropped from $1.25 a day in the earlier part of the decade to eighty cents in 1877. By April of 1877, the situation appears to have reached its nadir. On the morning of 5 April 1877, some 300 workingmen assembled on City Hall Square calling for "Work or Bread".[43] Subsequent demonstrations produced crowds estimated at 600. The demonstrations indicate that, in a city of 25,000, a good portion of its workforce was at the end of its resources. Most workers had families, most had been out of work since the previous autumn, most had subsisted: "Hans Shourdiz, a German said he had been living on soup since Christmas. On Christmas he got a good square meal, but since that time his stomach has been a stranger to meat." Another man said he had earned nothing since the previous August, "George Gilmour supported two children during the winter on $10; Alexander Stewart furnished food for two children without doing any work at all; . . . Michael Forbes supported a family of five children during the winter on $13.50."[44]

Prices, that winter, ran about $5.50 for a cord of wood and twice that for a ton of coal. Rent for a modest Lower Town dwelling was about $8 a month. A four-pound loaf of bread cost eleven cents.[45] Even for those workingmen fully employed the year round, existence was marginal. One study estimated $468 as the average annual income for an Ottawa worker. This was only about $9 more than required for basic living expenses.[46]

The city, then, despite the stabilizing force of the civil service, the presence of MPs and cabinet ministers, who made $5,000 a year, rested on a rather large labouring force, which led a marginal existence at the best of times, and was subject to impoverishment when times were difficult. At least one-quarter of the population would have been subject to this regimen: at the edge of starvation in winter and depression; and tied to the twelve-hour days of the wage-earner when employed.

The influence of labour reached a peak around the turn of the century, and is here displayed in a Labour Day parade at Dufferin Bridge in 1907. Dufferin Bridge, like Sapper's Bridge before it, linked Upper and Lower Town. From the earliest days to the present it has been the site of public demonstrations, whether riots, parades, or protests.

These were the able-bodied poor. Yet another group were unable to work. These were the men who were maimed in the frequent accidents in the mills, on construction, and in the bush; or who were killed, leaving widows to fend for themselves, usually by remarrying as quickly as possible.[47] Yet others were handicapped, lunatic or old, or infirm from disease, often tuberculosis. And finally, Ottawa had its share of the undeserving poor: the professional mendicants, the drinkers, and the "fallen" women. It seems that these were as often pregnant servant girls as they were prostitutes.

As for their welfare, a certain James Haberlin was to be the least likely of heroes. In 1859 he became the first object of permanent public welfare in Ottawa. His case established the limits of public policy in the city for two generations.

Sometime prior to September, 1859, City Council had provided funding for a man named Finn to provide temporary care for Haberlin and, on 29 September of that year Finn returned to city council to ask for more aid for this "poor creature".[48]

> Whilst admitting that it is a hardship on Finn…still it can hardly be expected that this council can agree that he should be forever maintained at the Public Expense: there are charitable Institutions in the City delivering aid from Government and in the opinion of Your Committee such cases are fit subjects for their protection.[49]

Council agreed to pay Finn $30 on behalf of Haberlin for what they said was to be the second — and last — time.

Before the Haberlin case was put on its plate, council had avoided the inevitable. It refused to fund a Citizens Relief Committee in the difficult period of 1849-1850, on grounds the city did not have statutory authority.[50] It grudgingly paid the board for two orphans, whose maintenance the provincial government in 1848 had thrust on it.[51] But made sure other support for orphans was temporary, after which they went into the homes provided by the private sector. Faced with a request for relief to support a foundling "deserted by its unnatural [sic] parents" the councillors dug into their own pockets for a dollar each toward support of the child.[52] It provided coffins for paupers, but only after determining that there were no family or friends to do so. It provided one week's support (five shillings) of "an infant child found on the street", one dollar a week to a widow to support a child left with her when her mother was put in jail,[53] temporarily rejected a request for a dollar a week

to one Thomas Green for support of a child left at his door until satisfied as to "need."[54]

All these *individual* emergencies, and more, were handled on a case-by-case basis and were treated as such — in other words, as emergencies of short duration. A number of *collective* crises were handled in a similar fashion, like the arrival in June, 1852, of a group of "distressed female emigrants" from Ireland. A voluntary committee requested £10 "until places can be found for them." Similarly, in 1858, a group of some twenty-five or thirty people were sent to the jail "…by the City authorities without any provision being made…with reference to Beds and bedding." At the request of the jailer, the council purchased ten pairs of blankets. The jailer also asked "…whether this Corporation would become good for the board of those 10 children that were thrown into Gaol along with their Mothers to prevent them from Starving in the Streets, as they had no home…" and to reimburse him for the clothing he purchased for them as they "was almost naked." Council agreed to the latter request and recommended a reasonable allowance "for their keeping."[55]

Haberlin, however, posed a special problem. He was "truly" destitute and "forsaken by his Family." He was also severely crippled and unable to care for himself without assistance. Council could not resort to public institutions: "…as the Petitioner is incurable, he cannot be admitted." Ottawa had no house of refuge. He was left to "the mercy of the Public." Probably the only thing that induced council to take him under its wing, was the belief, in keeping with its philosophy, that Haberlin could be considered a short-term if not quite, emergency case: "….being an aged man, in all probability, from his sufferings, together with his decline in life, he cannot long be a burthen on the community."[56] Council decreed that Haberlin be found "….some place where he can be attended to at as low a rate as possible."

Haberlin, however, proved more resilient than council supposed. He lived seventeen more years at council expense, moved around from foster home to foster home. He died 13 December 1876, at the last in the St. Charles asylum for the elderly. Council had to find four dollars for a coffin.[57]

Haberlin, for nearly two decades, and beyond, reminded the city of the perils of engaging in works of individual charity, except on a strictly emergency basis. Its chief activity, with respect to social welfare, tended to be confined to employment-related matters. Its

Two women at their cell doors in the local jail, 1895. In the nineteenth century, indigence as well as crime could lead to imprisonment.

Amanda Leveille, age 15, an employee of the Russell Hotel, 1898. The Russell Hotel was the premier hostelry of the Upper Town and a favourite of the politicians of nearby Parliament Hill. Its staff, many recruited at an early age, generally came from other parts of the city.

Sister Superior, Elizabeth Bruyère, in 1872. She arrived in Bytown in 1845 at age 26, leading five other nuns. The community she founded, known as the Grey Nuns or Sisters of Charity, established the first hospital (the "General"), the first girls' school, and the basic welfare services of the Catholic community. Photograph by W.J. Topley.

policy in this area was once again rooted in the 1850s and evolved by precedent through the nineteenth and into the twentieth centuries.

With the grant in 1855 of tax relief to a group of women, mostly widows, "in consequence of extreme poverty,"[58] it began a series of practices that constituted — almost until the depression of the 1930s — its unemployment relief policy. The remission of taxes and other fees, for example, that of the licence fee to a butcher's stall in the market to a woman ".... on account of her indigence consequent upon her husband's insanity and the support of a large family,"[59] was one of the chief measures used to deal with poverty. A second basic element of the policy was to give potential charges on the city their fare out of Ottawa, usually only as far as Brockville. The Ottawa press was asked to keep the policy secret. A third device, most commonly applied to the resident, male unemployed was relief works. The practice seems to have begun at least as early as 1875, when in the depression of that year, the Board of Works was instructed "... to consider the employment of such of the old residents of Ottawa as they find distressed for want of work, and if desirable, to employ them at such rates of remuneration as they may deem equitable."[60] By 1881 it had become "customary," at the beginning of the year, to provide work for the unemployed in stone-breaking, in order to provide supplies for the year.[61]

The hard times of the 1870s also appear to have tossed a number of other straws in the wind, including the provision of wood "for relief of the poor of the city,"[62] a gesture rejected on the first petition. Council also began providing small sums for various charitable organizations: $100 for each of five in 1875.[63]

As for the private or voluntary sector, there were few collective ventures until the arrival in 1845 of the Grey Nuns, led by Sister Elizabeth Bruyère, and the establishment of the Grey Nuns' Asylum, which accommodated the sick, provided a charity school for the education of pauper parents, and acted as an asylum for foundlings.[64] Their activities precipitated, in that same year, the Society of Ladies of Charity, comprised of middle-class women both Protestant and Catholic. Such joint efforts lasted a year. In 1846 the "ladies" went their separate ways, the Catholic women organized as the St. Elizabeth Society, the Protestant women into the Bytown Benevolent Society, and the Ladies' Benevolent Association.

And, as with the first of the charitable institutions, so with those that followed: they were denominational (Catholic and Protestant)

Elderly women, 1918, at the refuge branch of the Protestant Orphans' Home, the first Protestant facility for aged females. The elderly were divided by sex, the men sent to Abbotsford House and the women to a section of the orphans' home.

and often racial (French and Irish often, but also Scotch and English and, in the twentieth century, Jewish). The private welfare sector in Ottawa developed in as fragmented a fashion as the city itself, the Roman Catholics usually somewhat ahead of the Protestants and triggering countervailing institutions: the (Catholic) General Hospital producing the Protestant General Hospital; the Catholic orphans homes (for French and Irish) producing, in 1864, the Protestant Orphans' Home.

But at the centre of social relationships in Victorian Ottawa was the notion of obligation on the part of the wealthy or the church, and of deference on the part of the poor. A profound sense of cleavage and conflict, however pronounced among the various language and religious groups, was formally absent along class lines. Bitterness wasn't, as one workman sarcastically told his *confrères*:

> ... he would counsel them not to be down-hearted, nor [sic] despondent for a brighter, happier day was coming. In the meantime, the kind and charitable people of Ottawa would likely give them all the run of a moral hash foundry and with that assistance and the help of God they could dig through the mind of depression and keep the stomach of the little orphan from being lonesome and the barefooted boy from shuffling off this mortal coil.[65]

If Erskine Bronson is to be believed — and he and his family were prominent in Protestant voluntary charity throughout the Victorian period — society should be based on collaboration between capital and labour, and on a sense of stewardship with respect to the deserving poor. He had a strong faith in the virtues of agrarian life, and was concerned by the growth of cities. He believed firmly in personal responsibility, and in obedience and adherence to authority.[66] Capital and Labour, he was sure, could be reconciled "... by the adoption of a policy of mutual forbearance ... there need be no conflict between these two factors, without whose harmonious and concerted action commercial prosperity is impossible."[67]

THE URBAN LANDSCAPE

Between Confederation and the new century Ottawa assumed the garb of a modern city. Much was off-the-rack and had a stuck-on aspect, as new buildings and technology were grafted onto the old commercial city, or insinuated themselves through the streets and into the gap-toothed façades of the streetscape. By the end of the century, Sparks Street in Upper Town, had established itself as the "Broadway" of Ottawa, complete with asphaltic paving, street lights, tangled wire, Victorian "skyscrapers," and its "eternal tramcars." Lower Town was almost unchanged, apart from new market buildings. There, the low, stone buildings of the old mercantile community, the churches and church buildings, and the "frontier vernacular" of the tradesmen and workingmen, still dominated. LeBreton Flats retained its look as the community of the industrial workingman, only it was bigger, and less mixed: the wealthier of the lumber barons had moved, for the most part, to their fine homes along the cliffs of the Ottawa, or into the prestigious areas of Centre Town and Sandy Hill. In these areas, the beneficiaries of government — public servants, retail businessmen and professionals — established the quality residences that continue to mark these areas.

Ottawa's buildings, like much else, seem to have arisen as a function of its peripheral location, big "industries," and punctual communities.[68] There was evidently much concern in the nineteenth-century city to be up-to-date. On the frontier, this could be translated to mean what most other places and most other architects were doing, but — for reasons of cost or temperament — doing it in plainer fashion. A received tradition in building form and style was widespread. There was little in Ottawa, except perhaps the Parliament Buildings, that could not be found elsewhere in Canada in more dramatic form.

The stylistic prestige of the Parliament Buildings, termed civil Gothic in the argot of the day, also created some local mimesis. The *élite* churches at the western end of Upper Town were rebuilt in the 1870s in the Gothic style, though that was perhaps commonplace for churches anyway. It was, however, the Second Empire features of the Parliament Buildings that were more typically borrowed, appearing in the Market Annex (1875), and in a cluster of buildings at the eastern end of Upper Town.

But the punctual nature of the architecture in Ottawa most reflected and informed the character of the city. Ottawa's buildings were not so much those of a single city, but of three or four small communities. For example, the buildings of Lower Town that were built in its halcyon days before 1860 reiterated prevailing classical forms with an admixture of what has been called the Quebec tradition. Originality was mostly absent, but the French Canadian flavour still distinguished the area from the rest of the city. After

Snow removal, Sparks Street, 1890s. The arrival of the electric streetcar (see tracks) made snow removal mandatory. Previously, only sidewalks were cleared, the snow being heaped in the middle of the street and flattened with huge rollers to provide a surface for sleighs and for the horse cars.

Foote Paugh's circus, c. 1900, going over Sappers' Bridge, the ceremonial centre of the city. The proliferation of wires — power, telephone, telegraph, and streetcar — was typical of the turn-of-the-century city. The parade is emerging from Sparks Street, the "Broadway" of Ottawa, to the left of the Post Office Building. Wellington St., more sedate, is to its right.

27

Wellington Street opposite Parliament Hill, in the latter part of the nineteenth century, looking eastward. This corner of the city was distinguished by its "Second Empire" buildings.

Central Chambers, at the corner of Elgin and Queen, was built in 1890 to accommodate professionals, especially lawyers, who made this corner of Upper Town a favorite location. It was close to the growing government business of the "Hill," the booming commercial enterprise of Sparks Street, and the registry office on nearby City Hall Square. Central Chambers remains one of the most elegant examples of Victorian architecture in the city.

1860, as the Lower Town declined in importance, it turned to diluted mimicking of Victorian revivals by a stagnant and generally poor community, attempting, nonetheless, to conform to the architectural fashion.

More successfully fashionable was Sparks Street, whose late-Victorian buildings were floated on the surge of Upper Town people and the prosperity brought by the arrival of government. Most were five or six-storey "skyscrapers" in the latest style, some quite elaborate. But Sparks Street was still the main street of only one of the city's communities, however prosperous it was, and its character was thus that of the main streets of modest Ontario cities, not of its metropoles.

The modest commercial and office buildings, whether of Upper or Lower Town, were then at odds with the structures put up by government and industry. They paled beside the Parliament Buildings or the vast agglomerations of mills at Chaudière. Likewise, there was some incongruity between commercial Ottawa and residential Ottawa. For size and style, the *élite* residences of Upper Town, Sandy Hill, and the river cliffs much overshadowed the commercial and institutional buildings of the Victorian city. It is not to be wondered at, for these were often the homes of those grown wealthy on lumber or government. Their homes were as detached from the city as their businesses.

This sort of architectural non-congruence was most tested when a city facility was in the works, and was given its most peculiar expression when it came time in the 1870s to build a new city hall. There were disputes over the location, the financing, the architects, the contractors, the cost, and the inaugural celebrations. The funding for the new building, and its Upper Town location, was committed in 1873 by a city council with a Tory bias. But, after a political upheaval, the architect and contractors were hired by a council with a Reform bias. The resulting building, which seems to have been a compromise of both cost and style, either pleased everyone or did not especially offend anyone.

The cornerstone was laid on 20 July 1875 after a dilatory council committee directed to organize a ceremony missed several deadlines. Lack of interest, rather than civic pride, seemed to be the prevailing emotion.

> The magnanimous City Clerk, unwilling to allow the event to transpire without some celebration, order[ed] two dozen of ginger beer and a cocoa nut, which the assembled crowd disposed of in a remarkably short time.

The ceremony was about to go ahead with only the clerk, the architects, and a number of other civic servants, when Ald. Heney, chairman of the Board of Works "chanced by", and was asked to officiate. "Much astonishment was expressed at the absence of the Aldermen of the city who were not even made aware of the fact of such a thing going to take place." And at the opening ceremony 18 June 1877, city council simply trooped from the old city hall to the new one to the beat of a band playing "Auld Lang Syne", "The Girl I Left Behind Me", and other "popular airs". After brief speeches from the mayor and the clerk, they sat down to regular business, including a matter of arbitration between the city and the sureties of the failed contractor over final costs, which had grown to some $90,000 from a budgeted $60,000.

After 1867 the city also grew in area. In the 1880s — the bait typically was municipal services — it embraced New Edinburgh to the east, and Rochesterville to the west. Both areas served lumber manufacturing sites, the former at Rideau Falls, and the latter at Chaudière, and, in effect, attached company towns to the city proper. Mixed classes and cultures, in mixed dwellings, were marbled with the apparatus of the lumber industry: rail lines, lumber piles, bark, chips, sawdust, and noise. There was always the threat of fire, but because most mills used hydraulic, not steam power, there was somewhat less industrial dirt.

What industry didn't supply in the way of dirt, the railways did. Worse, the railways encased the city in a girdle of steel, and congested its heart with lines, yards, and stations. In part, the growing city flowed over and beyond pre-existing rail facilities. But fragmented communities within the town encouraged separate railway-based growth poles. Railways, jealously competitive, made no objection.

In this way, a tangle of rail-lines, yards, and stations became one of the most prominent features of the urban landscape, overshadowed only by the Parliament Buildings, and the mills and lumber-piles of Chaudière and Rideau Falls. The city was cut into pieces.

The city also moved past the stage where a "juvenile police" was sufficient to rid the streets of cows and pigs; where carters were sufficient to supply water; and an annual spring clean-up and liberal spreading of lime fully served the needs of public health. Growth, congestion, and the pretensions of being a modern capital all demanded the provision of modern services: gas, street lighting, water, sewers, roads and sidewalks, telegraph and telephone, garbage collection, horse-drawn trams, and electric power. It was in

Toward the end of the nineteenth century a neighbourhood of elegant middle-class homes developed in the area of Queen Street and Bronson Ave., at the western end of Upper Town where the escarpment falls off to LeBreton Flats. Many were the homes of the wealthy industrialists, notably Erskine Bronson, who had earlier lived near their Chaudière mills.

The "old" City Hall. Nicholas Sparks provided the site for the West Ward Market in an unsuccessful effort to spur the development of his property at the west end of Upper Town. Unable to compete with the By Ward Market, it was made over into a town hall by a Tory council which included Sparks.

In 1877 the "old" City Hall was replaced by this building, located on the original site, facing Elgin, between Queen and Albert, on what was known as City Hall Square. It burned down in 1931. A central police station, fire hall, and registry office were built behind it to form a civic complex that dominated the centre of the city. It is now the site of the National Arts Centre, to the southeast of Confederation Square.

Thomas Ahearn, inventor and driving force in the organization of the utilities monopoly, Ottawa Light, Heat and Power (purchased by the City of Ottawa in 1950). A prominent Liberal, he was appointed in 1927 by Mackenzie King to head the new Federal District Commission, which was instrumental in assembling the land for Confederation Square and Park, effectively removing a municipal presence from the centre of the city and replacing it with a federal one.

Ottawa, as elsewhere, the age of urban infrastructure. And it altered civic government as much as it altered the city landscape, producing in its wake — not only a modern police force and fire department — but an expanded and more professional "civic" service, to manage and regulate a city converted to "gas and water socialism". An expanded local government quickly filled the new city hall.

Gas, the horse-car line, electric power and traction, all developed in Ottawa as private monopolies, controlled by the most powerful of its economic and political *élites*. Their access to money and to politicians at the senior levels of government, and their influence in municipal government, generated a running battle between the city and its service-monopolies for nearly two generations. As for the public monopolies — roads, the market, sewer and water — their development reflected cleavages between the rich in property and the poor, and inevitably revolved around racial and religious divisions.

Civic experiments with electric street lighting, for example, were made as early as 1882 when power, generated at the city waterworks, was applied to a bank of carbon arc lamps, attached to a tower or "mast", overlooking the Flats. There was apprehension among some members of the community regarding the effects of turning "night into day." The light was "brilliant" enough[69] "...but the difficulty in its efficient working appears to be ample steady power for driving the dynamo machine."[70]

City Council was still, by 1883, somewhat ambivalent about moving into the light business. There was risk, though also the possibility of profit. And there was, even in the Victorian's enthusiasm for innovation, skepticism. "In short," said Mayor C.H. Mackintosh in an 1891 report, "day light has been such a cheap blessing hitherto, that the payment of $150,000 per annum for a little more of it, will scarcely meet with the approbation of those who take a practical view of the subject."[71]

A range of influences — including the opinion of the city engineer, and possibly the new mayor, C.T. Bate — tipped the council in the direction of the private sector, when two offers to light the city were placed before it on 15 September 1884. One was from the Royal Electric Co. of Montreal, the other from two local entrepreneurs, Thomas Ahearn and Warren Y. Soper, who in 1882 had incorporated a partnership to carry out electrical engineering and contracting. The latter, after some nimble and murky politicking,

Rideau Street, 1898, the north side, looking west. By this time the old commercial centre of the city had been supplanted by bustling Sparks Street and distinguished Wellington. The modest buildings of Rideau reflect earlier glories.

Francis Clemow (1821-1902), merchant and Senator (1885-1902), c. 1867.

won the contract in the name of the Ottawa Electric Light Co. (OEL).

In May, 1885, electric lighting commenced. The fire and light committee reported at year's end that "... the city is the best lighted one at the present time, being the only city in Canada that is entirely lighted by electricity."[72] It is to be noted, however, that Francis Clemow, long-time manager of the gas company, the displaced supplier of street lighting, was by 1888 managing director of the electric company.

On the strength of the street-lighting contract and the franchise awarded by the city, Ahearn and Soper and their partners — like Erskine Bronson — would build an empire, consolidated in 1908 as Ottawa Heat, Light and Power, and, in doing so, generate a running battle with City Council, which for twenty years would itself be divided over public versus private power.

The city's chief method of checking the OEL was to franchise competitors. The OEL's counter-strategy was to buy them up. It struck a rock, however, on Consumer's Electric (1889), which the city had tried to protect by making sale to OEL impossible under the charter. Ahearn, a political Liberal, was well connected with the Liberal government in Ontario and lobbied successfully to have the clause removed. But just before the removal became legal, the city in 1905 purchased the company for $200,000. With a distribution network, but no generating plant, it formed the core of the Municipal Electric Department, and subsequently Ottawa Hydro.

As for electric traction, at the end of the 1880s and through the early 1890s it became "....apparent that the use of horses as a motive power for street railway purposes is to be gradually superseded by that of electricity...."[73] It was also clear that the city, "in view of the anxiety expressed by many to have a street railway constructed,"[74] wanted electric traction. Moreover, the existing "horse-car" franchise was in the hands of the unsatisfactory Ottawa City Passenger Railway (OCPR); while the "electric" part of the formula that equalled the streetcar was dominated by the OEL Co. Municipal operation meant tangling with two private utilities.

Once again, following some byzantine politics, Ahearn and Soper obtained in 1890 the franchise for an electric street-railway. They subsequently formed the Ottawa Electric Railway Co. in 1891, and on 25 June, 1891 led a procession of five streetcars through the city. But the arrangement was far from satisfactory, since the city's old bugbear, the OCPR, with its "perpetual" charter,

The horse streetcars of the Ottawa City Passenger Railway operated in the city between 1871 and 1893, their original intent being to join the railway terminus of Lower Town with that of LeBreton Flats. In summer, horses pulled the cars along tracks; in winter, shown here, the rail wheels were replaced by sleigh runners. In the muddy, in-between season, "Spring equipment" or wagon wheels were used.

In June 1891, the streetcars of the Ottawa Electric Railway first paraded through the streets of the city. At the controls of the first car was Thomas Ahearn, who, with his partner, Warren Y. Soper, combined electrical expertise with complex politicking to bring electric "traction" to the capital.

still controlled the best routes in town, especially Sussex and Sparks. Horse-power and electric power co-existed. Council's refusal to permit OCPR conversion to electric power did not drive it out of business, but into the hands of Ahearn and Soper. Soper was installed as president of the OCPR in 1891, but representatives of the old board of directors — most associated with enterprises at Rideau Falls — were very much in evidence.

Council's spine was stiffened, however, by property owners on Sparks and Sussex, the major business streets of the city, who, after thirty years bad experience with the OCPR on their narrow throughfares, favoured no street-railway — electric or horse — at all. And there was the more general concern regarding control of the streets, denied for the first thirty years by Ordnance and the next thirty by the OCPR. Terms with the city were eventually settled in 1894. The perpetual charter of the OCPR, and the twenty-year electric railway franchise was surrendered to the city in exchange for a thirty-year charter, expiring in 1923, when the city had an option to purchase. Tax exemptions were replaced by an annual, per mile fee, with a bonus for paved thoroughfares. Rates for tickets were established, and the city's responsibility for snow-clearing abandoned by the companies. Standards of construction were stipulated.

Another group of services, however, remained in city hands. Water, of all the nineteenth-century utilities, generated the most ambivalence in terms of public-versus-private approaches. Water, at the outset, was a private matter, at least for drinking and cooking. So long as demand was low and quality not critical, the problematical wells of the city, and the private water-carriers, who toiled up the hills from the Ottawa River, could service the town.

Proposals in 1855, 1857, and 1859 failed, despite reports, complaints, high insurance rates, petitions, public meetings, repeated editorializing over waterworks, and promotion of a private scheme in 1866.[75] Finally, in 1869, resort was had to T.C. Keefer, a prominent engineer, who came to city council armed with new technology,[76] the high pressure, or "Holly" system, and this, with urban growth, and threat of fire, became the proximate trigger for undertaking the new scheme. Social and geographical biases provided the underlying impulse.

The old private suppliers, the water-carriers, appear to have come mainly from Lower Town, which by the 1860s, was still one of the low growth areas, and inexpensively built, with much of its property already heavily depreciated. Lower Town was, predictably, opposed.

The great impetus for the waterworks would seem to have arisen in those communities whose growth was most contingent on the construction of the Parliament Buildings: Upper Town and Sandy Hill. Both were places of rapid, expensive, and recent growth, and both were ill-protected. In the view of the first "chief" in his 1867 report, the most endangered area was St. George's Ward (effectively, Sandy Hill), especially the section "...that has within the last 3 or 4 years been so exclusively built upon, most of it very valuable property, and very little means of obtaining water in case of fire, except by Carters."[77] He claimed that Wellington Ward or Upper Town was "...if possible in worse condition."[78] In one entire large area there was "...not a public well, and when it is taken into consideration the large amount of valuable property lately erected in that locality...this state of things should be remedied as quick [sic] as possible."[79]

The third major problem, which added impetus to the demand for a waterworks was created by the Chaudière lumberers, whose piles of drying wood covered LeBreton Flats, and presented as much a hazard as a profit to the town. The danger was underscored in the dry summer of 1870, when fires swept toward Ottawa from Carleton County, and threatened to engulf the city. The lesson of the great Chicago fire of 1871 appears to have given the final spur to a waterworks scheme. It was launched in March, 1872, under the direction of an elected board of water commissioners, an innovation "borrowed" from Hamilton. The scheme also incorporated, from Montréal, a "fire alarm telegraph" and the reorganization of the fire department. In June, 1872, planning for a "grand main sewer" as an adjunct to the waterworks was begun, and actual sewer construction started in 1874, the year the waterworks began operating.

The waterworks commission was largely drawn from the Anglo-Protestant élite of the city, under a $4,000 franchise for electors of the Commission. Lower Town, cut out of the Commission, persistently sought to eliminate it, and to bring the waterworks under the direct control of the council. Twice they failed — in 1875 and 1877 — but ultimately succeeded in April of 1879. By then, the utility was operating. It had been generated and built by the blue-ribbon communities of the city, largely for their own protection.

Provision of an adequate water supply implied a fire department

Though the city was surrounded by rivers, its location on a high bluff made the supplying of water a problem. In the early days, water was usually drawn from the Ottawa River and brought up to town in horse-drawn puncheons such as those depicted in this watercolour by John H. De Rinzy (active 1874-1908).

capable of using it effectively. The earliest fire-fighters in the city were volunteers, organized around the equipment they had paid for, as much for social purposes as to protect the city. Fire companies were always prominent at civic functions, ceremonies, parades, and the like, since, with the militia, they were among the few bodies in early Bytown capable of gathering an organized and somewhat disciplined group in one place. They were also, almost immediately, in financial trouble, for while capable of finding capital to purchase the equipment, they could not find operating funds. Almost as soon as the town was incorporated in 1847, the fire companies offered their equipment in return for an annual operating subsidy.

The deal was done, but equipment was neglected,[80] and, by 1849, was "in a very inefficient" state.[81] An 1851 Report of the Fire Committee congratulated

> ...the inhabitants of the town upon the remarkable immunity from accidents by fire...ever since the first stone was laid in its construction—at the same time they had to add that particularly for the past year this must be attributed rather to the Special intervention of a Beneficient providence than to any precautions on the part of those whose duty it was to provide Such. Especially to the lower town is this remark applicable....[82]

Voluntary brigades were called out by bells rung from a number of locations in town. Response was highly dependent on the enthusiasm and organization of the fire companies: there was a marked reluctance to answer calls at night or in inhospitable weather. Dead heats inevitably precipitated arguments, since the first company to arrive normally assumed supervision of fire-fighting. This problem alone led to pressures for a fire "chief", a job held for a time by the chairman of the fire committee.[83] Once at the scene, there was no guarantee of water. Wells were inadequate, and the city's water-carriers were less reliable than the fire companies. As "premiums" were awarded to first arrivals, quarrels were frequent. Should fire-fighting actually begin, equipment often proved suspect. Leather hoses, especially, were easily rotted and subject to failure, often by being run over and trampled on. Maintenance of most equipment, especially that stored outdoors, was minimal. Of the fifty-seven fires attended in 1867, forty-seven resulted in complete destruction. Depressed finances and a certain reluctance to take over the unwieldy fire brigades persisted through the early 1860s, even though St. George's Ward engine house burned down in the meantime.

A number of serious fires in 1872, brought the Montréal fire underwriters — who handled most of Ottawa's insurance — to the city, and their report was predictably critical of the management of the fire brigade.[84] Insurance underwriters could make insurance costly, or refuse to write it. It was a problem that most affected those with something to lose. The city began to move toward a full-time brigade. In 1874, the fire and light committee told council it was "...of the opinion that owing to the advanced completion of the Water Works and...Fire Alarm Telegraph system...the time had now come for the reforming and reorganization of the existing Fire Department of the City...."[85]

There were different problems with sewers or "drains." The city's first sewer, begun in 1872, was a combination storm and sanitary project, designed to make streets and homes both drier and more salubrious. It did put an end, where connected, to excessive impounding of water, especially in the basements of the nation's capital. But in the first years such connections were not widely made. And where they were, residents in their homes — including the Prime Minister — and the public on the streets, discovered the evil smell of sewer-gas and, sometimes, its explosive effects. Aldermen, on a preliminary sewer inspection in 1873, were driven prematurely to the surface by noxious gasses. A number of bizarre experiments, including use of sewer-gas for steam heating, and the provision of charcoal filters on the manholes, were attempted to mitigate the problem,[86] but until sewer connections were properly trapped and vented the problem persisted. That process implied a plumbing inspector, among the first of that tiny and often maligned group of inspectors who would be a major factor in ensuring the welfare of a growing and congested urban centre. Public coercion also followed in the trail of the sewer, where connection in due course became mandatory, and made possible the campaign to rid the city of the back-yard privy.

Public health became critical in Ottawa, as elsewhere, in the second half of the nineteenth century, when urban congestion and urban filth began driving up death rates, chiefly from infant mortality and contagious disease.

A health establishment was set up only in 1874. It consisted of the part-time Medical Health Officer (MHO) and two inspectors, whose chief task was to oblige households to clean up their yards and premises.[87] It was a task that amounted to incessantly nagging a city still insouciant about the garbage in which it was drowning.

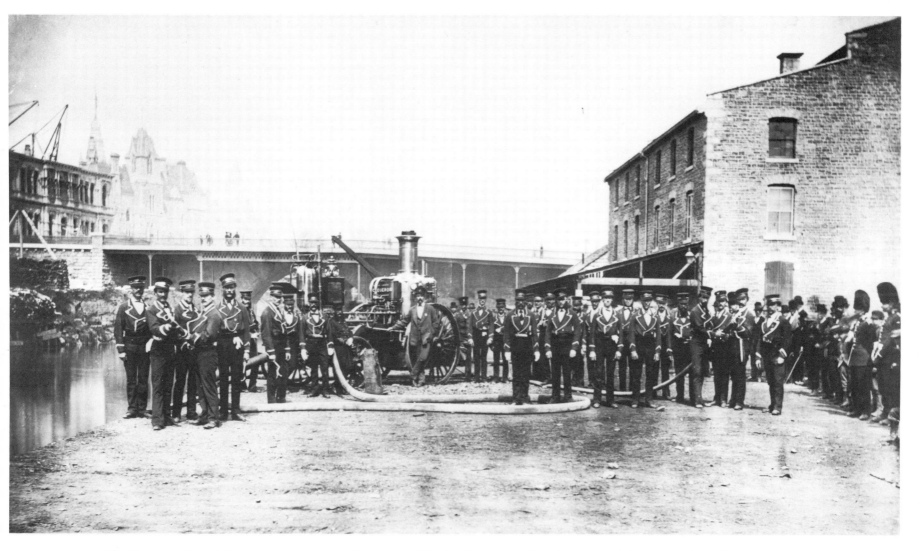

The "Conquerer," one of the early steam pumpers, with members of the fire department, 1874. Construction of the water-works in the 1870s made most of the steam pumpers, operated by voluntary brigades, obsolete. The works also precipitated the organization of a full-time fire department.

The two inspectors averaged some thirty clean-up notices a day, close to 10,000 a year, numbers that would indicate a complaint about practically every property in the city. Probably accounting for most sanitary problems were the totally inadequate mechanisms for cleaning properties and privy vaults. There were no public dumps, and arrangements for scavenging were individual. Of filth, there was no short supply in Victorian Ottawa. "We cannot shut our eyes to the fact that in this city large quantities of household refuse and garbage are constantly thrown upon the thoroughfares...."[88] Pools of stagnant water were everywhere, especially before the completion of the main sewer in the 1870s, and these pools were often filled with "decaying animal and vegetable matter and filth."[89] Even after the sewer was completed "In the spring and in the rainy season, stagnant pools of water are to be seen everywhere...."

Slaughter houses repeatedly upset health officers:

> ...all...are constructed of wood, and unprovided with trough, gutter, or reservoir of any kind. In utter violation of public rights, they have openings in the floor, or slides, through which blood, offal, and fecal matter are covertly dropped into the water of the Rideau River. The latter is largely used in the neighbourhood for domestic purposes and hence the supplies of ice for summer use in the city are mostly drawn.[90]

A smallpox epidemic in 1875, which prompted inspection of infected households, revealed the almost unspeakable domestic conditions in which the poor of the city lived. "On one occasion," the medical health officer reported, "I was notified of the outbreak of the disease in a house on Murray Street, and on proceeding thither, found that five of one family were attacked."

> The dark wooden tenement in which they lived was situated in the rear of the street, and was in a most disgusting state of filth. The family were lying on the floor, shunned by their neighbours, and attended by the only untainted member, a wan looking child of about seven years of age. Not one of them had been vaccinated; and the contaminated atmosphere in which they had evidently long been living, as well as their utter neglect of cleanliness, personal or domestic, had so vitiated their systems that on the appearance of the disease they fell ready victims to it. The father, mother, and three children died in quick succession, but the remaining child, who I had speedily vaccinated, was saved, and, through the benevolence of a member of Parliament from New Brunswick, has since been suitably provided for.[91]

Prior to the 1880s, the city fathers had at least a plausible excuse for inaction: science of the day was unclear as to the cause of disease. Yet in Ottawa an understanding of the germ theory of disease did not lead automatically to prevention. At best, public health in the nineteenth century was a matter of policing.

Regulations and bylaws to suit a growing city were not enough. They had to be enforced. More people implied more policing. A police "force" was first proposed in 1853,[92] but only with the repeated need for the militia in 1863 and 1864, the return of prosperity, and the arrival of government was one established. There was much resistance, especially from Lower Town, where a number of aldermen were "very strongly opposed" to the force,[93] which would deal not only with "disorderly characters" but enforce "sanitary precautions." Cost seemed to be the major objection. But as Alderman Friel argued, it was about time.

> He was sure there was no city in Canada or elsewhere with our population without a Police force. People who needed a force were not always those who asked for it. He did not particularly refer to the gentlemen around the board. (Laughter.)[94]

In 1866, men were appointed, ranks established, uniforms ordered, and "Nippers" (presumably handcuffs), and a desk purchased for the detective.[95] The first force consisted of a "Chief of Police" ($600), a Detective ($440), two Sergeants ($440 each), and six policemen ($360 each). The ten-man force cost $4,080, and, in its first year of operation, obtained 452 convictions that produced a revenue of $1,932.92.[96]

Though the police were occasionally involved with a spectacular crime, the most notorious perhaps being the assassination of D'Arcy McGee, the bulk of their arrests were for drunkeness, fighting, and prostitution. Much of their time was also taken up with tasks to ensure the regulation and smooth operation of a growing city. They were required to attend and assist in the fighting of all fires. For a time, the police chief was also the supervisor of the market, and responsible for leasing stalls and collecting rents. The police were truant officers and humane officials: they saw to the retirement and proper treatment of horses, and prevented cruelty to livestock in the market, whether "relieving" chickens with their legs tied up, or "relieving" cows by milking them. They were also for a time the "sanitary police", and each spring, under the supervision of the Medical Health Officer and city engineer, inspected and ordered the clean-up of the yards of the city. They

The modern Victorian city demanded modern policing, and the officer with his bicycle, in front of Poulin's Store on Rochester Street, was the epitome of modernity at the end of the last century.

also protected property and enforced building regulations.

The force grew slowly to the 1890s, and was something of a poor sister in the city. The police station, at the old city hall in Upper Town, was in highly questionable condition. The "chief" in 1882 termed it "...in a very foul state, and I think it a positive cruelty to compel the men to inhabit it. I always notice that the state of health of those who have been on station duty for a couple of weeks at a time becomes very much impaired...and it takes a few weeks on street duty before they recuperate...."[97] Council's effort to move the force and its "lockup" to a renovated Baptist church nearby was blocked, as was an effort in 1886 to put the Ottawa force under the jurisdiction of the Dominion police.[98] Plans were prepared in 1888 for a new police station (with a Fensom elevator). It, with the central fire hall, was located next to city hall in the heart of the city.

More modern policing arrived in 1896 with a new chief, William F. Powell. He began, in 1897, an "occurrence book" and a registry of convicted criminals; asked for a camera, and a patrol wagon, and praised the purchase of four bicycles. He demanded more presentable uniforms, began a program of exercise, and requested room for "a gymnasium, which I consider to be a very important necessity...."[99] The principles laid down by Powell, especially record-keeping, served the Ottawa force until the post-Second World War period.

Provision of urban infra-structure — gas, power, traction, water and sewer — proved to be the major activity of the city in the late Victorian period. Its major implication was that the City Council — whether utilities were in private hands, like traction, or public hands, like water — would be engaged in the regulation and control of the physical development of the city. Inevitably, politics and politicians at every level of jurisdiction were engaged in the process.

POLITICS AND COMMUNITY LIFE

Politics, at all levels, was fundamental to Ottawa's nineteenth-century ambitions, but politics in Ottawa was oriented less toward common goals and more toward the prerogatives, jealously guarded, of deeply entrenched economic and cultural communities. More to the point, these communities were sufficiently numerous and sufficiently strong that no one of them could set and carry out an agenda, whether in its own interest or that of the collective city.

Most activities played out in the political arena, as a result, ran in a tangled fashion into the city's various economic and cultural communities. These — French and English, Catholic and Protestant — remained extremely powerful, especially at the local level of politics, where every election and every issue was evaluated in cultural terms, if only to claim that "Sectional feuds were forgotten,"[100] or that a matter was resolved "...without any reference to... creeds or nationalism...."[101]

Chief among the economic communities at Confederation, were the lumber interests, particularly those at Chaudière, who "...did not allow a competitive business spirit to prevent their combination on matters of mutual benefit."[102] By the 1890s, lumberers' interests had extended to pulp and paper manufacturing; transportation associated with the woods industries, including Booth's railway; and certain utilities, including traction, power, and gas. All required a good deal of political sanction, and at all levels of government, federal, provincial and local. The lumberers, or their political agents, thus figured prominently, between 1867 and 1900, in the political process.

The lumberers, the utilities promoters, and their agents appear to have had a particularly strong grip on political representation at the senior levels of government, usually on the government side. Senate representation included the lumberer, James Skead (1867-1881, 1881-1884), and the lawyer Richard W. Scott (1874-1913), who as MPP and senator was the agent of the lumbering interests. As Senator, he was on two occasions in federal Liberal cabinets as Secretary of State. On the Conservative side of the Senate, Skead's place was taken in 1885 by Francis Clemow, director and manager of the Ottawa Gas Works, alderman, prominent citizen, and head of the commission that built and initially ran the city's waterworks. Joseph Tassé, senator from 1891-1895, and Conservative MPP from Ottawa City (1878-1887) was a newspaper man who wrote extensively on the economic future of the Ottawa Valley. A relative latecomer, W.C. Edwards, who took over the Rideau sawmills in 1893, provided a strong voice in the councils of the federal Liberals, both as an MP and, from 1903, as a Senator.

Federal ridings in the Ottawa area, when not being used as Ridings of Convenience (Macdonald, Laurier, and Borden all used Ottawa-area ridings after electoral losses), tended to be dominated by men associated with lumbering, milling or utilities, as were their provincial counterparts. The federal riding of Ottawa City seems to have had another peculiarity. It was a single-member riding from

Erskine Henry Bronson: lumberer, entrepreneur, politician, philanthropist, president of Bronson and Weston Lumber Co., c. 1895.

1867 to 1872, and a two-member riding thereafter, until 1930. But, by convention, or plumping, or some other informal process, one member represented the English community west of the canal, and the other member, with a few exceptions, the French community east of the canal.

Ottawa City, "west of the canal", was represented federally by J.M. Currier (1867-1882), lumberer, and former alderman; C.H. Mackintosh, (1882-1887 and 1891-1896), newspaper editor, editor of the *Parliamentary Companion*, president of the Ottawa Colonization Railway and the Gatineau Railway, and former mayor; W.G. Perley, (1887-1891), lumberer, promoter with J.R. Booth of the Canada Atlantic Railway, and father of G.H. Perley, the longtime MPP from Argenteuil and cabinet minister, director of the Bank of Ottawa, and vice-president of the Canada Atlantic; and W.H. Hutchinson, (1986-1900), managing director of McKay Milling, director of the Ottawa Electric Railway Company, and former alderman.

East of the canal was represented — after the 1872 acclamation of J.B. Lewis (former mayor, police magistrate, and prominent Tory) — by Dr. Pierre St. Jean (1874-1878), a Reformer; Joseph Tassé (1878-1887), prominent Conservative publicist and subsequently Senator; Honoré Robillard (1887-1896), Conservative contractor and former Reeve of Gloucester. After 1896 — regardless of what happened west of the canal — the Lower Town generally sent Liberals to Parliament Hill, beginning with N.A. Belcourt, (1896-1908), former Clerk of the Peace and Crown Attorney for Carleton County.

In Carleton County, the lumberers' connection was with John Rochester, (1872-1882) an Ottawa brewer, lumber manufacturer, and mayor, who was apparently forced aside in favour of John A. Macdonald (1882-1888), at a nominating meeting rigged by John R. Booth, with the collaboration of James Skead.[103] The seat was subsequently held by G.L. Dickinson (1888-1891) a Manotick miller, whose more famous father, Moss Kent Dickinson, lumber manufacturer, "King of the Rideau", and Mayor of Ottawa, represented adjacent Russell (1882-1887). Apart from Dickinson, Russell also sent to "Ottawa", among others, Robert Blackburn (1874-1878), managing partner in the New Edinburgh Woollen Mills, director of the Bank of Ottawa, vice-president of the "tram" company, director in the Ottawa Electric Co., and sometime reeve of both Gloucester and New Edinburgh, before they became part of the city; and W.C. Edwards (1887-1903), lumberer, director of the Bank of Commerce, and, from 1903, senator.

On the Québec side, Ottawa County was represented continuously from 1867 to 1891 by Alonzo Wright, a "farmer" with continuing interests in lumber, who through his marriage to Mary Sparks, forged an important link with the Sparks family in Ottawa. More directly, E.B. Eddy, the lumber manufacturer, represented Hull in the provincial assembly from 1871-1875, and was mayor of Hull (1870-1873, 1881-1884, and in 1887 and 1891). He was paralleled on the Ottawa side by Erskine Bronson, former city councillor and MPP for Ottawa from 1886 until 1896, and minister without portfolio in Mowat's government from 1890.

Though many of these representatives to the senior governments had previous local experience, and their agents, like Levi Crannell, were prominent local politicans, their primary economic interests tended to put them at odds with the local government. As indicated, their interests in sawn lumber manufactured for export, and utilities monopolies tended to conflict with the ambitions of the dominant local community for metropolitan status, and for a manufacturing base.

There was, then, a certain friction between the local and senior political representatives. As has already been shown, the city fathers repeatedly proved unsuccessful in influencing federal or provincial governments in matters ranging from horse-car franchises to national railways. Ottawa could never rely on the disinterested intervention of its economic cum political élite. Its social élite, dominated by federal politicians and senior civil servants, and headed by the rather exotic governors-general, were not much interested in the city of Ottawa, or probably even the city fathers.

As well as these considerable disadvantages, the city fathers faced serious problems of their own. At the end of the Victorian era they had still not worked out a way to successfully represent the cultural communities in the city. Dreams of metropolitan status, a great railway and manufacturing centre, and a partnership — more or less equal — with the federal authority in the city were repeatedly frustrated. Only railways and utilities (and preserving the cultural and class balance) seemed to admit to some progress, and they thus became the major, if uneasy, focus of city politics.

The uncertainty of politics in the period was to some extent compounded by changes in city council structure. In an effort to obtain better aldermanic representation, the provincial parliament legislated in 1866 an indirect system of electing the mayor, who was to be chosen from and by the fifteen aldermen (three from each of the city's five wards). The system of two aldermen and two councillors implemented in 1855 was abandoned. Aldermanic terms were also changed to three years, one third of the board elected each year. Without the mayoral contest, and the limited number of aldermanic contests, voter interest dropped off dramatically. The indirect system was abandoned in 1873, when the mayor was once again "returned to the people", and all aldermen, three in each of the five wards, were elected annually.

Differential growth of the city and its annexations were also to create new wards. Efforts to divide the growing Wellington Ward, which was grossly under-represented, were begun as early as 1879, but repeatedly failed, due to Lower Town objections and those of the Liberal provincial legislature. Lower Town votes were also largely responsible for delaying the annexation of New Edinburgh, a mixed community to the east of the city, something like Victoria Ward, and of Stewarton, to the south, a natural extension of Upper Town. In 1887 and 1889, the annexations were accomplished in two bites. A new ward, New Edinburgh was created for the 1888 elections, and expanded and named Rideau for the 1889 contest. Wellington Ward was divided for the 1889 elections along Bank to create two Upper Town Wards, Wellington and Central, and a new ward, Capital, was created to embrace the growing south-central area. Another new ward, Dalhousie, was also created to accommodate the growing west side of the city, in the neighbourhood of the lumber yards. There were, then, nine wards with three aldermen each. A property franchise, with the added rider that taxes had to be paid up, persisted. At least as early as 1891 a "labour man" was running for office. "Ladies" voted in the 1891 elections,[104] a practice recommended by City Council as early as 1883.[105]

At the electoral level in civic politics questions of cultural balance were paramount. "Issues" were always in evidence, but representation invariably took precedence. Only when it was settled, could problems be addressed, and when they were, their solutions inevitably had a cultural coloration, and sometimes a class one. There was much questionable government. As one eight-year resident of the city put it in a letter to the editor:

To me, Ottawa has ever been Ottawa — that is, taxes and desolation. True, this metropolitan city has its advantages. Parliament buildings, flourishing bailiffs, countless bankrupts, and 'rings' compared with which both Saturn and New York are 'nowhere'.[106]

Mayors of Bytown and Ottawa, 1847-1907. The old and new city halls are shown at centre. Mayor H.N. Bate is missing.

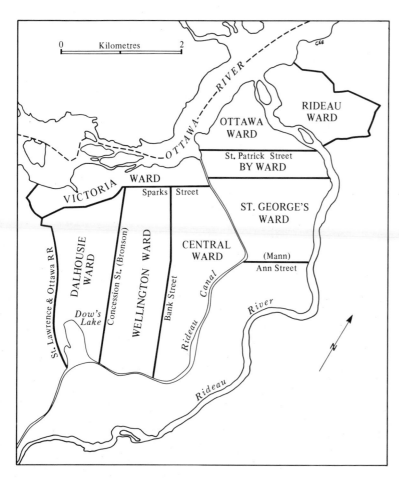

6 Wards, 1889: Government and lumber powered the late-nineteenth-century growth of Upper Town and LeBreton Flats. It was reflected in greater political influence, with the former represented by Wellington and Central wards and the latter by Victoria and Dalhousie wards. Rideau Ward represented newly annexed New Edinburgh.

The final civic election of the century, in 1899, almost symbolically gathered in most of the motifs of the late Victorian age: Lower Town vs. Upper Town; Conservative vs. Liberal (or Reform, as it was known in Ottawa); the utilities or "insiders" interests vs. the civic reformers or "outsiders"; the French vs. the English. To some degree, the influence of the Crown in the town was evident, as was the influence of organized labour.

Ostensibly, the forces of monopoly and civic reform were to do battle. The former was represented by Robert Stewart, alderman, insurance, and financial agent, supported by the "electric interests" with the full strength of the Reform or Liberal organization at his back.[107] Its chief agent in Ottawa for many years was Erskine Bronson. Stewart was "....regarded as the candidate of the Ring whose influence has been exerted in this election to the fullest extent to retain control of the City Council."[108]

W.H. Cluff, active as a reformer alderman, was the "outsider" candidate for mayor. He was charged by his opponents as a "first-class fault finder" who "could never see ability in anyone else,"[109] and was exposed to considerable personal attack, as he had been throughout his career as a reformer (but not "Reform") alderman, and one of the leading figures in the struggle against the power and traction interests, the contractor interests, and what were evidently rather questionable procedures in the management of the city treasury.

But the Lower Town, and particularly the French Canadians, recognized that a battle in the Upper Town provided a golden opportunity for them to prevail. They put forward Thomas Payment, who could not only claim to represent the French, but to represent labour, much of it also French, in both Lower Town and in lumbering wards of LeBreton Flats, Victoria and Dalhousie. He was the official candidate of the Allied Trades and Labour Association.[110] The English-language press saw Payment as a candidate who would distract voters from the central concern (as seen from Centre Town) of issues, to those of *cultures* and, even worse, of *class*. The *Journal* while recognizing that it was the "turn" of a French Canadian to be mayor, argued that "Ald. Payment was not a representative French Canadian,"[111] while the *Citizen* claimed in a post-mortem that Payment was not "...elected on his merits, but because he is representative of a class of citizens rather than of the whole city."[112]

From the voting pattern in the election it is evident that class and

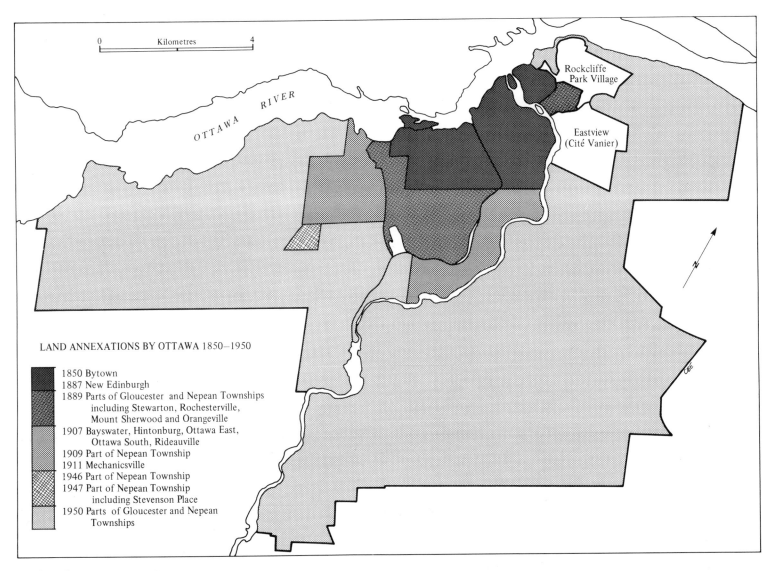

OTTAWA RIVER

Rockcliffe
Park Village

Eastview
(Cité Vanier)

LAND ANNEXATIONS BY OTTAWA 1850–1950

1850 Bytown
1887 New Edinburgh
1889 Parts of Gloucester and Nepean Townships
 including Stewarton, Rochesterville,
 Mount Sherwood and Orangeville
1907 Bayswater, Hintonburg, Ottawa East,
 Ottawa South, Rideauville
1909 Part of Nepean Township
1911 Mechanicsville
1946 Part of Nepean Township
1947 Part of Nepean Township
 including Stevenson Place
1950 Parts of Gloucester and Nepean
 Townships

7 Land annexations by Ottawa, 1850-1950: For much of Ottawa's history, adjacent communities were annexed as the city's need for land met the "suburbs'" need for services. The huge annexation of 1950 was intended as a final solution to the old incremental expansion. By the 1960s it was proving inadequate, but at this point regional government rather than more annexation became the preferred course.

This well-known 1876 view of Ottawa and Hull (bottom centre) shows a full-blown lumber town harbouring a national capital. Within a decade, however, government would begin its inexorable move from the bastion of Parliament Hill and from the parks on Major's Hill and Nepean Point which straddle the canal headlocks. Lithograph by Herman Brosius.

culture prevailed over issues in the election of Payment. He took narrow majorities in culturally mixed, but generally working-class Victoria and Dalhousie Wards; a solid majority in culturally mixed, but generally middle-class St. George's Ward (now serving Liberal masters on Parliament Hill); and, as expected, staggering majorities in By and Ottawa Wards in Lower Town. Cluff and Stewart sawed off the remaining vote all over the city, but especially where it counted, in heavily-populated Wellington and Central wards of the Upper Town. Payment was acclaimed, as usual, in 1900. His election set a pattern for the twentieth century. He was a "Populist" surrogate for the cultural *and* class minorities in the city.

In a broad sense, local political life in Ottawa at Confederation pivoted on a traditional and finely-balanced representation of race and creed, each element usually associated with a specific "territory". That is, the social structure of the city was the paramount consideration, and a common agenda for the city, whether for economic development or social improvement, was almost a practical impossibility. Equally, the balance of forces made it next to impossible, as was the case in many other centres, for a dominant *élite*, identified with the city, to strike an agenda and successfully prosecute it. In Ottawa, none was dominant. There were also a number of other, prestigious *élites* — the lumber barons, the federal luminaries, and the utilities magnates — who operated in the context of corporate enterprises, and who were not organically identified with the city. In a very real sense they used it. They had economic power, social prestige, and, with their connections at the senior levels of government, sufficient political power to compromise local government. The ambitions of the city were in this way contingent on the initiatives of such corporate enterprise. And civic ambitions and corporate ones were rarely coincident in Ottawa.

This depiction by C.M. Manly of a timber slide at Chaudière, with Parliament in the background, was published in the Toronto Art League's souvenir calendar of 1903. The slide, considered the greatest innovation in the timber trade, admitted the passage of cribs. In 1904 the last of these passed Chaudière. Afterwards, the future of the city would rest with the "magnificent pile of stones" on the Hill.

Chapter Four

A Narrowing of Options (1900–1940)

INTRODUCTION

In the first half of the twentieth century, Ottawa began to assume its contemporary and one-dimensional character as a government town. Its turn-of-the-century ambitions for economic complexity — rooted in a balance of lumber, government, and electric-powered manufacturing — melted away.

As the numbers in lumbering and manufacturing slipped, the growth in government compensated, although by the Second World War it had not come to dominate. The Civil Service grew steadily from the early part of the century, as the federal government faced the task of running an increasingly complex, expanding nation. Occupational profiles altered dramatically; religious ones only slightly.

Government also assumed a more significant role in the urban landscape. For government there was greater need for accommodation, and new government buildings proliferated throughout the downtown area. Government also began to change the city in its image. In the first years of the century the "Pittsburgh of the North" struggled with the "Westminster of the Wilderness" and it was by no means clear, at the time, which would prevail.

Though the city made provision before 1900 for a basic urban infra-structure — roads, sewer, water, transit, and the like — it had still made little progress in providing a structure for human security: pure water, public health, garbage collection, housing or welfare services. Equally, the city had only partially solved the educational needs of a "mixed" population. These too were on the twentieth-century agenda.

Politics and community relations at the turn of the century involved a *mélange* of groups — industrial, labour, public service, professional, French, English, Catholic, and Protestant — more or less contending on equal terms. Each, it seemed, had its design for the future, much of it reformist in bent. By the end of the 'thirties the Anglo-Protestant element in the central wards of the city had come to dominate politics, but its earlier reform impulses were exhausted, and most of the other groups had either disappeared, or had withdrawn into garrisons of their own in a curious form of institutional segregation.

ECONOMY AND METROPOLITAN GROWTH

Ottawa's economic prospects at the beginning of the twentieth century were as promising as any city in Canada as the "Lumber — Water Power — Government" capital of the Dominion. They rested on the twin pillars of the old sawn lumber industry and the Civil Service. Barges and steamboats still plied the lower Ottawa and John R. Booth's Canada Atlantic Railway had proven a considerable economic success. Production of pulp and paper had grown rapidly in the 1890s. The Laurier government sought to revive, on a grand scale, the Ottawa-Georgian Bay Canal Project. The city fathers and the Board of Trade, meanwhile, pursued efforts to attract smaller manufacturers on the basis of plentiful, cheap power.

But all these buoyant hopes eventually stagnated or failed. A cheap supply of sawn logs was exhausted; pulp and paper proved a limited source of growth. Hydro-electricty failed to attract industry. There were few local sources of capital, and, it seems, few local innovators, except, notably, men like Thomas "Carbide" Willson. Government did not fund the canal scheme. Booth sold his railway to the Grand Trunk. The manufacturing sector grew little through the twentieth century, buoyed up somewhat by an expansion in the printing and publishing business, led by Rollo Crain's innovations in the production of paper business forms.

A slowly crumbling industrial base was, however, compensated by a rapid expansion in the civil service. It occurred in two sharp phases. From about 1900 to 1910 numbers nearly tripled from the tiny Victorian service of 1,219 to 3,219 by 1910-1911, a gain of some 2,000 "headquarters" employees. The second, driven by the creation of new government departments, occurred in the following decade, to 1920-1921. The 3,219 civil servants of 1910-1911 had become 8,434 by 1920-1921, a gain of some 5,215. Through the 1920s and 1930s, total numbers, which included both the "permanent" and "temporary" employees, rose some 2,000 up to 1939.

The increase in public service employment and stagnation in the manufacturing sector produced significant changes in the city's industrial profile. For men, many jobs in manufacturing persisted (there were 5,203 males in manufacturing in 1911, 5,366 in 1931, and 7,200 in the 1941 war economy). For women it was quite different. The turn-of-the-century Ottawa woman often had a "career" before marriage in the service industries, particularly as domestics, but increasingly turned to the civil service. In 1911, the CS absorbed only 11 per cent of the female work force. In 1931, this figure had risen to nearly 23 per cent and, by 1941, to more than 34 per cent. It settled, after the war, at about 30 per cent. Female participation rates jumped dramatically from 32.8 per cent in 1911 to 63.16 per cent in 1941. Apart from the CS, new jobs were apparently in communications and commerce.

While women were making gains in the CS, however slow and discriminatory, the position of the francophone in the public service appears to have been deteriorating significantly. In 1867 numbers of francophones in the CS correspond to their numbers in the population generally, and they were distributed reasonably equitably through all ranks,[1] protected, it seems, by political patronage. But CS reform in 1908, and especially in 1918, when the Civil Service Commission was reorganized, substituted merit for patronage in headquarters operations. "Merit" emphasized education and discounted French. Francophone participation "declined precipitously."[2] In 1918, francophones numbered some 22 per cent of all public servants, but only 13 per cent in 1946. Among those earning $6,000 or more per year, their representation dropped from 25 per cent to 10 per cent.[3] The French had access to the civil service only by being English.

The place of women in the late Victorian civil service exercised public officials far more than the place of the French. There was the rare exception, like the deputy superintendent general of Indian Affairs, Frank Pedley, who argued (unacceptably to his contemporaries) that superior positions are not filled by women as "...the result, very largely, I think, of the experience that the superior positions have hitherto been filled by men and not by women."[4] Most bureaucrats, however, at the turn of the century, accepted widely-held stereotypes about women in the CS.

> When girls enter first...they are inspired with the idea either of getting married or of something happening that they can get out of the service. They do not usually take the same interest in their duties that a man does who feels that it is his life's work and he is going to remain at it.[5]

Women were seen to have limited upward mobility, not because of a lack of education, but "because they would not be good to control or manage" others,[6] because they lack a certain "business" sense that men had, or because "you cannot confide outside business which would be done by a man having their knowledge."[7] Basically women were different from men: "you cannot put a woman at the same class of work that you could put a man at."[8]

Given the expansion in the Dominion in the early twentieth century, coupled with considerable pressure to place the CS on a technical and professional basis, there was a powerfully felt need to attract promotable young men. But the private sector was outbidding the public. It was not, however, outbidding the public sector for the services of women, who by 1908 were flooding the lower ranks of the CS. In what seems to have been an historical accident, salaries on entry to the CS were the same for men and women, while in the private sector, higher for men and lower for women. Women, because of sexual stereotypes, were not deemed promotable, but because of the non-discriminatory wages, were drowning out the pool of "promotable" males.

The strategy, after the Borden reforms of 1918 and the entrenchment of the Civil Service Commission, was to use the merit principle (and veteran's preference) as a means of both hiring and promoting able young men — preponderantly anglophone — instead of women, who often had the educational qualifications but were by nature unpromotable, and instead of francophones, who were by nature promotable but by education not qualified. These distortions would be reflected in the Ottawa community: the decline of the French and the restriction of women as social forces.

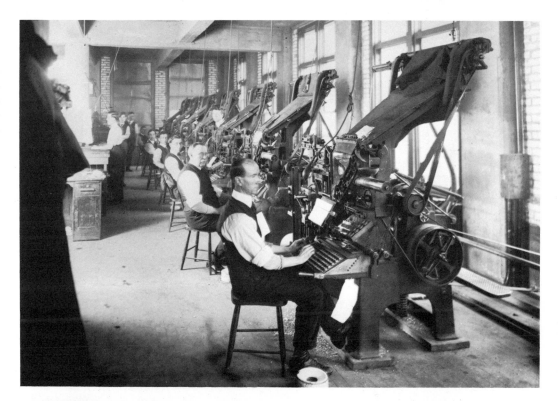

Linotypes and their operators at the Ottawa Free Press, 1908. With the growth of a government market in the twentieth century, printing and publishing rose to become an industry of the first rank.

Bookstore of James Hope and Sons, 35 Sparks St., about 1900. It was retailers like these, along Sparks and Bank streets, that most benefitted from the arrival of government and became the leaders in the Centre Town community.

The Edward P. Connors house, 166 Huron St., is one of the fine examples of the architecture of Francis G. Sullivan. The house shows his familiarity with the work of Frank Lloyd Wright, with whom he was associated before World War I.

Not only was the growth of the civil service important to the city, but the very way it grew. The arrival of government from the outset had proven a support to the Upper Town, and government expansion was reflected in the expansion of the Upper Town area of the city, especially the retail areas on Sparks and Bank and the residential areas stretching southward from the Upper Town core. And the CS was increasingly English, like Upper Town. Inevitably the political balance of the city was altered, as it was, equally, by the relative decline in the industrial areas of LeBreton Flats.

Perhaps the greatest impact from the decline of private sector manufacturing and the growth of the public sector was on the metropolitan ambitions of the city. In effect, the government became a huge corporation, autonomous from the city and committed not to city growth, but to itself. Government responded to the national demands and compromises faced by whatever party was in the Commons. The connection between the growth of individual fortunes and the commensurate growth of the city was broken in Ottawa. Rather, starting in the 1920s, the federal government began re-moulding the capital as a national symbol. Boosterism took a strange form as the city's economy between 1900 and 1940 was revolutionized.

DEMOGRAPHY AND SOCIAL RELATIONS

From the beginning of the century to the First World War, Ottawa experienced one of its most rapid periods of growth. Its population rose from about 60,000 to more than 110,000, an increase of more than 3,000 people per year. Not only did a deceptively healthy economy attract people: a healthier city increased them. Ottawa began to feel the impact of public health measures, expressed in a steady drop in the death rate, especially infant mortality. "Natural increase" boosted the population. Annexations between 1907 and 1911 also added a few thousands of people (and much land) from adjacent townships.

The First World War, at the outset, proved no particular blessing. With the depression of 1913, the decline of the woods-based industries, and the departure of numerous Britons who, in 1914, flocked to the colours, the population of the city actually declined, until about 1917. The government then seemed to discover a nation at war, and began to fill wartime and post-war agencies. Apart from a

Off to War, 1914, from the assembly area at Lansdowne Park. Successful recruiting, combined with a depression in the early part of World War I, resulted in an absolute drop in the population.

slump in population growth in the mid-1920s, probably due to continued problems in the woods-based industries, growth of population, through the Depression of the 30s and into the Second World War, was steadily upward, at just under 2,000 people annually.

Ottawa after 1867 was uncharacteristic of most Canadian cities. Its rather steady growth, rather than boom and bust cycles, was almost unique. Nor was it a recipient of much of the European immigration from the Laurier boom. A mosaic, chiefly Germans, Italians, and Jews, grew only haltingly, and a small Chinese community also emerged. The Germans formed the largest group (1,248 in 1901), but until the post-1945 period the least distinctive. Acceptance into the English community was perhaps easier, and the two World Wars provided apparent incentive for assimilation. Certainly numbers in the German community declined in these war years. Its institutional expressions — churches, clubs, and the like — were small in numbers, discrete in size, and fairly widely scattered.

The case for the Italian (305 in 1901), and Jewish (398 in 1901) newcomers was quite different. Though both were smaller in number than the Germans, they were clearly identified as distinctive groups, the Jews in the market area of Lower Town, the Italians around St. Anthony's church in the "Village", at the southern end of LeBreton Flats. Both, unlike the German, appear to have started poor, and both, where middle-class status has been acquired, have retained greater cohesion.

In 1890, Ottawa's Jewish community was tiny, numbering some forty-six souls.[9] It was led by Moses Bilsky, who, after an adventurous youthful career that took him to the Cariboo and into the American Civil War, settled in Ottawa in 1869 as its only Jew, and prospered as a watchmaker and jeweler. Only by 1892 had the community reached a size sufficient to found a synagogue. The bulk of Ottawa's Jewish population, however, were probably from the towns and *shtetls* of Russia and Lithuania,[10] driven across the Atlantic with thousands of others by the European pogroms at the turn of the century. Many of the early migrants to Ottawa were pedlars, and though the story may be apocryphal, were attracted to the city and its ten-cent licence fee, as opposed to Montreal, where the fee was $25.

By 1900 there were two synagogues in the Lower Town market area. A third was founded in 1911, on James Street, at that time near the end of the Bank Street retail strip. The community quickly developed Hebrew schools and benevolent organizations, including, by 1899, the Ottawa Young Men's Hebrew Benefit Society and the Ottawa Ladies Hebrew Benefit Society, and by 1910, a loan society and burial society.

Many members of the community prospered and were solidly established — generally in merchandising — by the First World War. By almost any measure they had risen rapidly up the social scale in the course of a generation.[11] But the Jewish community, itself, imbued with a strong ethic of mutual self-help,[12] appears to have made a major contribution to the prosperity and well-being of its members. Its homogeneous nature may have been of some assistance in this regard. In the early years, it was solidly orthodox, and it was not until 1938 that a conservative synagogue was established and only in 1966 a reform one.

The Jewish community was, at the same time, autonomous, and fairly well accepted in the larger Ottawa society, though the friendship of its leaders with the Liberals did little to alter Mackenzie King's mind with respect to inter-war Jewish migration. Equally, there were occasionally nasty incidents, notably the anti-Semitic libels of an Ottawa policeman in the depression,[13] and a rather cool reception to Jewish membership in the *élite* clubs of the city. But on the whole they found a niche in the larger society, and did so without compromising their own integrity. To some extent, this accommodation was due to the fragmented nature of the pre-existing Ottawa community, itself almost a federation of relatively closed groups.

Unlike the Jews, Ottawa's Italians existed in relative isolation until the post-1945 period. Some thirty-six people of Italian origin were enumerated in 1881, and by the turn of the century the population had grown to about 305. Original settlement appears to have been in Lower Town.[14] "They worked as labourers, and at a number of skilled trades. Some were fruit vendors, using pushcarts, who in time moved indoors and opened small stores,"[15] But the bulk of them — apparently migrants from the south of Italy — had concentrated in the early twentieth century on the southwest fringe of the city, later Dalhousie Ward, where they worked in labouring occupations and maintained small vegetable gardens. It was this latter concentration that prompted the establishment in 1913 of St. Anthony's Roman Catholic church in the area, under the Servite Fathers. The church, the first and only national parish for the Italians, in turn became the focal point for the community, which was a much beleaguered one before 1950. It had little economic

Merchants and shoppers in the By Ward Market area. In the background is the newer Byward Market Annex (burned 1926).

strength to begin with, and held a minority place in the "ethnic" structure of Dalhousie Ward, where until 1945, English Protestants, and the French and Irish Catholics predominated. Sources of additional migration were cut off after 1920. In the Second World War, when Italy was a belligerent, Ottawa's Italians faced, in addition, forced acculturation.

The post-1945 migration of Italians, however, added considerable strength to the group, both in terms of numbers and leadership, while older members proved upwardly mobile and took positions of influence in the larger society. In addition, the Italians in Dalhousie Ward retained a certain coherence and managed to make social and economic gains compared to other groups, which suffered a series of dislocations in the twentieth century.

Of all the wards in the city, Dalhousie, created in the 1880s, was perhaps the most complex in its development. It was, in broad terms, the southward extension of LeBreton Flats, and like it was focused on the Chaudière sawmills. In the late nineteenth century, it was dominated by Anglo-Protestants, mainly located along the higher ground in the eastern part of the ward. But these were displaced by French and Irish Catholics, who in turn remained strictly apart, to the point that ". . . at no time have the French and Irish ever shared church facilities."[16] "The basis for this conflict was a combination of linguistic and theological differences in the degree of liberalization between the religious sub-groups."[17]

Sectarian conflict, as in the rest of the city, played an important role in the early development of the ward. French and Irish Catholics contended with each other, with the Italian Catholics, and, in turn, with the Protestant and often the Orange groups as well. Up to the 1930s, at least, open conflict would occur on ceremonial occasions, when Catholic processions were harassed by Orange militants. In addition, the ward was clearly a centre of activity and support for class-based and populist politics at least at the local level.

Throughout the city, cultural facts of race and religion continued in the new century to dominate those of class. The numbers of Irish — and census-takers made no distinction between Protestant and Roman Catholic — fell steadily as a proportion of the city's population: from 37.2 per cent in 1871 to 30.3 per cent in 1901 and to 20.9 per cent in 1941. It is conceivable that many Anglo-Irish were assimilating into the English population, for it grew steadily from 17.3 per cent in 1871 to 26.8 in 1941. The proportion of French, 33.0 percent in 1901 and 31.0 in 1941, and the proportion of Roman

Catholics, 53.0 percent in 1901 and 49.4 per cent in 1941, remained relatively unchanged. The Irish Catholic community and the French persisted, though the French became even more concentrated in the Lower Town wards, while the Irish Catholics continued to scatter throughout the city.

But if the Irish Catholics diffused, the English and Scotch (and probably the Anglo-Irish) did not. They tended to concentrate in the wards down the middle of the city: Central and Wellington (the old Upper Town), and Capital and Riverdale (the more recently annexed areas to the south). These wards were characterized in the twentieth century, as in the earlier periods, by high educational levels and generally superior living standards. And they were expanding.

St. George's Ward also retained its wealthy, English-French character, though many of Ottawa's *élite* began their drift from here to Rockcliffe Park Village in the period. Dalhousie and Victoria, the industrial and working-class wards, were the potential source for class-based activity, but the stagnant industrial sector of the city seemed to vitiate them.

Most working-class Ottawa, in the twentieth century as in the nineteenth, led a hand-to-mouth existence, unprotected by social security nets. Those at the bottom end of the ladder, like the maids who came from Lower Town, LeBreton Flats, or the countryside, were completely exposed.

> You did everything, you'd do the washing on a scrub board, and the ironing, and clean, and do the cooking, and anytime they wanted something in the evening, you'd do it. There was no limit to the hours. I don't remember ever being sick, or if I was sick I worked.[18]

On Thursday, "maid's day off", there was release for half a day, and perhaps a weekend every two months. Privileges were removed for failure to clean a knife. Pay was $7 to $9 a month. Recreation was a ten-cent movie or a "walk in the park, and along the Driveways."

Life was only marginally better in other women's work. In the 1920s department store cashiers and telephone operators started at $8 a week. Those with some education could work as supervisors, accountants and nurses at from $16 to $25 a week. Hours were long and sickness ignored. Recreation centered on the movies, the walks, and occasionally a streetcar ride out to Britannia Bay or Rockcliffe Park.

For men, like women, the old paternalist system had a powerful grip on the Ottawa community. Along with the decline of industry,

Celebrations were common in Ottawa. Here is an element of the St.-Jean-Baptiste Day parade of 1913, the fête of the French community.
The Catholic Irish would have their own on St. Patrick's Day, the Protestant Irish on the "glorious twelfth," the various English
communities on the days of their patron saints, and the "Government" on July 1.

it was probably a second major factor in the failure of industrial labour organization to emerge in the city.

Jobs were often obtained through contacts with relatives or friends, and seventeen- or eighteen-year-old lads were introduced to the workplace through a mentor. Work usually began at the bottom, as a sweeper, cleaner, or runner for about fifty-five cents an hour in the inter-war period. Those with some education could enter clerical trades at about $70 to $80 a month to start. Long, faithful service generally brought promotion to foreman or supervisor, and better pay. But security was minimal. There was no compensation for illness, and the lay-off notice, without compensation or pension, was common for men in their fifties.

And as always, the racial and religious divisions in the city seemed to work against a common consciousness. Though job experiences, whether those of French or English, of Protestant or Catholic, have marked similarities, these do not seem to have been communicated across the lines of race and religion. Working people, too, tended to hive off, even more so than the *élite*, in residential enclaves distinguished by attachment to religion and language. The experience of the place of residence overpowered, it seems, that of the place of work.

Ottawa's punctual communities, including the government presence, played a powerful role into the twentieth century in both the shaping and vitality of its "culture", whether sports, arts, architecture or letters. Culture was clearly a reflection of social relations: certain activities tended to be confined to certain groups, in certain areas. And their vitality was inclined to correspond to the vitality of their sponsoring groups. At the turn of the century, sports was perhaps the most lively activity, a reflection of the interest of both the Upper Town business community, and the vice-regal and civil service groups of the government corporation.

On a cold evening in early 1903, for example, a bundled crowd gathered to watch Ottawa's ledgendary Silver Seven play hockey against the Winnipeg Rowing Club. Among the spectators was the governor general, Lord Minto and his wife. The venue was the new Aberdeen Rink (1898), a wooden, vaguely Moorish construction of romantic, late Victorian parentage. The location was Lansdowne Park, recreational testimony to the influence of the Centre Town community, and marking its southern boundary. The best of three series was for the Stanley Cup. Ottawa won it, one of nine times between 1894, when the cup was presented, and 1934, when

Ottawa, as the Senators, dropped out of the National Hockey League, never to return. The crowd left the arena about midnight, nearly all, doubtless, striding forth with a gait labelled the "Ottawa Step", acquired, it seems by skating. "Skating...gives grace and firmness of step, acquired in no other way, and since all Ottawans skate—as in no other city is it so general—it follows that the Ottawa Step is unique."[19] After the game, the Mintos would repair to Rideau Hall, just beyond the eastern boundary of the city, and many in their entourage, politicians and senior civil servants, to Sandy Hill. Few would set out for Lower Town, especially as the Ottawa team was "...composed of young men of the highest circle in the city..."[20] Few games, apart from lacrosse, engaged the community. Similarly, few in the crowd would have found their way to LeBreton Flats, home to the industrial workers of Chaudière. Most of the hockey crowd would have made its way into Centre Town, by the turn of the century the preponderating community in the city. Many would have been business or professional men. Almost all, whether Protestant or Catholic, would have spoken English.

The Irish, however, were more likely to be found attending "Rugby Football", the game "which will make an Ottawan forget his dinner," the game that "has made Ottawa famous all over Canada."[21] Football in Ottawa also tended to speak English. It was also played with vigour. The city team acquired the name "Rough Riders" in 1898, taken from Teddy Roosevelt's Rough Riders of the same year, although a different sport. The label had been used by a Hamilton sports writer to condemn Ottawa for rough play. Only one forward was praised for being manly: "He punches in the face and does not kick from behind."[22] The team was known briefly as the "Senators" from 1925-1927, and from the time Lord Grey presented the Grey cup in 1909, Ottawa won it nine times. Unlike the hockey team, it survived.

Other sports also reflected all the strengths and weaknesses of the Ottawa Society.[23] Winter snow, summer heat, and the rivers and hills of valley were nature's great "nursery", not only for skiers, but for skaters, rowers, canoers, and runners, and a variety of team players. The city and valley provided a rich environment and much opportunity for the budding athlete. But as much as specific sports grew from the legacy of nature, they also grew out of a discrete social *milieux*. Nor was there the sort of personal wealth that could underwrite a major sports undertaking. Nevertheless, the Ottawa communities provided sufficiently strong platforms to produce

Ottawa Hockey Club, 1903. "Champions of the World" and holders of the Stanley Cup.

Ski jump at Rockcliffe, 1921. The area was a favorite for recreation, winter and summer, and site of one of the city's first parks, later managed by the Ottawa Improvement Commission. The jump is now gone.

world-class individuals in sports, and the city and valley have sent a legion to the top in skiing, tennis, canoeing, rowing, figure-skating, and shooting. The city and valley also nurtured, through their junior, semi-professional and university programs, a string of first-rate athletes in team sports, including hockey, football, rugger, baseball and lacrosse. In hockey, Frank McGee, Fred Taylor, Alex Connell, Harvey Pulford, Frank Nighbor, and Bouse Hutton (who played on three championship teams in the same year: hockey, football and lacrosse), as well as Bill Cowley, Syd Howe and King Clancy. In football, there was Tony Golab, and various members of the Southam clan. There were runners like Johnnie Raine, batches of tennis players and paddlers; "all rounds" like the Ross family (The *Journal*), R.T. Shillington, and Tom Birkett. The city was a source of numerous marksmen, and a long tradition at Bisley.

The early twentieth century was the heyday of national class teams: men's hockey (to the 1930s); the Ottawa Alerts, Canadian women's hockey champions in 1923; the Ottawa Rough Riders' football team. It is particularly significant that the Rough Riders, and the early hockey teams, were among the rare beneficiaries of local government largesse in support of athletic or cultural activities. It was not that hockey and football transcended divisions in the community, but rather that their chief supporters were to be found in the Upper Town fragment, which, in the twentieth century, dominated the city council. They were in turn allied with rural Carleton county, which was instrumental in the development of the Central Canada Exhibition and Lansdowne Park.[24] The city owned the park, while the Central Canada Exhibition Association (1888) owned the buildings and managed activities in them. The grandstand and playing field, in later years, were used by the Ottawa Rough Riders, and when the "Civic Centre" was finished in 1967 — through a major contribution from the city — it provided not only new stands for the Rough Riders, but a hockey rink for the newly-formed Ottawa 67s. Ownership of the Silver Seven, as with the Rough Riders and the 67s, was rooted in the Anglo-Protestant business community of the central and western part of the city. It is only they who have been the beneficiaries of city patronage in the provision of sporting facilities, and only they who have generated national-class team sports.

Ottawa's one other important gift to sports was, perhaps, its early swimming pools. But that was unintentional. It was part of a campaign for "baths for the boys", an aspect of a later nineteenth-

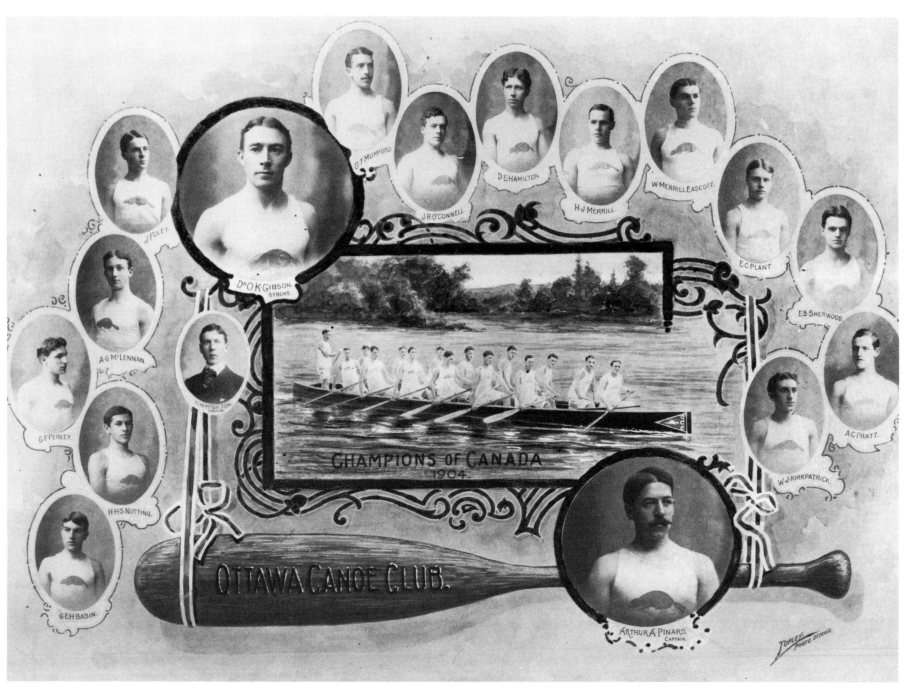

Ottawa Canoe Club, Champions of Canada, 1904. The Rideau Canal and the Ottawa River provided wonderful opportunities for rowing and canoeing, both competitive and recreational. Both sports also carried a certain social appeal, being predominantly the recreations of the English-speaking community.

Lansdowne Park, about 1950. These buildings, in a sense, symbolize the collaboration of the anglophone communities in the city and surrounding Carleton County. The grandstand in the foreground was home to the major sports teams of the city, largely supported by the Centre Town business community. The Aberdeen Pavilion (upper left) contained the hockey rink. Both facilities were used for the annual Central Canada Exhibition, held each summer, which had its roots in the rural county.

century public health movement, that ultimately produced the Plant Bath for working-class Dalhousie ward. It was named for Mayor Plant, a surrogate of the anglo-working-class, and the Champagne Bath, in Lower Town, was named for long-time alderman, controller and Mayor, Napoleon Champagne. Ironically, for sanitary reasons, the facilities could not be used as baths, so they were converted to swimming pools. The *élite*, in the twentieth century, swam in the pool at the Château Laurier.

Those whose tastes ran to more genteel or intellectual diversion — the bulk of them from the middle ranks of the CS — might more likely be found, during that first decade, in the core areas of Upper or Lower Town, or Sandy Hill. But Arts and Letters, from the outset, divided into two streams.[25] Few figures could comprehend both. The French community worked though *l'institut canadien français d'Ottawa,* and the College (and later University) of Ottawa, where a range of dramatic, musical and literary activities had been carried on for two generations. The English community was more associated with the Mechanics Institute and Athenaeum (1853), and the Natural History Society of Ottawa (1863), which, with overlapping memberships, merged in 1869 into the Ottawa Literary and Scientific Society. The naturalists spun off again in 1879 as the Ottawa Field Naturalists Club, under the leadership of James Fletcher. While the naturalists survived to the present, the OLS died in 1907. Much of its role — especially lectures and intellectual intercourse — was subsequently assumed by the Arts and Letters Club, which survived until 1937. It appears to have drawn its membership largely from the Anglo-Protestants and members of the CS, since, at the time, neither group was served by a post-secondary institution, as were both the French and Irish Catholics. The history of the city was kept alive by the Women's Canadian Historical Society of Ottawa.

But intellectual life maintained a fragile existence in the city of the day. It was, possibly, as President Otto Klotz, of the Ottawa Literary and Scientific Society, claimed in 1906

> ...that the great mass of the people is not hungering for intellectual development but rather in search of amusement, entertainment or such forms of diversion as involve little or no mental exertion and stimulate only the more primitive faculties of the mind.
> ...all public meetings and addresses that have an educational object are patronized by a very much smaller number than is to be found at a football match.[26]

Whether "high" or "popular", intellectual or material, Ottawa's cultural activities, too, were a reflection of its essential dynamics.

Culture, at the turn of the century, was typically "stuck on", frequently by the Dominion government, so the city's intellectual reputation owed much to government and its employees. Some native sons, like Elkanah Billings, found in government a vehicle for talents that would otherwise have been frustrated. Billings — a member of the pioneer Billings family — was a moody failure as local farmer, lawyer, and newspaper editor, but from 1856 a reclusive success as a world-class palaeontologist with the geological survey of Canada.[27] More often, of course, the cultural life of the city was nourished by adopted sons and daughters, who came to Ottawa as government employees. Among the scientists were W. T. Macoun, James Fletcher, the Saunders, and Sanford Fleming. In the literary and intellectual world were Archibald Lampman, D.C. Scott, W.W. Campbell, W.D. LeSueur, Lawrence Burpee, A.D. De Celles, Errol Bouchette, Leon Gerin, J.C. Glashan in mathematics, and the Frechettes.

Also notable was the vice-regal influence up until the First World War. The enthusiams of British governors and their wives, coming from what was seen as a superior culture and a superior class, were signal. They lent their benediction to a National Gallery, a Royal Society, Music, Drama, Figure-Skating, Tennis, Cricket, and Skiing.[28] But their enthusiasms lasted only as long as they were present, and the permanent community had to pick up the pieces and carry on after they had gone. They were, to be generous, catalytic. Often the form and the direction of the institutions established, based on British models, were inappropriate. But the further problem with vice-regal patronage, apart from the fact that it was "stuck on", was its intellectual and athletic hi-grading. Rideau Hall drew to itself, for social purposes, the talents and energy of the city *élite*. Not only was Ottawa divided among its communities, but it also had to compete with Government House.

Individual stardom, flowing from the punctual communities inside the city, and achieved in venues outside it, meant that heroic accomplishments — and they have been numerous — and the myths surrounding them, have rarely been embedded in its historical memory. Local heroes were often lost. Nor were they available to help establish a community consensus, whether to boost or promote the city, as occurred in Edmonton,[29] or to contribute to social amelioration, as was the case in Winnipeg.[30] Social or com-

Members of the Ottawa Field Naturalists' Club on an outing in 1901. This club, which can trace its origins to the 1850s, still thrives because of a large community of natural scientists in the city, and because of the city's easy access to "nature." In earlier periods, clubs such as this, along with the churches, appear to have been important for the mixing of the sexes.

William Dawson LeSueur has been called the most impressive Canadian intellectual of his generation. He came to Ottawa in 1871 to work in the Post Office Department, and with other civil servants became central to the cultural and intellectual life of the city. He was a mainstay in the upper-class Literary and Scientific-Society, successor to the Mechanics' Insitute and Athenaeum.

Archibald Lampman (1861-1899): unambitious clerk in the Post Office Department and in the first rank of the "Confederation poets." Like many in Ottawa's cultural scene, he was partly in government, partly in the city, and mostly in neither.

Elkanah Billings, a member of the pioneer Billings family, (1820-1876). Beginning as an amateur naturalist, he came to have an international scientific reputation as the first palaeontologist of the Geological Survey.

Otto Julius Klotz (1852-1923), in 1901. Klotz, an astronomer, was keeper of the intellectual life of Anglo Ottawa, and godfather of the Ottawa Public Library. In 1917 he was appointed director of the Dominion Observatory.

munity meaning in sports, arts, and letters, popular culture or architecture, was frustrated, or narrow.

Ottawa, because of its internal divisions, was more like three or four small cities, rather than a single large one. As a result, its cultural establishments were often small or fragile, and often combined amateur and professional. Supporters, too, given the nature of the city's wealth — salaried — bought tickets with enthusiasm, but could rarely underwrite capital costs. Music was a typical example.

Small organizations of amateurs, and military bands, supplemented from time to time by travelling aggregations, were staple fare for Ottawa audiences before the 1890s. Taste, too, was mainly confined to selections that were short and light. Only in 1894 did the city get its first full-size symphony orchestra, directed by an employee of the post office, F.M.S. Jenkins. It consisted of amateurs with occasional soloists, after 1897 from Montréal and New York. Predictably, financial difficulties appear to have been behind its demise in 1902. It was replaced in 1903 by the Canadian Conservatory String Orchestra, renamed the Canadian Conservatory Orchestra when it got woodwinds, and in 1910 again renamed the Ottawa Symphony Orchestra. It, too, was an amateur and professional ensemble and in 1920 introduced Ottawa audiences to their first complete symphony. Again, financial difficulties, and the departure of the conductor to Toronto, finished the orchestra in 1927.[31]

A series of aggregations kept concert music alive until 1941. There was a wartime hiatus, until 1944, when the Ottawa Philharmonic Orchestra was established from elements of the Air Force Band and aggregations of the Civil Service Recreation Association, the National Film Board and some professional players. It seemed to have been the recipient of the first city cultural grant, one of $1,000. It fell apart in 1960, when the fifty-one professional musicians and management deadlocked over salary.

Dramatic, operatic, and choral groups, likewise, were mainly based on skilled amateurs, supplemented by professional performers, and often by professional directors and producers. They were backed by enthusiasts in boards of directors, and by ticket-buyers. But community support appears not to have been widespread, and certainly that of the city council was not generous. Ottawa has yet to build a first-class cultural or sporting facility.

The fragmented nature of the community, and its curious corporate economy, frustrated the development of first-rate venues for its cultural activities. Various groups, from the Ottawa Philharmonic Orchestra to the Ottawa Choral Society, and the Orpheus Operatic Society, have performed under a variety of roofs, including the Capitol Theatre, high school and collegiate auditoriums, and the city's churches. Only the Ottawa Little Theatre, organized in 1912 after an unsuccessful effort to establish a National Theatre in Ottawa, made a home of its own. In 1928, after Church Union, it purchased the redundant Eastern Wesleyan Church, on King Edward, and performed there until the building burned in 1970. A new theatre subsequently replaced the old "church".

Finally, there was a certain austereness or even crudeness in the Ottawa product. "Rough Rider" is not a misnomer. In the arts and letters, this aspect emerged in an odd form of puritanism. The free play and experimentation of a large community addressing its culture and cultural problems in the context of an understood cultural memory was mainly absent. With rare exceptions, external standards, often dogmatized, prevailed. Even the Ottawa Literary and Philosophical Society put itself out of business in 1915, and reorganized as the Arts and Letters Club of Ottawa in order to get rid of "heterodox members", who "...persistently attempted to turn the society into a means for the propagation of a species of Atheistic Socialism."[32] And in the various literary and scientific societies, the topics of discourse always were stiffened by a certain amount of uplift.[33] These societies, English or French, were, after all, only a sermon away from the numerous churches that brooded over Ottawa society. Not much escaped them. Dark corners of innovation were little tolerated. Perhaps that is why poets like Archibald Lampman, as well as governors-general, took to the wilderness in canoes.

Cultural life apparently began with "civil servants" and amateurs: such as the British soldiers from the 15th Regiment stationed on Barracks Hill, who in 1837 performed the *Village Lawyer* for charitable purposes.[34] A dramatic club was organized in 1850 and played in the old Town Hall on Elgin: a professional troupe first arrived in 1854. It pointed up the need for a proper theatre, and a local syndicate generated $7,500. in subscriptions to build "Her Majesty's Theatre" on Wellington, seating 1,000.[35]

Her Majesty's Theatre was a major venue for a variety of dramatic, choral, and musical groups produced by the pre-government city, the musical and choral groups usually having a link to the

Arrival of government brought national showcases to Ottawa. The Royal Canadian Academy of Arts Building, founded under vice-regal patronage in 1880, was the predecessor of the National Gallery. Such national institutions were a mixed blessing in the city: while local artists benefitted from their proximity, local efforts were often put into the shade.

Ottawa Amateur Orchestral Society, 1898. It was founded in 1894, and its guiding hand was again a civil servant, F.M.S. Jenkins, a member of the Post Office Department.

The Ottawa Philharmonic Orchestra, about 1948, playing in a hockey arena. Like those that came before and after, it was an ensemble of amateurs and professionals that played under whatever roofs were available. It was disbanded in 1960 following a dispute with its professional players, to be succeeded by the Ottawa Symphony Orchestra, counterpoint to the National Arts Centre Orchestra, the "national" as opposed to the "local" ensemble.

The Ottawa Choral Society, 1898.

organists and choirs of the city's churches.[36] Arrival of the civil service gave an added support to the cultural scene. It was likely their patronage that led to the construction, in 1874, by the seven Gowan brothers of Gowan's Opera House (on Albert Street) in Upper Town. Ownership changed and so did the name: to the Grand Opera House. But for a generation it was the centre of the city's cultural life. Its influence declined after the opening of the Russell Theatre in 1897, and it turned to popular entertainments, including motion pictures. It ceased operation after a fire in 1913.[37] Its successor, the Russell Theatre, was located on Elgin again in Upper Town. It again was destroyed by fire in 1901, but immediately rebuilt, and remained the cultural centre of the city until 1928, when appropriated by the Federal District Commission as part of the Confederation Square development. Much of the activity within the French community was centred, after 1876, in a small theatre in the home of the *Institut canadien français* in Lower Town.

Movies came to Ottawa early, largely due to the efforts of the Holland Brothers, Andrew M. and George, though the first movie "theatre", C.W. Bennett's Vaudeville Theatre, the "Unique", was opened only in December, 1906, and combined, as was common, regular showings of movies with live acts. It is unclear whether Ottawa went through the rather disreputable "nickelodeon" stage that had given early movie places a bad name, since Bennett's Theatre provided "...regular showings of moving pictures to Ottawa under the patronage of the Governor General, Lady Laurier and the Mayor."[38] For fourteen years it was the premier vaudeville house in the city.

But from 1928, culture was without a home, except for Loew's Theatre (later and better known as the Capitol Theatre), built in 1920 for motion pictures. It was one of the great "movie palaces" of North America and, in the minds of some, one of the finest.[39] The Capitol, with its large seating capacity (2,353), huge stage, and elegant appointments assumed the premier position from the 1920s. It showed not only movies, but was also the stage from which Ottawa saw the world's major performing artists, many brought by the impresario, Antonio Tremblay. It became a centre of the city's cultural and social life. But it was, all the same, a movie palace and that was its main business. From the expropriation of the Russell House Theatre (1928), until the construction by the federal government of the National Arts Centre (opened in 1969), the city had no first-class venue for live performance. Indeed, the Capitol stayed in operation only until the NAC opened, and was then demolished.

The genesis of the Ottawa Public Library is an almost archetypal illustration of the growth of a public cultural institution in the city. Efforts to supply the town with a library date to 1838, when "newsrooms" were located in the British Hotel in Upper Town and McArthur's Ottawa Hotel in Lower Town, each apparently servicing their respective communities. In 1841, Alexander Grey, a jeweler and bookseller, opened a circulating library which collapsed the same year. By 1844 only one of the two newsrooms was extant. Libraries were subsequently attached to the Mechanics Institute and continued to be maintained when it evolved into the Literary and Scientific Society. From 1852, and into the twentieth-century, *l'institut canadien français,* despite three fires, maintained a library for its members. City Council from time to time provided nominal sums (the maximum seems to be $200 in 1893) to the Literary and Scientific Society to support its Library.[40] By 1895, it seems to have been in storage at the YMCA.[41]

First initiatives toward a free public library were likely taken by the Local Council of Women. The local council, backed by P.D. Ross of the Ottawa *Journal,* successfully petitioned the city for a bylaw to be presented to the ratepayers on January 6, 1896. The council campaigned hard for the bylaw, and enlisted the support of, among others, Lord and Lady Aberdeen, Mayor Borthwick, ex-mayor McLeod Stewart, and E.H. Bronson, the lumber baron. Leading figures in the project were Mary Klotz and her civil-servant husband, Otto. In the midst of the campaign, the Wellington Street home of the lumberer, George Perley, was donated to shelter the library.[42] It was an Anglo-Protestant initiative.

The bylaw, put forward at the end of a depression, was resoundingly defeated, failing to receive a majority in any ward, though opposition was particularly strong in locales with a preponderance of French voters. Activists in 1897 convinced city council to establish a library *board,* but council in 1898, and again in 1899, rejected its petition to establish an actual library. In frustration, Otto Klotz in 1901 independently wrote to Andrew Carnegie, steel magnate and library benefactor, for a donation, stressing the city council's dilatory performance. But one day after he sent his letter, Mayor W.D. Morris and Wilson Southam, proprietor of the *Citizen,* sent a similar one. They, too, emphasized the tight finances of the city and chose as their scapegoats, first a federal government that did not

Interior of the Grand Opera House, 1899. Arrival of government inspired this edifice, which was the premier showcase of the city in the latter part of the nineteenth century.

Interior of the Russell Theatre, 1899: Ottawa's finest theatre from the turn of the century until 1927, when appropriated by federal authorities to clear the way for Confederation Square. After some forty years, its cultural descendant, the National Arts Centre, was built nearby, on the former site of City Hall.

pay taxes, and second a French community that had allegedly defeated the 1896 plebiscite. Carnegie offered the mayor $100,000 for the new library, provided the city would ensure $7,500 a year in operating funds. Klotz never got a reply.[43]

City council, after vociferous resistance, accepted Carnegie's offer. Enabling legislation was not approved until 1902, and only in 1903, after protracted wrangling, did council approve and purchase a site in the Upper Town on Maria (now Laurier) and Metcalfe. Council almost abandoned the project in May, 1903, when Carnegie was quoted (he claimed erroneously) in the *Iron Monger's Journal* that "Canada has no future except as a part of the States..."[44] Construction problems also created problems, including, ironically, the "failure" of the contractor for the "steelwork".[45]

The new library, with its French books still not purchased, was opened in April of 1906 by Carnegie himself. His presence was somewhat embarrassing as "Ottawa Public Library" had been inscribed on a marble tablet in the lobby and chiseled on the external cornice. The former was covered with a brass plate inscribed with "Carnegie Library", the latter covered with bunting and union jacks.

Most of the luminaries in the city attended the opening ceremony. Not invited was ex-mayor W. D. Morris, the man who had solicited Carnegie's money in the first place. He watched proceedings from the veranda of a house across the street, "A Modern Zaccheus".[46]

Like most of Ottawa's institutions, there was little support from the community for the capital costs, whether from the wealthy or from local government, whose members saw it as a "needless luxury"[47] or, in the case of those from Lower Town, as an institution more favourable to the Upper Town and the English. Discretion in the choice of location (at the eastern end of Upper Town), and a commitment of funds for books in French was required to somewhat mollify the French community.

THE URBAN LANDSCAPE

At the turn of the century, the youthful Mackenzie King described the business part of Ottawa as "small and like that of a provincial town, not interesting, but tiresome." It was "not a pretty place save about the Parliament Buildings."[48] Four generations of growth had been directed by government, the lumberers, and a variety of

railway interests. Around these, a multitude of smaller decisions had created the urban landscape in all its confusion and complexity with only "the elementary conception of an ever extending checker board."[49] The lumber piles of Chaudière, which more than once threatened to incinerate the town, remained prominent, as did the railways that carved it up and caused great obstruction to the traffic as well as annoyance and injury to the health of the residents in the vicinity." Ottawa was newly beset by the blighting wires of the telegraph, hydro, and tram companies, and their monopoly arrogance, and — by the twenties — with the automobile.

Aided by tramcars, the growing population spread rapidly, especially to the south and west, leap-frogging the industrial areas, and breaching the boundaries of the Victorian city. More than 1,600 acres to the south and west were annexed in 1907, another eighty in 1909, and a final 119 in 1911. By 1913 the streetcars were carrying some twenty-four million passengers per year. Streetcar travel had increased sixteen times in the twenty-one years up to 1913; population only two and a quarter times.

The impact of the streetcar was twofold. It tended to reinforce patterns in the older parts of the city, while in the newer areas tended to dictate to development, in particular "... the Bank Street line, the Experimental Farm line and the Britannia line did much towards distributing the city's population...."[50] On the commercial front, "the advent of the streetcar transformed Bank Street."[51] Whereas in 1881 there were fewer than fifty businesses along Bank Street, by 1932 there were more than 600.[52]

In Centre Town by 1900 the bulk of the commercial operations was clustered at the east end of Sparks Street. The rest of the area, down to the CAR tracks at Catherine Street, was mainly residential and nearly 87 per cent British in origin.[53] By 1925 governmental, commercial, and office buildings stretched across the northern end of the area in a band nearly three blocks deep. They had mushroomed along both the Bank and Elgin streetcar lines, and were sprinkled among hitherto solidly residential streets.

Much of the displacement of Centre Town residents appears to have been to the Glebe, along Bank, but south of the cross-town rail lines. It was so called as much of it was a glebeland of St. Andrew's Presbyterian Church, the flagship of the Upper Town Scotch. It was developed for the most part with the prestige homes of the well-to-do, Anglo-Protestant community.

East of the canal, much remained as it had been. Lower Town,

The fire that burned the Centre Block of the Parliament Buildings in 1916. Many at the time believed it to be the work of Axis saboteurs.

Pavilions such as this, on the grounds of Parliament Hill, were a prominent feature of efforts to improve the National Capital in the early twentieth century. The tower of the Centre Block, burned in 1916, is seen in the background.

Sparks Street, looking east to the Russell Hotel, 1900. Paved, lighted, and beset by its "eternal tram cars," it was known as the "Broadway of Ottawa."

View from the Centre Town home of photographer Samuel Jarvis, 161 Gilmour. Now part of a re-gentrified section known as the "Golden Triangle," this was a developing area in 1899.

solidly French, remained in stasis; the fine residences of Sandy Hill attracted yet more; New Edinburgh, in the shadow of prestigious Rockcliffe Park Village, began its slow conversion from a mixed industrial area to one of the more sought-after addresses.

The area between the canal and the Rideau river was added to the city with the annexation in 1907 of the Village of Ottawa East, much of it working-class and associated with the rail-yards and warehousing of the area; and Rideauville, which became known as Ottawa South, a rather less prestigious extension of the Glebe.

Expansion was complicated by the Rideau river, the canal, and the tangle of rail-lines, which together cut the city up into distinct areas, and militated against interaction or blending. Such obstacles also created serious problems of engineering and traffic flow. In 1915, within a five-mile radius of City Hall, there were 112 dead-end streets, seventy-eight level crossings, and fifteen grade-separations. Bridging, whether rivers, canal, or railways, was a central concern at City Hall. The alternative was to eliminate the obstacles: removal of rail-lines; filling in the canal. Both were suggested.

Obstructions to the city's streets became even more crucial when the automobile and truck began to play a role in its development. A steam-car was apparently demonstrated in 1891 at the exhibition, and in 1900 Mrs. Thomas Ahearn drove a electric Stanhope buggy down the newly-paved Sparks Street. The first automobile with an internal combustion engine appeared on Ottawa's streets a year later. But before the First World War the automobile was largely a rich man's toy, a fact underlined by the 1916 Holt Report on the planning of the capital. It ignored the automobile as a factor in its discussions and recommendations: there were only some 400 autos in 1912, though in 1910 drivers had been fined for speeding.

By the 1920s, the automobile and the truck could no longer be ignored. Eleven years later, in 1931, automobiles in Ottawa numbered some 23,000 and trucks 3,200. By 1923 traffic problems were reported as serious.[54] The police, too, were motorized, with a two-car fleet in 1912 and a motorcycle in 1918.

Concerns with growth, with the amelioration of health, housing, and traffic problems, and with the development of Ottawa as a national capital, led to an especially heightened agitation for planning at the turn of the century. But as the issue of planning emerged, there also emerged, as the city made the transition from lumber town to government town, the critical question of whose plan.

In effect, there were, at the beginning of the century, three planning visions: the old one of the city as a place to do business; the newer one of Ottawa as a national symbol; and finally, under the urging of a number of municipal and health reformers, the vision of the capital as a living place.

The planning vision rooted in business growth, probably reached its peak in the early part of the twentieth century. It was chiefly concerned with promoting a healthy business atmosphere, especially for the retail trade, from which most of its advocates came. The chief "planning" dimension, however, was the development of the "city efficient": good water and sound roads, cheap energy, and capable local government. There were successes, chiefly the municipal power movement that created Ottawa Hydro, and the good government movement, successful in 1908, in the creation of the Board of Control, seen as parallel to a corporate board of directors, efficient and businesslike. But this planning vision was still narrow.

As planning for growth reached a peak in the early years of the century, a parallel movement, aimed at providing a city in which people could live, as well as do business, emerged. It embraced a number of city reform politicians, but its chief driving force appears to have been a number of professionals, like Dr. Charles Hodgetts, concerned with a "salubrious" city, a number of architects, concerned with the aesthetics of the capital, and, of considerable importance, its only professional town planner, Noulan Cauchon, a dress reformer — he advocated the wearing of shorts (by males) to expose the body to sun — and former railway surveyor and engineer.

As early as 1910, Cauchon had conceived of a comprehensive plan for city and capital, one that was widely publicized in Ottawa.[55] He argued for the rationalization of the railway mess;[56] called for a segregated industrial area in the east end of the city;[57] put forward a plan for Parliament Hill and area;[58] urged improvement of internal transportation, including electric rapid transit;[59] and advocated the "great Circle Parks", now the Greenbelt.[60] City Council endorsed this comprehensive scheme in 1912.

Through the agitation of Cauchon, a number of sympathetic aldermen, professionals, and businessmen, and with support of the newspapers, Ottawa set up its own town planning commission in

Numerous plans were drawn up in the twentieth century to create a "city worthy of the capital." This one, by the Chicago planner E.H. Bennett, was proposed in the report of the Holt Commission, 1916. It looks north along the line of the Rideau Canal. Holt's report ignored the automobile as a factor of city life.

1921. Cauchon was chairman, and remained so until his death in 1935. The new OTPC, "persuasive" in nature, was the first city planning instrument. With a small complement of sympathizers on the aldermanic board, and in the atmosphere of post-war city planning enthusiasm, it re-affirmed Cauchon's 1912 plan for the National Capital,[61] rejecting Sir Herbert Holt's 1916 version, which was sponsored by the Federal government. It quickly embarked upon the development of a zoning plan.[62] At a practical level, it spent much time "rounding corners", to speed traffic along the streets.

But the city fathers, when it came to actually doing anything, showed little enthusiasm. Reform was exhausted by the mid-20s and planning with it. By the 1930s, the council was totally uninterested. Though the OTPC lasted on paper until after the Second World War, it was, by the time the Depression arrived, effectively moribund. As Cauchon himself observed on the matter of planning "the Council has deemed it wise to proceed with much caution in this matter, both with regard to expenditure and legislation."[63]

Ottawa's city fathers had a particular excuse not to plan. They felt the federal government and its pocketbook should play a central role in developing the city as a capital. To begin, it should pay its property taxes. But the Dominion's obligations went further: "The government may reasonably be expected to contribute in addition such sums as are necessary to make a Capital worthy of the nation."[64]

> In all great countries the spirit of the nation had found expresssion [sic] in the capital city. Further the national spirit of the people has been unified and stimulated by the creation of a stately and magnificient capital. If Canada is to be a great nation the capital of Canada must in dignity and beauty be made worthy of a great people.[65]

But apart from Laurier's 1893 promise to create a "Washington of the North", little was done about capital planning. In 1896, two city alderman, Fred Cook and Robert Stewart, convinced city council to undertake a study of national capitals, especially in their relations with local governments and with respect to capital beautification. Their findings, embodied in an 1897 petition from the city, prompted the federal finance minister, W.S. Fielding, to prepare legislation providing for capital improvement from the national budget.[66] The result was the creation in 1899 of the Ottawa Improvement Commission (OIC). The city was to receive the cosmetic of capital improvement. It was for the nonce a token gesture, or as Thomas Ahearn later put it, the OIC chairmanship "...was more or less a pleasantry on the part of Sir Wilfrid"[67]. Nonetheless, an agency of the federal government would participate directly in the development of the city, an "imperium in imperio", as one man put it. The OIC, with its small budget ($60,000) and limited powers, carried out, in the early years, what amounted to a program of urban brush-clearing and prettifying. It also paid the city $15,000 for services, like fire protection, supplied to government.

In the early part of the century the federal government, itself, became more prominent in the urban landscape. Prior to 1896, its chief impact had been the creation of the Central Experimental Farm in 1886, on some 465 acres, much of it a farm owned by J. R. Booth, and the construction in 1885 of the Langevin Block on Wellington Street. But with the beginning of the Laurier boom, there was a boom in government construction. Between 1896 and 1913, eleven new government buildings were erected, including showcase structures like the Public Archives, Royal Mint, and Victoria Memorial Museum. Most were in the core area.

More important, the national government (and in particular its prime ministers) developed a special interest in the affairs and the appearance of the city. In the nineteenth century the city was urging the national government toward schemes of improvement; the roles were reversed in the twentieth. The government had made some identification with the place. It would often conceive of it as its own. It required only the active intervention of Mackenzie King in 1927 to establish the planning supremacy of the federal authority.[68] There was delay due to the war and the reconstruction of the Centre Block, which had burned in 1916.

King's instrument was to be the Federal District Commission (FDC) of 1927. It was, in the main, a simple successor to the OIC, and continued the OIC tradition of spending the bulk of its efforts in park and driveway developments. King, however, placed at the head of the FDC the Ottawa utility magnate, Thomas Ahearn, a man used to getting his way. Much local representation disappeared with the new commission. As well as the aggressive chairman, the name "federal district" also held much significance. For the first time the instrument for planning the capital was formally to move across the river into Hull. Ottawa was losing its monopoly as capital. And King asserted the federal presence in the core, with the development of Confederation Square and Park, in the heart of

Prime Minister William Lyon Mackenzie King at Kingsmere. King was an enthusiastic landscape-planner of his Gatineau estate and of the city. A large federal presence in the Ottawa core owes much to his efforts.

Upper Town. In 1927 he winkled a $3 million capital appropriation for the project from Parliament. It was the first investment on such a scale for the "improvement" of the federal capital.

In a broad sense, the activities surrounding the development of Confederation Square had the effect of squeezing the city out of its own centre, including its City Hall. King had determined that the area of Confederation Square — for two generations the heart of the *city* — would assume a new role as the heart of the *capital*.

The burning of city hall in 1931, and the removal to temporary offices (as it turned out, for more than twenty years), seemed to demoralize the elected politicians. They were in the nature of orphans adrift in their own land. As the city's planning impulse died in the 'thirties that of the federal government was renewed, when King hired the French planner, Jacques Gréber, to advise on planning the "Parliamentary Precinct". The war interrupted the prosecution of these plans, but as will be described later, they were revived afterward on a much larger scale. A somewhat demoralized city faced an active and determined federal government across a somewhat shabby urban landscape.

THE URBAN COMMUNITY

In the years before the Second World War, Ottawa confronted the large issues of education, health, and welfare. Though the city built a range of modern institutions — schools, hospitals, health and social service facilities — and established a supply of pure water, its deeply-rooted social fragmentation conditioned their evolution and dictated their form. Institutional separation was established as the formula for community life. But in politics, where separation was not possible, the groups first contended, and were then dominated by the Anglo-Protestant Centre Town community. Politics, unlike the community, became one-dimensional.

Church, state, and school — all intertwined — were the chief institutions that sought to mediate the affairs of the urban community after main force was abandoned in the rubble of the Stony Monday Riots of 1849. By the turn of the century, however, the elementary school as an institution, bent and twisted in the wind of racial and religious controversy, had ceased to play its role of social control and mediation. It had, rather, in the separate schools controversy, become the centre of the storm.

Educational controversy emerged at the outset with the passage of Ryerson's Common School Act of 1846. Prior to that time, children were taught by parents, tutors, or in private schools like James Maloney's "English Mercantile and Mathematical Academy" (1827-1879), or in the bilingual institution established in 1845 by the Sisters of Charity.[69] Debate in the early years swirled around a proposed linguistic and sexual division of the public school system. These divisions were firmly rooted in religious sensibilities. Bytown's Common School system was originally to have been English only, and sexually mixed, a protestant or "New England" innovation. An immediate effort was made to obtain a French School on grounds "that it is but just and reasonable there should be in Bytown a school in which the French language may be taught, as a large portion of the inhabitants are of French Canadian origin, and of right are entitled to Educational privileges."[70] There was also to be settled the "question regarding Schools for the education of Females,"[71] a matter of great importance to the Catholic Church in Bytown.

The two men who pressed these issues, J.E. Robichaud, a French Catholic, and Henry Friel, an Irish Catholic, were a two-man minority on the seven-man board of education. Robichaud could achieve only a limited compromise. After a talk with the Bishop of Bytown, "whose opinion I considered valuable" Robichaud said that:

> ...instead of...putting motions which I knew very well would fall to the ground, — I seconded a motion giving Fifteen Pounds to the French Teacher, which was also carried by a casting vote of the chairman. As to the French School for Femals [sic], the proposition would not be listened to. In the first place, some members of the Board considered that the allowance to the Sisters of Charity would effect that object; and, in the second place, a majority would be against it.[72]

Matters were much different by 1850. Between 1850 and 1855 the Lower Town and largely Catholic population (under the 1850 charter, gerrymandered in Reform interest), had gained political control of the town. Catholic education was funded, including that of Catholic girls.

Much would change again on January 1, 1855. The newly-chartered city was carved up into five wards that gave the Protestant sectors of the community a narrow preponderance, of which they immediately took advantage. There followed the municipal offices bloodbath of 1855. It extended to the school board. Its new chairman, James Cox, insisted that the French schools be closed. As well, he announced that Roman Catholic children would no longer be segregated by sex in the Lower Town school.

> The town until lately was entirely under the control of the Roman Catholic priesthood, who, as you are aware, are strenuously opposed to education of every form.
> The division of the town under its late municipality, gave to Roman Catholics the preponderance in the board of school trustees, and as a consequence they carried every measure to suit the views of the priesthood.[73]

The Roman Catholic population of Ottawa, in response, moved quickly to take advantage of the provisions of the provincial Separate Schools Act of 1853 and the Taché Act of 1855. By December 25, 1855, there were boards of separate school trustees in every ward. The separate school position was further consolidated by the Scott Act of 1863. Under this act, separate elementary schools could receive a share of municipal as well as provincial monies.

Institutional segregation of Protestants and Catholics proved a satisfactory, if not uncontroversial, solution to elementary education for some twenty-five years. Then new controversy erupted, this time on linguistic lines.

In Ottawa, from 1856, there were two linguistic systems operating under the single Roman Catholic Board, guaranteed by the *understanding* that one French and one English trustee would be elected from each ward in the city. By the 1880s, there was a rising tide of language-based militance in Québec, and it was carried into Ontario communities. This activity served to frighten English Catholics, mostly Irish, who began a campaign, to the delight of the Anglo-Protestant language extremists, to put an end to "bilingualism" (the buzz word for French schools) within the Roman Catholic Separate system. No more than in Ottawa did Ontario's English-speaking Catholics (also mostly Irish) feel trapped "...between the upper millstone of French-Canadian nationalism and the lower millstone of protestant bigotry."[74] The result was that they "...chose primarily the language option, thus indirectly siding with the Protestants...."[75]

It was particularly galling inside the Ottawa separate system. The French controlled the Catholic vote in the city wards, and, from time to time, there was "bi-lingual" (that is, French) "intervention" in the elections that put the Irish in a minority. It occurred in 1886, again between 1903 and 1906, and again in 1914. English-speaking Roman Catholics in Ottawa, their influence on the board problematical, attempted from the 1890s to counter French strength by the use of provincial regulations and inspection, charging, for example, that the Christian Brothers, who provided the male, "bi-lingual", elementary teaching in Ottawa, neglected English, contrary to law. A provincial regulation, requiring Ontario teachers' certificates, was used to hoist the Christian Brothers (who had theirs from Québec), out of the Ottawa system. The dispute erupted again in 1904, when the French-dominated board, through "intervention", attempted to give a ten-year contract to the returned Christian Brothers. The English portion of the separate board obtained a court injunction to block the move, and urged the Conservative government of Ontario to take action. In 1910, it appointed Dr. F.W. Merchant as a one-man commission to look at the "bi-lingual" issue. His report was critical: "bi-lingual" teaching was mostly French, and mostly poor. The government responded by strictly applying Regulation 17, aimed at upgrading the "bi-lingual" system through making it English. French, as a language of instruction, was prohibited, except in the first two years. Thereafter it could be only a subject of study. Teachers without sufficient English to teach the public school curriculum would be barred.[76]

The resistance was ferocious in Ottawa, where the newspaper, *Le Droit*, was founded in 1913, to defend the French in Ontario. When the Separate Board, dominated by "French intervention", in 1914 determined to hire the Christian Brothers, the whole separate system was closed down, and in 1915 placed in the hands of three provincial commissioners. The Irish launched a lawsuit against the closure (and were successful), and the French against the commission (also successful). There was more.

> ...sacraments were refused to Catholics who sent their children to public schools; children walked out of the Garneau School when the inspector insisted on questioning them in English; parents and children demonstrated in the streets: and riots broke out at the Guigues school in opposition to the teachers provided by the official commissioners.[77]

The issue inflamed politics at all levels, including national, but at the local level it seemed to commit the French even more resolutely to their Lower Town garrison. And, from the time of the Separate*

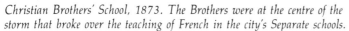

Christian Brothers' School, 1873. The Brothers were at the centre of the storm that broke over the teaching of French in the city's Separate schools.

The Ottawa (later Lisgar) Collegiate Institute, about 1880. This was the flagship of the city's secondary system, which was English-speaking, non-denominational, and run by a board appointed in the main by City Council.

Prospective teachers toiling in a garden at the Normal School, or teachers' college, June 1909. Built in 1879, it was the province's second such college. Its functions were moved to the University of Ottawa in 1978.

Schools issue, they remained an entrenched minority.

In the 1920s the French found new allies among a number of Anglo-Protestants, who formed a "Unity League". Working closely with the French Canadian Educational Association, they linked French language rights to national unity, and urged a national identity based on a bi-lingual culture. Meanwhile, within the Ottawa community, efforts at reconciliation between the French and Irish communities were successfully carried out by Rev. P.J. Cornell, an Oblate and Pastor of St. Joseph's Church. He negotiated in 1918 an institutional division of the Separate Board, once again into French and English committees. It was the traditional and largely successful compromise. Social realities in the Ottawa community were, by the 1920s, solidly entrenched in the institutional separation of elementary education. A public board ran the English and non-confessional system. A Roman Catholic Separate Board ran a parallel system, confessional in nature, but divided into French (or "bi-lingual") and English sections. Secondary education in Ottawa was more class-bound.

From the establishment of the Dalhousie District Grammar School in 1843, until the consolidation of secondary education under the Ottawa Board of Education, January 1, 1970, public secondary schools in Ottawa were run by an *appointed* Board of Trustees.[78] Funding was mainly private and provincial until 1871, when local tax support was legislated. The public secondary system was English and non-confessional. It was also for the wealthier.

Secondary education in French was, by and large, provided by schools operated privately by religious orders. Only in 1968, did the Ontario government permit public secondary education in the French language to Grade X, and in September of that year the Collegiate Institute (or secondary school) Board assumed responsibility for seven French-language schools, with some 3,500 students.

Tax-supported elementary instruction in French, though frequently threatened, was available in Ottawa from the outset. But public secondary education in French was not. Nor was that education confessional. On both grounds of language and religion, the French Catholic community faced barriers at the secondary level that restricted subsequent job access, and access to universities. Only the wealthy could afford the additional tariff of the private school. For the English Catholic the problem was parallel, but less formidable. Whatever the qualms about entering a secular system,

there was not the additional barrier of language. Public funding of Catholic separate schools to Grade X was subsequently legislated, and in 1984, in principle, extended to Grade XIII.

Federal bilingual policies, dating from the 1960s, sent a shock wave through the Ottawa community. In effect, a bilingual capacity was for the first time in 100 years an advantage for mobility within the public service, the biggest game in town. It implied a major revision within the Ottawa school system, especially the initiation of a French immersion stream, beginning in kindergarten, in the public system.

As for post-secondary education, it was traditionally obtained by the Anglo-Protestant community from Queen's, McGill, and the University of Toronto, despite the presence of the University of Ottawa in the city. Only in 1938-1939, did a committee of the YMCA begin to discuss a non-Roman Catholic institution. War caused a discontinuation of these efforts. They were revived in 1942 under Henry Marshall Tory, with the support of much of the original committee, now designated the Ottawa Association for the Advancement of Learning. From these beginnings, Carleton College was organized in 1942, along with an Institute of Public Administration in 1943, the latter subsequently brought under the umbrella of the college, which in turn became Carleton University. The committee that, in 1938-1939, initiated Carleton had noted that "while the Roman Catholic population was served by the University of Ottawa and St. Patrick's College, the somewhat larger non-Catholic population had no institute conducting college work . . . ."[79] Carleton College and University, in that sense, corresponded at the post-secondary level to the Ottawa Public system at the elementary level. It completed an English and protestant system.

The Roman Catholic community had long possessed an institution of higher education in Ottawa, in the form of Ottawa College, later the University of Ottawa. But its parochial foundation was unacceptable to the protestant community. It was largely run by the Oblates, who formed much of its teaching staff. Like the Catholic elementary system. it was much divided by the language controversy. In its early years it was primarily a French-language institution, but became largely English (more properly Irish Catholic), in the latter third of the nineteenth century. They were superseded, in turn, by the French community in the latter nineteenth and early twentieth centuries, and ultimately the Irish

Convocation at Carleton University in 1954. Shortly after this picture was taken, the university moved southward to a new campus near the intersection of the Rideau River and the Rideau Canal.

Tabaret Hall at the University of Ottawa, nearing completion in 1903. A statue of the Rev. Father J.-H. Tabaret stands in the foreground. In 1853 Tabaret had been placed in charge of the university's predecessor, The College of Bytown, and he oversaw its move from Lower Town to its present site in Sandy Hill and its erection as a university.

Roman Catholic community sought a solution in institutional separation, almost on a pattern of the elementary system.

In 1929, the Irish Catholic community announced the opening of a new English-language institution, to be called St. Patrick's College. It was to have an ambitious program in the liberal arts and sciences, and plans for the applied sciences. Chronic financial problems in the post-war period eventually led in 1967 to amalgamation with Carleton University.[80] In the same period, the University of Ottawa secularized and developed its present form as a bi-lingual institution, rather than a Catholic and French one.

In health, as education, coercion, not conviction, led after thirty years to the conversion. Coercion and conversion were precipitated by two typhoid epidemics.[81] The first swept across the city in January of 1911, and when it ended in March, some 987 cases had been reported and eighty-three had died.

It was not as if the city were taken unawares. The epidemics of the 1880s (1,500 cases in 1887) were distant, but remembered. The waterworks as a source of disease had been pointed to by the MHO in 1900. And the city itself had, in 1910, hired a waterworks consultant, who had recommended general water treatment, including chlorination, or alternatively, a pure supply from the nearby Gatineau Hills. Nothing was done. In 1910, the health department estimates were only $3,000, and its staff was almost unchanged from 1875. Granted, some of the earlier tasks of the health department had been assumed elsewhere. In 1902 the Strathcona or Isolation Hospital was opened, chiefly to accommodate young patients with the contagious diseases of childhood, such as diphtheria. A smallpox isolation facility was maintained on Porter's Island, in the middle of the Rideau River, consisting of a shack and a tent, but was little used since subject to spring flooding. In 1907 systematic scavenging, paid for by the city, but contracted out, was launched under the direction of a protesting city engineer who preferred it under the health department "where it properly belongs".

Provincial pressure in 1911 appears to have been critical in causing the overhaul of the city's health department. Reform of the health department was also good politics. It gave the appearance of action, and was seemingly cheap compared to the typhoid epidemics, which had cost the city $20,000 to care for and compensate victims. And the publicity of the provincial and federal inquiries was clearly causing some economic distress. It was one reason the mayor "declared" a subsequent typhoid epidemic at an end. There was concern that visitors would stay away from the annual Central Canada Exhibition. The epidemic, paying no heed to the mayor, continued.

The events of 1911 "... resulted in placing the department on a most substantial and practical basis. The health officer ... is now assisted by a competent chemist and bacteriologist, a chief food and dairy inspector and assistant, a chief sanitary inspector with a number of assistants, whose duty it is among other things to patrol the shores of the Ottawa River to prevent as far as possible the ... contamination of the river above the intake pipe." The report added that the thirty-two meetings held during 1911 established "... a record unequalled for many years." The majority were sessions "replete" with sanitary subjects.[82] The budget proposed for 1913, compared to the $3,000 for 1910, was indicative of the change: $15,000 was proposed for general operation, $24,000 for salaries, and in addition some $61,000 was allocated for the operation of the isolation, smallpox, tuberculosis, and chronic care hospitals in the city.[83] A full-time medical health officer had been hired by 1913, and he was supported by a four-man bacteriological department, four food inspectors, six sanitary inspectors, two plumbing inspectors, a disinfector, and an office staff. New programs included a modified milk program, and by 1918, an annual baby contest at the exhibition. These were followed after the war by the establishment of well-baby clinics and ultimately a scheme of district nursing, as well as a veneral disease clinic. By the end of the 1920s, typhoid had practically disappeared as a killer, tuberculosis was under control, and infant mortality had dropped dramatically, from a 1904 rate of 170.7 per 100,000, to one in 1939 of 39.26.[84]

But while the overhaul of the health department had been rapid, the solution to the critical problem of pure water proved to be a protracted one. The 1911 epidemic was traced to Nepean Bay, polluted by raw sewage and human waste. It should not have been a factor, since the city's water supply was drawn from the middle of the Ottawa River, and carried under the Bay in two large intake pipes. But it was discovered that in periods of low water, like January of 1911, emergency intakes on the shore of the bay were opened to provide necessary additional flow for fire prevention. In effect, the city was pumping raw sewage through its mains. These emergency intakes were ordered closed and sealed after the 1911 typhoid outbreak. The Medical Health Officer resigned, due to stress.

But 1912 started badly. A provincial health inspector visiting the

Shack and tents on Porter's Island, near the mouth of the Rideau River, served at the turn of the century to isolate people with contagious diseases, such as smallpox. Spring flooding often made its use problematic.

Taylor McVeity. His efforts to get to the bottom of the typhoid epidemics that beset the city in 1911 and 1912 cost him his job as city solicitor, but won him the mayor's chair.

city encountered a major smallpox epidemic (224 cases and two deaths). He scored the city for its inadequate procedures and facilities, including the new smallpox isolation facility, and threatened to close down the entire city. Smallpox was followed in July by the second, and more severe typhoid epidemic, with 1,378 cases and ninety-one deaths. The cause, given the reforms of 1911, was held to be a mystery. But an apparent cover-up was revealed when a curious supreme court judge, acting privately, discovered that the source of the epidemic was a poorly engineered and leaking intake pipe, once again drawing the polluted water of Nepean Bay into the city's mains. It was ordered closed, leaving the city with a single (and its oldest) intake pipe. A judicial inquiry was ordered into the health and engineering departments. It eventually resulted in the resignations of both the city engineer and new MHO (who had earlier taken a leave of absence as a result of a nervous breakdown). More significant was the effort of the City Solicitor, Taylor McVeity, to show at the inquiry, collusion between the city engineer and the mayor. He was unsuccessful, and in the process was fired.

The city for nearly two years limped along on a one-pipe water supply, while local politicians ferociously debated alternative schemes. Eventually, the much reduced pressure came to the attention of fire underwriters. In November, 1914, they termed it inadequate, imposed a surcharge on existing policies, and refused to write any more. Fire protection was thus linked to health protection.

Early 1915, the Ottawa Board of Trade hired its own consultant. He recommended supply be drawn from the middle of the Ottawa River, subjected to basic treatment on Lemieux Island, and then sent by two huge pipes on a bridge *over* the polluted Nepean Bay waters into the city's system. A first pipe was in operation by 1917, and a second to complete the system only by 1919. It remains a current source of supply.

But the critical factor that explains both the long-term resistance and the precipitate plunge toward solution appears to have been socio-economic, mixed up, as usual in Ottawa's case, with geography. Poverty, disease and death had long been associated, but in Ottawa these factors had a pronounced racial, religious, and locational dimension. Mortality in Victorian and early twentieth-century Ottawa was persistently higher among French and Catholics, and therefore also in French, Catholic, and poor areas,

Repeated typhoid epidemics were traced to intake pipes drawing water from polluted Nepean Bay on the Ottawa River. The solution, shown here, was to run the pipes over the river from the purification plant on Lemieux Island.

(see Table VIII), but not in the English and protestant areas that controlled council.

Public health meant, in effect, taxing the property of those who were already healthy for the sake of those who weren't. But worse, in Ottawa, it meant taxing the Anglo-Protestant community for the benefit of the Catholic one. Epidemics, fortunately, proved bad for business. They also cost. Property had to be taxed to compensate victims. At that, a pure water supply might have been a long while coming had it not been for the demands of the fire-insurance underwriters. Lack of insurance most affected those with much property.

The influenza epidemic of 1917 triggered the birth of final major health facility of the period. In 1924, the 500-bed Civic Hospital was opened. It was under-written by the city and merged the Protestant General Hospital (1849), the Ottawa Maternity Hospital (1894), and St. Luke's General Hospital, (1898). It incorporated a School of Nursing. With 850 students, it was the largest in Ontario in its time. It was the protestant counterpoint to a Catholic system already in place.

As the chairman of the Board of Health was to put it in 1919:

"...public health is very largely in the nature of a purchasable commodity: that, along with firefighting appliances, pavements and sewers, it must be, within rational limits, bought and paid for."[85]

Social welfare, like public education and health, reflected the tensions among the various Ottawa communities, and between the private and public sectors. Only in the twentieth century was some resolution effected. The division between the public and private sector was rationalized in the 1920s; the division among the Ottawa communities in the 1930s. And perhaps only in the post-Second World War period did charity and welfare cease to be considered a special vocation of women.

In somewhat *ad hoc* fashion the Protestant community had set up by the turn of the century the YMCA and YWCA; the United Protestant Benefit Society; the Home for Friendless Women; the Ottawa Maternity Hospital; the Lady Stanley Institute; the Protestant Home for the Aged (men); and the Refuge Branch of the Protestant Orphan's Home (for elderly women).[86] More formal co-ordination seems to have emerged in the mid-1890s, with construction of a modern building in 1894 for the YWCA. The YW, in Ottawa as elsewhere, had begun as an organization to provide refuge for single working-girls, who were moving into the dangerous urban environment of the Victorian period. There they would be safe from the "white slave traders", as well as other temptations. But the YW in Ottawa as elsewhere — with a woman's environment run by women — quickly became a centre from which women's organizations were both launched and grew, and particularly so in the facilities offered by the new building, itself a creation of a funding campaign, largely organized and run by women.[87]

The other critical event of the 1890s was the arrival on the Ottawa scene of Lady Aberdeen, wife of the Governor-General. Lady Aberdeen was an aggressive and inspired Liberal, who in short order had provided the organizational impetus for the Local and National Council of Women, the May Court Club, the Victorian Order of Nurses, and the Associated Charities of Ottawa.

All of these organizations were intimately involved at the turn of the century in a series of public health and welfare campaigns, many concerned with child welfare — such as the "Milk Depots" — but perhaps, most significantly, with the campaign against tuberculosis, the great killer in the cities. The campaign against TB seems to have alerted many of the volunteer workers to the extent of poverty in the city, and the limits of voluntary efforts in its amelioration.

Contracting TB at the turn of the century was virtually a death sentence (of 1,975 diagnosed cases in Ottawa in 1907, 1,933 died).[88] The only known cure was rest, good diet, and fresh air, only possible for the rich, or for patients sent to the provincial sanitarium at Gravenhurst. TB beds in local hospitals were mainly reserved for the dying.

In 1905 the Ottawa Association for the Prevention of TB was formed and, in 1906, amalgamated with the local branch of the National Sanitarium Association. A nurse, supplied by the Victorian Order of Nurses, was hired in 1905 to find and track TB cases, which the association would provide with the equipment (tents, sputum cups, and the like) for home cure. A dispensary was operated by the May Court Club to ensure adequate diet. With the help of the Public Health committee of the Local Council of Women, school children were educated in the perils and causes of TB, and the committee agitated city council for enforcement of anti-spitting bylaws (the women took to raising their skirts so as not to sweep along the streets of a spitting society).

Agitation for a local sanitarium seems to have been the result of frustration with the home cure program. Among the poor, where

Lady Aberdeen, wife of the Governor General, was the catalyst for many of the city's early social agencies after her arrival in the 1890s.

Ella Bronson was one of the leading figures in philanthropy in Ottawa's Protestant community. She was noted for her work with the Protestant Orphan's Home and with the Associated Charities of Ottawa.

the disease was endemic, due to poor diet and poor living and working conditions, breadwinners who left their jobs to effect a cure only exposed their families, without income, to starvation. Mothers with TB struggled on, the only alternative to abandoning the care of their children:

> A mother with an infant, ten days old. This home is a small shack built below the street level.... On entering here I found the sick mother huddled up over a cook stove, where a meal was being prepared. Beside her on a rough board table her baby of 10 days old lay on a pillow, two other small children were running about the house...."[89]

Tuberculosis cure had social and economic ramifications that required at the least some sort of institutional support, as it was next to impossible for many of the poor to cure themselves at home. Voluntary efforts with some reluctant municipal support led to the opening of the Lady Grey Sanitorium in 1910, followed by the Perley Hospital in 1912-1913.

At the turn of the century, then, all strands of health and welfare were beginning to intersect and to be rationalized. Catholic charities had the church to provide general oversight. In the 1890s, under the aegis of Lady Aberdeen, the Charity Organization Society was founded in order to co-ordinate the activities of, chiefly, the protestant voluntary sector. It assumed a more elaborate form about the time of the First World War as the Ottawa Welfare Bureau (OWB), and had adopted the new professional thrust as a "casework" agency. Co-ordination was, in 1927, taken one step further in the form of the Ottawa Council of Social Agencies, which engaged the Catholic agencies and those of the Jewish community. After the 1932 Whitton Report, a community chest and council was established in the city, which engaged, only after much hard negotiation, and in the face of financial crisis, Protestant, Catholic, and Jewish agencies.

The city itself, until well into the twentieth century, resolutely maintained its limited role, supplying *ad hoc* relief and small contributions to the voluntary sector. But it, too, sought rationalization, and in the 1920s organized a Social Service Department (SSD), that carried out the city's statutory obligations with respect to pensions and provided limited outdoor relief.

In 1925, meetings between the puiblic and private bodies worked out their respective areas of responsibility, and they followed pretty much the lines decided upon by precedent in the nineteenth century.[90] The private sector OWB took care of unemployment, with the city providing food and fuel, as well as desertion, non-resident indigents, temporary disability, and severe family tension. The city's SSD took care of widows, the aged, the imprisonment of the male wage earner, the permanently handicapped, or those with a chronic inability to cope. That is, "indigence, not unemployment, was the chief criterion for receiving public assistance."[91] Unemployment assistance — or at least its delivery — was a private sector matter. The city did, from time to time, provide relief works.

The Depresion of the 1930s broke and reversed the pattern and Ottawa was typical of most places. The private agencies collapsed under the burden of delivering relief to the unemployed, and in Ottawa's case, the burden was transferred to the Public Welfare Department, organized in 1933, in effect out of the older SSD.

Ottawa's experience of the Depression was not atypical of other major centres in the Dominion. It, equally, seemed to follow the same pattern of beginning with relief works in the early years and later shifting to other forms of direct relief, initially script and relief in kind, and ultimately much direct relief in cash. Strict residency requirements were used, and special organizations serviced special categories of reliefees, like single men and single women. The private sector agencies, operating under a community chest by 1933, were generally employed in filling in the gaps in the public system, such as the provision of clothes. The work test was employed in the city. Under it the "able-bodied" had to perform occasional tasks at the civic woodyard and on various "boondoggles", as testimony to their willingness to work.

The Ottawa experience was also the same as other places in the sense that unemployment struck most severely at the weaker levels of the social stratum, centered in the Lower Town and Chaudière wards. In Ottawa's case it meant, additionally, that funds flowed from the Anglo-Protestant community to the French, and to a lesser degree Irish Catholic communities.

Such tensions triggered an investigation by the police into the city's unemployment relief administration, operated by the unique Public Welfare Department. It was determined that the department, headed by Bessie Touzel, staffed largely by women, and directed by a citizen-council board, was much too concerned with welfare of human beings rather than the efficient administration of relief. It was too soft. The Direct Relief Department was created, the women were replaced by a smaller group of men, Bessie Touzel

Demonstration in Major's Hill Park during the Great Depression. The facade of old Sussex Street is in the background.

resigned, and the Public Welfare Board was abolished. The department, built on the older Social Service Department, had operated from 1933 to 1936, and represented what one man called "...an experiment by the City in the principles of social welfare."[92]

Ultimately, the Depression and war experience produced Canada's version of the welfare state, and Ottawa, like other Ontarian and Canadian cities, would find its place in it largely as a delivery system, operating under provincial (and to a degree, federal) policy, and three-level funding. After the creation of regional government in 1969, the city's major welfare agency moved to the regional level.

URBAN POLITICS AND THE URBAN COMMUNITY

Urban politics at the turn of the century drew on a wide spectrum of the Ottawa community, most of the elements motivated by reform impulses of one sort or another. It was a time as confused as it was yeasty. Though power and traction, along with the economic future of the city, dominated the political agenda, they did not represent the whole of it. Big, new issues, centering on pure water, the delivery of social services, and planning were beginning to demand the serious attention of local politicians.

Ald. W.D. Morris, the merchant candidate "not of the wealthy classes, but of the masses,"[93] became, in the new century the leading enemy of the "corporate" vote.[94] Morris "...was up against a campaign of slander, misrepresentation and falsehood; everything possible was being done to secure his defeat." He "...had to fight the opposition of the electric interests, the gas company and the city official clique."[95] But in his victory in January, 1901, he offered "...a stinging rebuke to the scandalous campaign so relentlessly pursued against him by the Journal...and by the combines."[96]

It appears that the "People's Votes" did indeed "Declare for Morris". Morris's win represented a broadly-based middle- and working-class protest against the emerging utilities monopolies. "A wave of municipal reform," had apparently "swept over the city," and it was one that was characterized by the appearance on city council of two "regular" labour candidates (out of three who had run) and a total of fourteen (out of seventeen) in civic office who had been endorsed by the Ottawa Trades and Labour Council. Even in Wellington Ward a Labour candidate headed the poll. In a plebiscite, the "'people" had voted for a municipal telephone service, and civic aid to hospitals.

Precisely what constituted municipal reform in early twentieth-century Ottawa is rather unclear, but certainly at its core was the antipathy toward the utilities trusts. On this ground at least the urban *élite* and labour had a common view, whatever other differences might be evident. The result, however, was to pit most of the city, wrapped in the flag of reform, against the Catholic French of Lower Town, who remained the core of support of the Liberal-leaning utility promoters. Though the chief issue was, ostensibly, utilities reform, the election "offered a particularly tempting opportunity to foment a clash of racial and creed prejudices and unhappily it was taken full advantage of."[97]

In 1905 and again in 1906, the challenge to the power trusts from Anglo-Protestant Centre Town was met by the cultural solidarities of the other communities, especially Lower Town. The "trust" men, however, in 1906 lost not only the mayor's chair, but five of the six open council seats, which went to the municipal ownership group. Council was thus in a position to put on the ballot for 1907 two crucial plebiscites that embodied early twentieth-century reform: a power bylaw, and a plebiscite to bring in a board of control. Within this background, the 1907 election became a pivotal one, which was to largely condition the nature of Ottawa politics for two generations.

The power bylaw was approved overwhelmingly (7,262 to 3,095),and the Board of Control solidly (4,745 to 3,095). A city-owned utility was put forward, not as a device to destroy the monopoly Ottawa Electric Co., but to regulate it through competition. In a broader sense, the victory of the municipal bylaw was part of a bandwagon effect in Ontario, stemming from the campaign for Ontario Hydro and the People's Power. Municipal power was also a reflection of the strength of the Upper Town as the dominant, if minority, element in the city, and marked a point of clear decline of the chief industrial group of the city — the Chaudière lumberers and power monopolists — whose traditional political control, rooted in LeBreton Flats and Lower Town, was broken.

The Board of Control was Ontario's version of the city commission system, widely perceived in the early twentieth century as the mark of a progressive city. In Ottawa, opposition was expressed primarily in a racial and religious sense. The Franco-Catholic minority in Lower Town saw a Board of Control system — elected

8 Ottawa Wards, 1911 (top) and 1929 (bottom): Government grew and increasingly was English. Woods-based industries stagnated. The new streetcar suburbs to the south and the west were thus similar in character to old Upper Town, and, in their new wards, tended to vote like it. The Chaudière community was submerged in expanded Victoria Ward, and hived in Dalhousie. The French of Lower Town moved eastward to the Town of Eastview (now Cité Vanier). Southward expansion of Sandy Hill (St. George's Ward) was effectively blocked by railyards. Many of the wealthy and influential began their migration to Rockcliffe Park Village.

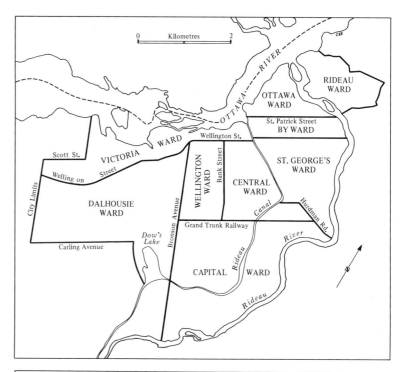

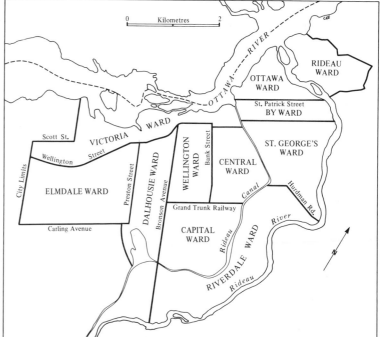

city-wide — as putting them into a position of almost complete impotence, and it was in the Lower Town wards that most of the resistance to the Board of Control system emerged.

Board of Control advocacy in Ottawa dated to about 1898, and a campaign for the change seems to have been triggered by a series of questionable activities in many city departments. A cashier in the water works department had been jailed for two years, following charges of embezzlement; nepotism was alleged in the city's finance department; instances of favouritism in assessment evaluations were brought to council; and collusion was charged in the award of contracts by the works committee. At least two of the city's departments were described in 1898 as being in a "semi-demoralized state".[98]

But apart from these matters of administrative efficiency, there was a concern on the part of a number of the city's more prominent citizens to provide the city with a strategic agenda: to give it some direction or a collective purpose. The people most closely associated with Board of Control reform were also those most associated with city boosterism, for example the publicity bureau, and with public power. Efficiency, public power, and promotion tended to be aspects of the same impulse. And just as public power was inclined to come from a middle-class Upper Town business group, so too did the advocates of efficiency and promotion.

As an institutional change, the creation of the Board of Control was crucial for local politics. The first action (after appointing a clerk) of Ottawa's first Board of Control (1908) was to ask City Council (now consisting of the Mayor, the Controllers, and the Aldermen) to abolish all standing committees, except the Board of Health.[99] The second action was a recommendation that the rules of order be amended "...so that the seats of the controllers in Council should be the first four on the Mayor's right,"[100] A real assertion of precedence was underscored by a symbolic one.

The Board also asserted itself as the "gate-keeper" on both policy and routine matters, some small, like charitable requests, and some large, like the budgets for the city and all the school boards. It also became the initial contact point for negotiations, including those for major developments like the Château Laurier and Union Station, the power and traction franchise, labour relations, and for annexations and amalgamations. The Board had to go to Council for approval of its recommendations, but in council, the Board, which itself made up almost a fifth of the council, could be its own

strong advocate and voting bloc. Since the Board seemed to act most of the time on the basis of consensus (there were few divisions in its deliberations), the Board tended to present a united front within council.

But perhaps the Board's greatest source of influence stemmed from its jurisdiction over the money and people that ran the day-to-day operations of the city. From the outset, the Board carved up the administration of the city among its members: on the first board, for example, one controller assumed direction of waterworks, property, and health; a second the board of works; a third, the fire department and library; and the fourth, finance and the city electrical department. At an operational level, the Board agreed to "...notify the heads of the several departments that in future no expenditures are to be made nor are any liabilities to be incurred necessitating expenditures of money without first having secured the sanction of the Board of Control."[101]. The Council may have had the last word on big policy, but it was through the Board that "the City Clerk was authorized to order a supply of notepaper for the use of the members of Council."[102]

The evident and real power of the Board thus served to narrow real representation in the city's political process. Like the race for mayor, that for Board of Control was citywide. In effect, that meant the Anglo-Protestant groups would dominate. Only by vigorous use of plumping could the French provide any counterpoint at all: usually a maximum of one member on the five-man board. But even that member was to some degree co-opted by the necessity to engage in administrative log-rolling — he could only protect his departments by obliging his fellow controllers with respect to theirs — and was to this extent co-opted by the necessity of presenting a united front to the city council. Conformity was a prerequisite for the exercise of influence.

The configuration of the representation on the Board of Control reflects these realities. Until it was disbanded, as a result of the reform impulses of the 1970s, the city generally elected three anglophone board members, usually from Upper Town or Sandy Hill. Vigorous plumping usually elected a francophone as the fourth member.

The events of 1907 and 1908 — public power and the Board of Control — while put forward as reforms, served most effectively to put anglophone Upper Town in the driver's seat. Public power represented the political eclipse, at the local level, of the Chaudière

The city's first Board of Control, 1908. This political and administrative body would shape civic politics for three generations.

Road construction on Sussex Drive, 1913. The Lower Town that it passed, once the chief commercial area, was by the twentieth century caught in time. But the street, a major link between Rideau Hall and Parliament Hill, was gaining in importance.

group; while the Board of Control represented the eclipse of other minorities in the city, chiefly the labouring and francophone enclaves.

The one rising group of potential influence was the civil service. But hobbled from the thirties by election restrictions — political office paying more than $500 (the alderman's honorarium), required job resignation — the CS made little impact. Between 1920 and 1950, only two civil servants were elected to the Board of Control, both before 1935. The city has yet to elect a civil servant as mayor. To that extent, the civil service did little to set an agenda for over-all city growth. [103]

Labour, an apparently rising force at the beginning of the century, and again just after the First World War, managed to place a sprinkling of candidates on the aldermanic boards (eight in the 20s and a similar number in the 30s), but rarely cracked the ranks of the controllers: one labouring man made it to the Board of Control in the 1920s for two terms and another in the 1930s for one term. There has never been a "regular" labour candidate in the mayor's chair.

The pivotal 1907-1908 elections also represented a precipitous drop in the influence of the francophones. The decline of French Canadian influence in the political life of the city is complex. The community had been at its most influential in the late nineteenth century in its alliance with the Chaudière lumberers and utility barons who had strong Liberal connections with Queen's Park. But the decline of the Chaudière lumberers as a force in the city's politics, the emergence of the public power issue, and the twentieth-century dominance of the Conservatives at Queen's Park all tended to reduce electoral influence. Finally, there was little opportunity for growth of the francophone community within the civil service, that great economic growth sector of the early twentieth century. It was reflected in the fact that the most eminent lobby group of francophones within the public service — the Jacques Cartier society — operated in the 1930s as a secret organization, whose membership and operations are still relatively unknown.[104] To add to these problems, Lower Town as a commercial centre stagnated. But of greatest significance was probably the separate schools clash. The resolution of this question in the 1920s, was institutional separation of the French, both from the dominant anglophone community and from their Irish co-religionists.

While the anglo *élite* had risen to pre-eminence on a "reform" impulse, this same was somewhat narrow in constituency and perspective. In 1916, at the height of the Canadian social reform wave, given energy by the war, the city approved plebiscites against drink, for proportional representation, for a city manager, and, narrowly, votes for women. It would later toy with the idea, ardently pressed by the Southam's, publishers of the *Citizen*, and by Controller Tully, of the single tax. As noted, and by the mid-1920s it had hired a planner, established a social service department, and created a plausible health service. At the end of the decade, the city launched its first public housing project.

The failure of planning, the overwhelming vote in 1926 to go wet, the degeneration of public housing into a public scandal, and the elimination, in the 1930s, of the city welfare department in favour of relief efficiency, seem to represent parts of a pattern in the drying up of conservative reform. In particular, the resolution in 1924 of the traction franchise matter removed the outstanding issue that had triggered the conservative reform impulse in the early part of the century, and had given Upper Town business some sort of reform legitimacy. But the structure that had gained power was so solid that neither scandal nor inactivity was sufficient to reduce its pre-eminence, nor did it admit new sources of people or ideas. When reform ran out, the governing *élite* simply became narrow as well as exclusive.

In a broad sense, the central political force of the city, from about 1908 until 1970, consisted of a group of merchants and professionals whose activities were centered in Upper Town, and in newer areas, directly to the south along Bank Street. They had come to power on a fairly strong reform and booster impulse, blending industrial promotion with anti-monopoly sentiments, and in the initial phases, did pursue these efforts. Anger or displeasure at their activities would emerge in the form of a periodic "populist" incursion, usually in the form of a mayor acting as a class *and* race surrogate; one or the other was not sufficient. That is, a charismatic figure, running for mayor, could from time to time generate a coalition from among the lower income groups, French, Catholic, and labour, and translate it into sufficient votes to become mayor. But such a populist could rarely widen his basis of support to embrace the Board of Control and the aldermanic board, or sustain his own success for more than one or two terms.

Blowing with the prevailing political wind seems to have been the basis of federal representation in early twentieth-century

Ottawa. From Confederation to 1896, the city elected only Conservatives; from 1896, it elected, with occasional exceptions, only Liberals. For the Liberals in the early twentieth century, two streams of influence seem to have been central. There was a Lower Town reform (and usually French) connection through men like N.A. Belcourt and E.R.E. Chevrier; and an English connection centered on the industrialists of Chaudière and Rideau Falls (Ahearn, Hutchison, and Edwards). In the late 1930s, however, there was a shift in the source of Liberal representation, one rooted in Liberal machine politics, with probable connections to Ahearn and Chevrier. Ottawa East was dominated from 1945 for more than twenty years by J.T. Richard, former general secretary of the Young Liberals of Canada, and a director of the National Liberal Federation; and in Ottawa West, for more than thirty years from 1940 onward, by George McIlraith, an early executive member of the Liberal Federation.

Provincial representation at Ottawa was more closely related to social and economic patterns in the city than to the prevailing political climate of the province, though it is very clear that in the late nineteenth and early twentieth century Liberal lumberers and their surrogates like R. W. Scott, Erskine Bronson, Lumsden (1898), G.C. Hurdman (1915), and one Conservative lumberer, C.B. Powell (1903), dominated political representation from the city. It was not surprising, given the prominence of the forest and hydro industry.

At the provincial level, as at the federal, some experience at the local level was an important preliminary to success at the senior level: Powell, 1903; McDougal, 1905; May, 1905; Champagne, 1912; Ellis, 1912; Pinard, 1915; Fisher, 1924; Birkett, 1927; MacKenzie, 1968; Cassidy, 1972; and Bennett, 1972. Why this pattern occurred in Ottawa is unclear, but it may be accounted for in the twentieth century by the dominating presence of the federal government. In some sense, the most prominent personalities in Ottawa were the elected federal members, who were not available to represent the city at, obviously, the federal level or the provincial. Equally, many of the other important or able citizens of Ottawa were civil servants, and restricted in their political activity. That is, prominence in the major enterprise in the city (government), did not translate into either a vested interest in politics or in an inclination to run. A political profile therefore had to be gained by other means, and the most plausible was through local political eminence.

Ottawa and Hull, looking northwest, 1979: the skyline of the Government City. Most of the land and buildings on both sides of the Ottawa River, as well as those of Chaudière, are government-owned. The same is true of Confederation Square (right centre), with the last of the "temporary" buildings coming down near the strip of the Rideau Canal. Visible in the upper centre, north of the river, are the new government office complexes, Térrasses de la Chaudière and Place du Portage.

Chapter Five

The City Transformed (1940-1980)

INTRODUCTION

War and post-war reconstruction, combined with the eclipse of a wood-products industry, confirmed Ottawa as a government town. But government was to do more. Under the guiding hand of prime ministers, Ottawa was to be turned into a National Capital commensurate with Canada's new status as a middle power. The city, willy-nilly, had thus to respond to two determinant forces: the sheer growth of government, its employees, its buildings, and its needs for services; and the perceived need to create a national and even international showpiece.

Between 1941 and 1971 the city faced, not only a threefold increase in population, but an almost five-fold increase in territory, all this apart from capital building and the clearing away of a backlog of projects put on the shelf during Depression and War.

In an economic sense, it had been almost totally transformed from providing for a "producer" community to meeting the needs of a "consumer" market, though service remained central in the local economy. It simply switched from lumber to government, from industrialists and their workers to middle-class bureaucrats. The city was thus compelled to re-tailor itself in its buildings, amusements, and amenities to conform to the tastes of a liberal-professional, relatively secure, and well-paid middle-class. The expanded role of government in the national economy and other facets of Canadian life, from sport to broadcast regulation, also attracted thousands who had "business with government". It was to turn the Ottawa airport, for example, into one of the busiest in the country, and its telephone and other communications systems into giants. Visitors coming to the city for business, combined with those attracted by the sights, soon made the tourist and convention industry second only to government. Ottawa became a one-horse town, though it was a mighty big and sophisticated horse.

In a very real way, the demands and the social structure of the government slowly became woven into the very fabric of the old city. Economic hierarchies within the federal structure were manifested in the social and the physical landscape. What one did in government found expression in the neighbourhoods. Lower Town, for example, rehabilitated by the National Capital Commission, and gentrified by the public service, had by the 1980s ceased to exist as a somewhat quaint francophone enclave. Similarly, as a consequence of federal demands for a bilingual public service, thousands of children from English-speaking homes were toiling in French immersion programs, and chain department stores were answering customer calls with "G'dday-Bonjoor".

Post-war secular changes, common to many cities, paralleled the emergence of the federal monolith, and made dramatic changes in the urban landscape. The core was "beautified" and "hi-risified", and by 1970 massive suburbs had spread into satellite communities and even into Hull. Growth of government and the demands it made for beauty, office space, homes for its employees, and city services generally, triggered a protracted period of private and governmental construction on a large scale. This set in train a demand for land use and other plans, thereby placing land and building development at the top of the agenda at city hall. Control of development through planning became the focus of post-war city politics, which, until the late 1960s, had still been operating in a pre-war sectarian mould. As development declined in the city and moved to the growing suburban communities, politics began to change again. By the 1970s they were re-focused on quality-of-life issues, and often had a neighbourhood base. In the forty years from the Second World War, a new city, quantitatively and qualitatively, was created.

Looking south over the Ottawa toward the Chateau Laurier, the canal headlocks, and Parliament Hill, 1946.

Alta Vista suburb, 1957. This area was part of the huge annexation of 1950. It is in many ways the southward extension of Centre Town and the Glebe.

ECONOMY AND METROPOLITAN GROWTH

In 1939, the demands of war altered the economic balance in the city, as it turned out, permanently. In the space of six years, the civil service tripled from the 12,000 or so in the "headquarters" labour force, to nearly 36,000 by 1945. Most were "temporary" employees, many others in military service. In fact, "permanent" members of the CS declined in numbers in the war years to a twenty-year low of just under 7,000. They were the base on which some 30,000 "temporaries" rested.

The city staggered under the pressure of the newcomers. Places had to be found to both live and work, often in ramshackled conversions, and in the so-called "temporary" buildings, intended for the "temporary" employees. There seemed to be an expectation that, in the wake of the war emergency, government would return to something like its pre-war size. But the Dominion, unexpectedly, emerged from the war as a major world power, with wide-ranging international obligations. And the trauma of depression set the government on a course of underwriting basic welfare and employment support systems, managing more complex tax systems, and regulating new and more complex technology. Again, there were the veterans to be accommodated by the state they had served.

The result for the CS was a relatively small (about 6,000), decline in numbers to about 30,000 in 1951, probably due to shrinkage in the armed forces, and smaller losses on the civilian side of the service. From 1951, however, the CS experienced rapid and continuous growth into the 1970s. The temporary employees of the war, like the "temporary" buildings that housed them, were converted to "permanent" use. Some of the "temporary" people, however, mostly women it appears, never made the conversion. They were replaced by men.

Overall, the growth of the CS during the war and its entrenchment afterward, ensured the dominance of government in the economy of the city. By 1971, some 32 per cent of the male labour force of the city and 28 per cent of the female, was in the federal public service industry. Other white-collar jobs reinforced the sense of a city devoted to "Service", whether public or private. By 1971 some 55 per cent of the male labour force was in the "Service" industry and some 65 per cent of the female. All other industrial sectors were diminished by comparison, particularly for males,

Development was driven by a huge expansion in the Civil Service dating from the war. Here are employees of National Revenue at work in the Connaught Building, January 1947.

who, more than females, had entered "Service" industries. "Trade", at about 12 per cent of the labour force for both male and female, represented the next largest sector. By 1971 the manufacturing sector represented only about 8 per cent of the male and 4 per cent of the female labour force, though it had been as high as 19.5 per cent of the male labour force in 1941, when local factories had been converted to war use. But that was a last fling.

In 1946 the Eddy company absorbed the Booth firm, and effectively eliminated industrial activity on the Ottawa side of Chaudière.[1] The Eddy operations were concentrated on the Hull part of the falls, and the source of much of its labour appears to have been the Québec community. A little more than ten years later, the Broad Street railway yards, adjacent to Chaudière, and those near the Union Station in the centre of the city, were removed as part of a rail-line relocation program to a new, integrated venue in the southeastern part of the city. Within a little more than a decade a major portion of the industrial and transportation sectors had disappeared from core area locations. The foundation of a major working-class community had been displaced, and at the end of the 'fifties, much of the community itself was removed, as LeBreton flats was cleared in a major urban renewal project.

Expansion of government continued to require space for both work and residence. As a result, the building boom was sustained in an almost unbroken fashion from the 1940s to the 1980s. With it came the emergence of a number of local construction firms, like Campeau and Minto, which had grown to almost international proportions by the 1970s. It was also with the contractors that the most important political intersections, especially at local level, occurred.

Though Ottawa lost some of its prestige after the war as a supplier of food and raw materials, it maintained — as it had for 150 years — pre-eminence in the Ottawa, Gatineau, and Rideau valleys as a supplier of wholesale and retail goods,[2] especially food and petroleum. Though clearly in the shade of Montréal, and to some degree Toronto (with about one-fifth of their activity), it clearly dominated the trade of its river valleys. Its wholesaling and retailing activities in the post-war period corresponded almost exactly to those of the early and traditional years as a lumber hinterland.[3]

The city, throughout its history, had also had a fairly strong local bias in its trading activities, and was one of the last of the major cities in Canada to be penetrated fully by the national chains, a major Sears store arriving in the 1960s, and the Bay only in the 1970s. The town and area were served by family-based firms like A.J. Freiman Ltd. (bought out by the Bay in 1971), and Charles Ogilvy Ltd. But, by the 1970s, the great service-chains began to dominate, particularly in the retail and hotel trade. Logos familiar around the world made their appearance in the city's streets, and more particularly in its shopping centres: the three largest dominated by Sears, The Bay, and Eaton. Indeed, the last, opened in 1983 in the downtown core was to be called the "Eaton Centre", until angry protests from the city and its residents forced a change to the more acceptable "Rideau Centre". Cosmetic name changes aside, government and external chains by the eighties controlled the city centre. Little of local flavour, including local government, was in evidence, the By Ward Market excepted. Even the great retail experiment — the Sparks Street Mall — was falling under the shade of Parliament Hill, and chain stores.

The Mall, which involved closing the premier street of the city to traffic, was apparently suggested by capital planner Jacques Gréber. The idea was executed, beginning in the summer of 1960, by the Sparks Street Development Association, and after six years of summertime experiment, became a year-round operation in 1966. The scheme, the first in Canada, in some respects represented the height of influence of the Upper Town retailers, who gathered political support and funding to both rehabilitate and to close the "Broadway of Ottawa". It was an almost recklessly bold experiment at a time when most cities were fixed on demolishing their Victorian downtowns in favour of steel and glass high-rises, and enlarged traffic corridors. And it was successful beyond expectation. But Upper Town or Centre Town in the immediate post-war period was at the peak of its influence in both business and political matters. As yet, it was not overshadowed by national chains, suburban shopping centres (the first was Westgate, opened in 1954), the activities of government, or the demands of neighbourhoods and community organizations. Centre Town, after 100 years of struggle, was king of the Hill. The Mall, in a sense, is its symbol and legacy to the city.

It was, however, a last hurrah. Expanded suburbs and shopping centres diluted traffic. Downtown was no longer the only place to go. And, in the growing, changing city, a share of the political, as well as economic influence, was being demanded by others. Chief among them was government. By 1965 it was well on its way to

LeBreton Flats and the Chaudière area, 1965. The demise of the lumber town was underscored in the late 1950s when an urban renewal clearance obliterated the lumbering community. Even the remaining rail-yards were soon to go. Wartime "temporaries" look down from the Upper Town bluffs (top centre).

controlling the centre of the city, and by the 1980s this control included ownership of the entire north side of Sparks Street. Government had become the pre-eminent landlord on the chief business street.

Elsewhere, too, the hardy independence of traditional Ottawa business seems to have been put to rout in the post-war period, as the huge market of the civil service and its stable salaries attracted more and more chains. Local autonomy in a range of businesses proved impossible to maintain. In the later 1970s and early 1980s, the Morrison-Lamothe bakery sold out, the Beach Appliance firm closed down, and the Ottawa *Journal* folded, leaving the newspaper field dominated by the *Citizen*, flagship of a chain begun by the Southam family. Other indications that national rationalization was affecting the city occurred in 1981, when Ottawa was removed from the trans-continental line of VIA rail services[4] and the last Gatineau passenger train ran in October of that year.[5]

Some considerable impetus to the Ottawa economy was provided from the late 1960s with the emergence of a high-tech industry, especially in Kanata, known as Silicon Valley North. The initial development probably occurred in 1969, with the establishment of Microsystems (now Bell Northern). In the 1970s some forty high-tech firms were established in the city, most of them Canadian-owned. The Canadian Advanced Technology Association was also headquartered in the city and, in the 1970s, thirteen of its fifty members were Ottawa firms. By 1981, three of the city's largest employers were the high-tech Bell Northern Research, Digital Equipment of Canada Ltd., and Mitel Corporation,[6] and more than 40 per cent of those employed in manufacturing in Ottawa by 1981 were working in these industries.[7]

Emergence of a high-tech manufacturing centre in Ottawa owes much to government. Growth was likely triggered by the presence in the city of the National Research Council and the Communications Research Council, both of which, after the Second World War, provided not only basic electronics research, but a demand for electronic equipment. Government itself, by the 1960s was becoming a major market for electronic equipment, in order to process the vast amount of data generated in departments such as National Revenue, Health and Welfare, and the Dominion Bureau of Statistics. More general automation of government offices began to grow in the 1970s. Federal buying power was probably the dominant reason for the presence of a high-tech industry.[8] But by the 1960s government had also provided a very attractive place to live. Ottawa had become in many respects an archetypal post-industrial city: clean industry, low density, and a pleasant life-style. It was, by 1980, almost the antithesis of the lumber town.

As vital as government's role had been, major contributions to the high-tech industry were also made by long-established private companies, such as Bell Northern Research and Computing Devices of Canada Ltd. Markets for equipment included the large aerial surveying and mapping companies in the Ottawa area. In addition, the two universities made major contributions in research, trained manpower, and entrepreneurs, as did one of the most highly-educated populations in the country. Finally, a location close to the major Canadian markets of Toronto and Montréal, as well as those in the Boston-Washington corridor, and in Europe, made Ottawa in many ways an ideal setting for the industry.

Though high-tech, with its exotic appeal and fast recent growth, has assumed a high profile in the Ottawa economy, the most rapidly growing sector up to 1971 was printing and publishing, also geared to service government. In 1951, with thirty-two firms, it was the second most prominent business in the city. By 1971 this number had doubled to sixty-four "...to become by far the most important single manufacturing activity in Ottawa."[9] And it was this industry that appears to have offset the decline in the food trade, which in 1951 had been the largest in the city and had fallen to fourth by 1971, with a loss of nine firms in the generation.

But for the most part the economy came to revolve around the services required by government employees, and perhaps most vital, given the prosperity and the increased use of the automobile after the war, the tourist and convention business.

In effect, the private sector treats government and its employees as a stable, internal market. Or as in the case of the tourist and convention industry, as the major attraction for a market. There is little in the way of an imperative to seek out external markets for city products, and this, to some extent, has proven a problem with the emergence of medium and high-tech industries in the area. They found an initial or basic market in government but, to be viable, had to compete internationally. They are also very "foot-loose", unlike lumber and government, and are not pinned permanently to one place.

Finally, the economy in all its aspects became regional, and less focused on the city. In the 1970s, the government determined to

Sparks Street Mall, 1977. The Broadway of Ottawa was closed to vehicular traffic in the 1960s, the first experiment of its kind in Canada. It proved a huge success.

build its first major office complex outside the boundaries of Ottawa, in Hull, Québec. It was one capable of absorbing some 25,000 public service jobs. This, coupled with smaller government operations in the region, has spread the influence of government. It is less exclusively that of the city. The city in the same period also reached the limits of its growth. The major annexations made in 1950 were effectively the last, and Ottawa proper confined by the Québec boundary and the greenbelt, virtually ceased to grow.

DEMOGRAPHY AND SOCIAL RELATIONS

After 150 years of nearly continuous growth, the city appeared to have reached its limits. Political decisions at the senior levels of government seem chiefly responsible.

Creation by the province of the Regional Municipality of Ottawa-Carleton (RMOC) January 1, 1969, removed the traditional bait of annexation: provision of services. When the city ran out of land in the 1970s, it could no longer cut off a new slice from its municipal neighbours. People moved into the surrounding municipalities; the city's boundary did not move with them. Large new communities — especially Nepean, Kanata, and Gloucester — grew up and proved indigestible. These three became cities in their own right in 1978, 1978, and 1981 respectively.

A provincial boundary down the Ottawa River had from 1867 prevented Ottawa encroachments on Hull, but, equally, the federal authority had adhered to the terms of the British North America Act that Ottawa "shall be the capital". Hull was denied a share of the government-generated economy, though small numbers in the Civil Service lived there, and in 1956 it became the location of the government Printing Bureau. But in 1969, the federal authority determined that it was going to help Hull "catch up",[10] chiefly by means of construction of two major federal office complexes: Place du Portage and Terrasses de la Chaudière. The offices, the expansion of French in the PS, or Public Service (as the Civil Service came to be called in 1969), and improved road and transit services across the Ottawa River, all made the Hull region a more attractive place to live. Its population grew.

These political decisions ensured the development of large, independent communities outside Ottawa proper, and limited the city's population in the long term. What is by no means certain, however,

is the effect of this limitation on the social mix inside the city. To 1976, population densities in Ottawa's core declined and shifted to the suburbs,[11] and a low income zone of transition developed just outside the core area. But the beautification schemes of the National Capital Commission, especially the removal of rail-lines, served to create an attractive and not too busy central city, still rich in "heritage" dwellings. Since the mid-seventies, many of its residential areas have once again attracted the city's professional middle-class. Extensive gentrification has significantly altered the social mix in Lower Town and, more recently, in the LeBreton Flats-Dalhousie Ward, traditionally working-class areas. Such middle-class bastions as Sandy Hill and Centre Town appear to be going through a process of "re-gentrification". In all these areas, traditional cultural identifications, whether the French Catholic of Lower Town, or the Anglo-Protestant of Centre Town, also seem to be undergoing considerable alteration.

As well as altering social location, political decisions in the postwar period dramatically altered social relations. Of central importance were the pressures within the Civil Service, the federal government, and the nation, to create a capital that functioned in French and English. Perhaps the first roadblock was removed in 1956[12] when, in effect, skills in both official languages were incorporated into the merit system. In 1962 bi-lingual cheques made their appearance,[13] and a year later French was made a working language in the Civil Service.[14] Subsequently, language bonuses were given to those competent in French and English.[15]

Effects of such indirect incentives were limited, and in 1967 the "B and B Commission" could still decry the English cast of life in Ottawa.[16] Pressures from the commission, as well as other sectors, produced much stronger affirmative action by the 1970s. In 1971 the National Capital Commission (NCC) was made the instrument of symbolic bi-lingualism in the capital, responsible for ensuring that signs and symbols on government land and buildings, and their planning, reflected and supported the two languages. More direct action was taken in 1975, when numbers of French in the PS were ordered to be doubled.[17] Two languages became essential to a public service career.

Ottawa City seemed to follow in the wake of federal initiatives. A draft bylaw to make Ottawa a bi-lingual city appeared in 1970,[18] and city council itself went bi-lingual in 1972.[19] Public education, too, responded to federal initiatives as English-speaking parents

Place du Portage buildings under construction, Hull, P.Q., 1975.

Tin House Square in Lower Town. Part of the effort of the National Capital Commission to recapture the flavour of one of the oldest sections of the city. The elaborate facade of the home of a Lower Town tinsmith was saved and mounted on the wall of the building at centre.

FAMILY EARNINGS, 1941

- $1750 and above
- $1000–1749
- less than $1000
- Non-residential, parks, unoccupied areas

9 Family earnings, 1941: The social landscape of the city on the verge of its transition to a government town. Portions of old Upper Town are becoming a lower-income rental community. The low incomes of Lower Town and the Chaudière district are evident.

realized that careers for their children in the Public Service — still the city's largest employer — would be heavily dependent on a bi-lingual capacity. Federal funding for French immersion programs decided the issue in 1971. As for the children of French-speaking parents, their opportunities were enhanced in the 1960s by the expansion of secondary education in French, culminating in a decision in late 1969 — amidst great controversy — to convert Champlain High School to a unilingual French institution.

The shift was enhanced by the impact of the Quiet Revolution in Québec, which emphasized, in both its outlook and educational system, a more pluralist and technical approach to the world. Many young professionals were attracted to Ottawa from Québec, and locally there was an increasingly great pool from which to recruit candidates whose mother-tongue was French.

The action on language appears to have shifted the class balances in the city. With the French speakers, particularly, there seems to have been a move from the old trades and labour pursuits to the middle-class and professional occupations of the civil service city. The overall result was a breakdown of the ghetto effect that had characterized it for generations. Francophones were moving into the secular, middle-class strata, so long alien, while young anglophones were gaining a passport into what had been a remote and often disdained culture.

But this trend is very recent. The polarization of French and English in Ottawa was still very powerful as late as 1971: "...a family's ethnic group affiliation remains the most influential in determining their choice of residential location."[20] By and large, the French in Ottawa continued to reside in the central and eastern part of the city, while the English lived in the southern and western areas. Economic status also remained closely tied to race and religion. Findings for 1961 showed that high average income per household in Ottawa correlated most strongly with home ownership and a Protestant religion, and not only weakly, but inversely with households that were French speaking only, or Roman Catholic.[21]

The effect of such movement on religion, coupled with more general secular trends, and ecumenical ones is unclear. But the general effect in Ottawa seems to have been a reduction in the religious bitterness and the distance that informed much of political and economic life from the time of the town's establishment. In a sense, French and English, Catholic and Protestant, have come to look much alike.

Major breakthroughs were also made by women in the post-war period. Many women had been drawn into the work-force in the war period, but it proved to be a temporary phenomenon and, following 1945, most seem to have gone back into the home and volunteer work, the traditional "careers" for most women in the period. As for the Civil Service, the opportunities for women proved somewhat similar to those for the French. Women, like the French, were disadvantaged by the merit principle. As previously mentioned, females were considered incapable of handling management jobs. But further — a practice not confined merely to the government — marriage meant resignation: in the nineteenth century by convention, and, later, by law.

The decision of the government in 1955[22] to remove restrictions on married women in the Civil Service was thus a landmark for women in Ottawa. Though in practice most of them remained at home after marriage, they were, after 1955, not bound to it. Through the 1960s, probably aided by the feminist revolution, the concept that women were incapable of management jobs began to dissolve, and, further, there then began a large feminine influx into the universities. By the 1970s, the elements were in place that would enable well-trained cadres of women to combined career and family. Also, affirmative action programs within the PS began to create opportunities within senior ranks. It remains clear, however, that the lower ranks of the PS are still dominated by women, and even in senior ranks progress has been slow. In the post-war period, then, formal restrictions on women that had created social inequalities were removed. The consequences are still unclear, though a strong female influence in the political life in the capital from the 1970s is evident.

Parallel to the movement of French and female sectors into a middle-class PS milieu, was the decline of industrial labour — or at least its blue-collar dimension — relative to the total population. Blue-collar Ottawa almost disappeared in the forty years from the Second World War. Of parallel importance, the CS in 1962 was given collective bargaining rights,[23] which generally seems to have had two important implications. Salaries, in the first place, were improved along with conditions of employment, and employment itself was made more secure. Of perhaps greater importance, the

Carleton University, 1973. It was begun during the war as a cap to an English educational system in the city, and to service the needs of a government town and returned veterans. This photograph looks northward to the city centre.

senior members of the CS ceased to act as the mediators and interlocutors between employees and the Civil Service Commission and, ultimately, between themselves and their political bosses. An ancient paternalist system was undone.

Class relations, in this sense, became more controlled by the strata within the government operation, as reflected in the differences among the public sector unions — for example the Public Service Alliance of Canada, as opposed to the Professional Institute of the Public Service — than between boss and worker. Equally profound differences emerged between those who worked within the large public service corporation and those who worked as, or for, independent capitalists outside it.

Ottawa also became a more polyglot community in the period following the Second World War. The traditional ethnic communities — German, Italian, and Jewish — clearly made important strides. All proved upwardly mobile, in both society and politics, and all managed to achieve a distinctive presence in the city.

Newcomers in the post-war period were chiefly from the Middle East and the Orient. The little Chinese community grew significantly and stamped a unique character on a small section of the west central part of the city. More recently, a Vietnamese community has established itself nearby. But probably the largest influx was that from the Middle East, particularly Lebanon, and in the last generation they have made a significant contribution to Ottawa life.

The overall effect of the shifts in the social strata and in the emergence of new communities, both in the suburbs and the core, was to create a new set of demographic and social relations less than a decade old and with consequences which, if now evident, are not entirely clear. Perhaps symbolic of the change was the virtual disappearance in the 1970s of the annual Orange parade, which as late as 1960 drew an estimated 50,000 spectators.[24]

Just as economic and social relations assumed a new orientation in the post-war period, so too did a host of other activities, like post-secondary education. The role of the two universities is still being defined in the new community. Carleton, only forty-odd years in operation, and the University of Ottawa, with its relatively new, secular, and bi-lingual format, are both still defining a place in a much changed city, dominated by the federal presence. Both, for example, have strong programs in public administration, and both have made efforts to collaborate in areas like "high-tech" and women's studies that over-arch historically rooted cleavages. But the universities must still respond to the communities that created them, as reflected even in the names of their buildings, like Paterson and Southam Hall at English-language Carleton, or Tabaret Hall and the Morriset Library at the University of Ottawa.

Cultural activities, too, feel government influence. In the early decades of the twentieth century, Ottawans had hoped to benefit from the capital function by creating a "national" drama school and a "Canadian" conservatory. In certain areas, the community, in typical booster style, sought to focus the activity of the nation on the nation's capital. The idea did not take. But it was picked up after the Second World War by the federal government. It expanded its cultural interests from a geological museum, a national gallery, and an archives, into museums of man, of technology, of war, and of aeronautics, the National Film Board, and a National Library, all of which had their chief showcases in the city. As part of a broader scheme to create a capital worthy of the nation, government even began restoring the buildings of the old lumber town for national purposes, ultimately accounting for the rehabilitation of Lower Town, and the "Mile of History" on Sussex Street, as well as current activities to restore part of the derelict industrial sites on the Chaudière islands. The "city's" heritage was appropriated for "capital" purposes. Government also played a critical role in building the National Arts Centre, which became home for the NAC Orchestra, and national theatre companies in French and English, the latter now defunct.

Government, too, in the twentieth century rapidly expanded its scientific research, which in the nineteenth century had been rooted in the Geological Survey and the Central Experimental Farm. The chief agency was the National Research Council, launched in the 1920s.

The two universities inevitably interacted with the federal cultural and scientific agencies, as always the biggest business in the city: the Steacie, Mackenzie, and Herzberg buildings at Carleton University are testimony to a long relationship with the NRC. The first two are named after NRC presidents, the last after a Nobel prize winner, who made his home in both places. But the government enterprise, unlike private undertakings in other places, generally will not directly fund local endeavours: it constructs institutions of national importance on its own. Local cultural and scientific endeavours then try to fit into the cracks, and sometimes fall into them.

One of the consequences of World War II was the concentration of much national activity in the hands of the federal government, and therefore in Ottawa. Some 30,000 federal employees were added to the wartime city. Here, in this still from the film **Grierson**, John Grierson (right), longtime head of the National Film Board, discusses advertising posters with graphic designer/illustrator Harry Mayerovitch.

The Ottawa Public Library had a painful birth; the City Archives is of recent genesis; the Ottawa School of Art is periodically homeless; and the only community museum, run by the Historical Society of Ottawa, is housed in a heritage building owned by the federal government. Local theatre survives in the Ottawa Little Theatre, and more recently, in the Great Canadian Theatre Company and the York Street Theatre. Music is kept alive in the Ottawa Symphony Orchestra, begun in 1965-1966. But all of these are very much in the amateur/professional and fragmented tradition of the city. In the shade of federal enterprise, local culture often remains pale, though as paradox, of course, much local culture is the product of people who work in the federal enclave.

Most cultural agencies in Ottawa — like the universities — were, from the post-war period, attempting to respond to their communities; to aspire to national or international standards of performance; and to live with the corporate culture generated by the federal government, as part of its perceived national purpose.

In sports during the post-war period, only the Ottawa Rough Riders survived as a "national" team, but one owned in Toronto, and a "provincial" junior hockey team, the "67s", was put together by local entrepreneurs. They both nurtured a number of local figures of "star" quality, from Russ Jackson to Denis Potvin. But most of the figures to reach a national or international prominence were rooted in punctual, local organizations inspired by the natural amenities of the valley: skaters like Barbara Ann Scott and Lynn Nightingale; skiers like Anne Heggtveit and Betsy Clifford; paddlers like Sue Holloway; shooters like Linda Thom.

As for popular culture and entertainment, it has taken some curious twists in the city. Its breeding ground, as in sports, has been in the dramatic and musical organizations associated with the limited communities of the city, like the Ottawa Little Theatre. From these have come "stars" like Rich Little, and Paul Anka. The international booking circuits on which they now travel have only recently found Ottawa an amenable stop, generally at the annual Central Canada Exhibition, or, since 1969, at the National Arts Centre. Previously such individuals were prone to book their acts into the clubs in the Hull area, where more generous hours of operation and a more lively atmosphere produced the best of night life in the capital region, from world-class jazz to country and western.

The federal government, too, in a curious way, has given new dimensions to cultural life in the city, most notably as an energizer

Railway lines flank the east bank of the Rideau Canal, about 1950. The Peace Tower of the Parliament Buildings is at left and Union Station, now the National Conference Centre, is at centre. For 80 years this was the railway entry into the city. The rail lines were relocated in the 1950s and 1960s as part of a capital beautification programme.

Aerial view from the Nicholas Street interchange of the completed Queensway, looking northwest over the Rideau Canal, the city, and the Ottawa River, 1969. Rail lines, rail-yards, and industrial operations had formerly filled much of the open space. Buildings of the University of Ottawa can be seen near the frozen canal's right bank (centre right).

and a market. Perhaps most notable has been the long life and international success of Budge Crawley and Crawley Films, winner of a 1977 Oscar for *The Man Who Skied Down Everest*. With the talent available in the National Film Board, Crawley has produced numerous outstanding efforts in film-making, especially in documentary and animation.

The architectural styles of the twentieth century also reflect the presence of government and the corporate private sector. External organizations and their architectural standards in the early twentieth century imposed themselves on the city with a vengence. The Grand Trunk Railway gave the city the neo-Roman-bath Union Station (1912), and the castle-like Château Laurier Hotel (1912). Much government building in the core area, in the early twentieth century and under the influence of the chief architects of the department of public works was in a castle-like style.

This imposition of corporate and branch-plant design, especially in Upper Town, severely limited local opportunity for twentieth-century commercial construction. Perhaps the only prominent example is the Daly Building (1905), and then only by fortuitous timing. It went up in the core of the city just before the federal authorities determined that "Confederation Square" was to be dedicated to the Dominion, not the local community. There was no further development of commercial architecture in the area, where building heights were also limited, in deference to the Parliament Buildings. Ottawa remains one of the few cities to have no prominent "wedding cake" structures, so typical of North American cities in the early twentieth century. Commercial styles, rooted in the local business community were strangled, and the corporate styles of government and railways imposed.

URBAN LANDSCAPE

As has been noted, federal government growth, in and after the Second World War, coupled with the disappearance of the sawn lumber industry, transformed the urban landscape. Beyond its core, satellite concentrations of government buildings abutted new post-war suburbs. And beyond them, the greenbelt encased the city and parts of neighbouring townships. Sandy Hill and Centre Town slowly succumbed to commercial and multi-residential penetration. Only Lower Town, the very oldest part, remained some-what intact. It had for years been preserved by neglect. The sixties had a different fate for it. But while the buildings were saved, the people weren't. The old Catholic and French centre was slowly being edged eastward and upward by rehabilitation and affirmative action. An economic class was supplanting a group previously identified by race and religion. An identifiable working-class area would cease to exist under the forces of gentrification, and of rising salary scales. The By Ward market persisted, however, increasingly surrounded by wine bars, boutiques, and heritage. Little-changed communities were those that remained independent of the city, like Rockcliffe Park Village and Cité Vanier (formerly Eastview), growing cheek-by-jowl in enclaves, rich and poor, on the eastern edge of Ottawa, each in a different way a tax-dodge municipality.

A new urban landscape, like so much else in twentieth-century Ottawa, emerged under the twin pressures of Town and Crown. The sheer physical presence of government (in its buildings), required huge commitments of money, and was a determinant element in the city's development. On two fronts, the "Crown" launched major planning initiatives, one concerned with accommodating the government enterprise, the other with creating a national metaphor.

As for the city, during the Depression and the war years, its control of planning and development slipped. The Depression, the death of the planning activist, Cauchon, in 1935, and the war, were sufficient to ensure that little was accomplished. The passing of the city as an industrial place and the narrowing of political vision at city hall seemed to demoralize further its control over its destiny. Only in 1957 did work start on an official plan, despite a huge post-war construction boom, and a huge annexation in 1950, that committed the city to major public works projects.

As the initial planning thrust dribbled out in the Depression, that of the federal authority was in many respects given its start. Mackenzie King was again the central actor. While visiting the Canadian exhibit at the Paris exposition in 1936, King met and was impressed with the French beaux arts planner, Jacques Gréber, whom he invited to Ottawa in 1937 to advise on the planning of Confederation Square and the War Memorial. Gréber, who was hired more or less personally by King, had no institutional connection to the Federal District Commission, the official agency of capital planning. What work he did was interrupted in 1939 by the war. In 1945, he was invited back to Ottawa by King to resume his

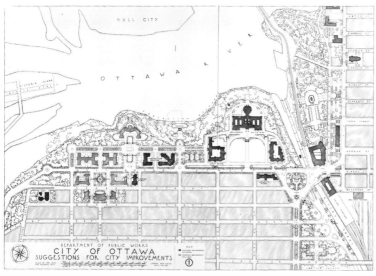

Jacques Gréber's 1937 plan for "improvement of the Parliamentary Precinct." Development was interrupted by the war.

Jacques Gréber returned to Ottawa after the war to direct the planning of the entire National Capital Region. Here, in 1949, assistants prepare a model of the plan, which guided federal development of the capital for more than a generation. The section in the foreground contains the Parliament Hill area; Hull is at lower left.

work.[25] This time, however, an institutional connection was provided to the FDC, and Gréber was mandated to provide a plan for the entire capital region. On March 8, 1946, a National Capital Planning committee was established under a bylaw of the FDC to "draw up a master plan of the National Capital District,"[26] designated in 1944 as a 900-square-mile area, embracing the city and its surroundings. The twenty-nine-member committee included representation from the local governments and engineering and architectural associations, as well as a heavy federal representation. Gréber was to act as consultant, with John M. Kitchen, who had been associated with Cauchon, and Edouard Fiset as associates.

The city, however it felt about planning, had additional practical cause to be satisfied with the federal authority. As a result of joint Senate and Commons report of 1944,[27] it began, in the 1950s, to pay the city grants in lieu of property (but not business) taxes that approximated a true levy on federal government property. In fact, the government became the largest taxpayer in the city. Though that would imply the federal authority might have some interest in how its taxes were being spent, no mechanism, even of consultation, was established, and if anything, city-federal relations soured in the decades after the grants were begun, to some extent over the matter of planning.

The idea that the city was to be taken seriously by the federal authority in planning the capital (though in effect it was adopting the city's turn-of-the century position) was swallowed only partially and piecemeal. The prominent Ottawa Liberal, George McIlraith, claimed in 1945 that the city's plans had nothing to do with the capital as a national memorial.[28] It was in part a problem stemming from the fact that "Sometimes it is difficult to draw the line . . . ,"[29] between planning for the city and planning for the capital, and, in part, from the insistence by the FDC that "a series of local demands" is no substitute for "the reasoned provisions" of the National Capital Plan.[30] But the difficulty also stemmed in part from the fact that while the planning expertise of the FDC was growing apace, as well as its authority, either through statutory mandate, budget, or control of property, that of the city was relatively weakening. This was partially through a failure to develop a strong planning department, and partially through the more general loss of local autonomy in the 1940s and 1950s. Of equal importance, the old sectional politics of Ottawa were inappropriate to the new, post-war city. But perhaps the greatest factor

psychologically was the fact that the FDC made a plan to which it became firmly committed, and the city and the surrounding areas did not.

The Gréber report was ready by 1950.[31] There were few surprises. Earlier studies, like those of Todd (1903), Holt (1916), and Cauchon (1921), had pin-pointed the obvious problems, and had posed most of the solutions. Chief among them remained the railways, and the intensified automobile traffic that was demanding new roadways. Among other things, Gréber suggested that abandoned railway rights-of-way be used to accommodate automobile traffic. He also expressed a great deal of concern about riverine pollution. But most of his recommendations were well-worn variants of earlier proposals, including an expansion of Gatineau Park, the creation of a greenbelt around the city, and perhaps most important, in the core area, the use of Confederation Square as the central ceremonial approach to Parliament Hill. To implement these proposals, the National Capital District was subsequently to be enlarged to 1,800 square miles, to embrace seventy-two municipalities in two provinces (done in 1959), and the FDC reformulated as the National Capital Commission (NCC) with a full-time chairman (also done in 1959). No provision was made for representation from local governments on the NCC.

By the 1950s, the FDC not only had the Gréber Plan, but was also heavily funded and strongly supported by successive prime ministers: King, St. Laurent, and Diefenbaker. It launched a major program of property acquisition, including the greenbelt (1958), that would enable it to pursue its primary operational premise: development through ownership of property. The FDC, in the 1950s, also began the crucial rail-line relocation program. The main thrust of its work was continued by its successor the NCC. By the late 1960s, the two agencies had put in place the basic infra-structure of roads, bridges, parkways, and the like, necessary to a national capital setting.

From 1936 to 1969, the chairman of the FDC/NCC had, except for three years, been an engineer, and the commission itself had largely been concerned with the practical problems of implementing (with modifications) the Gréber Plan. Relations with the city, if not always perfect, were at least practical. The city tended to accept, in general terms, the plan set out by the prestigious Jacques Gréber. And since much of the interplay between the city and NCC was at the technical and engineering level, accommodation could gener-

In recent years the National Capital Commission has turned from engineering to "people" activities, including support of the Gatineau 55, the only international loppet held in Canada. Some 3,000 skiers are shown at the start of this 55-kilometer race.

ally be found. Finally, the broad policies of the FDC/NCC included a "degree of interest" clause, under which the NCC could finance local works, according to the "degree of interest" the FDC/NCC had in them. It proved considerable in the fifties and sixties, and many basic city works, including major roads, bridges and water-treatment facilities, were heavily underwritten by the FDC/NCC as part of capital beautification.

While the city wanted sewers for its periphery, the FDC wanted to clear up the pollution that detracted from the beauty of the rivers. The result was shared costs for major water and sewer projects. The FDC wanted to remove rail-lines from the core; the city wanted a freeway. The result was shared costs (with the province) for the Queensway, basically on the old GTR/CNR right-of-way. The city wanted a bus system; the FDC wanted streetcar lines and wires removed from the Parliament Hill area. The result was a federal contribution in the "Parliamentary Precinct". The city wanted a new Rideau Canal bridge; the FDC wanted truck traffic out of Confederation Square. The result: the Mackenzie King Bridge. The FDC wanted a better connection to proposed office expansion at Confederation heights and, ultimately, to the airport; the city wanted better access to its southern reaches. The result was shared costs for the Bronson Bridges over the canal and the Rideau River (Dunbar Bridge). The FDC wanted better access to its building clusters in the west of the city; the city wanted a better east-west arterial. The result was the expansion of Carling Avenue (into six lanes) with federal assistance and provision of federal land.

Collaboration even included the matter of a location for a new city hall, which had been operating from rented quarters near Sussex and Rideau from 1931, when the old one burned. Despite strong feelings that the city hall should remain at the town core, the offer of FDC land on Green's Island, at the mouth of the Rideau River, proved too attractive to resist. A new city hall was opened in 1958. The heart of the city, as a result, belonged almost completely to the federal government.

Finally, apart from the FDC/NCC activities and the tax grants, the city also benefitted, in some respects, from the location in Ottawa of national showcases: the museums, National Gallery and National Arts Centre, which Charlotte Whitton termed "Fort Culture", opened in 1969 at a cost of $50 million.[32]

Prior to the 1960s, the three major agencies of development — the FDC/NCC, concerned with the "Capital", the Department of Public Works, concerned with Government and Civil Service accommodation, and the city and private developers, concerned mainly with housing and services — had operated fairly autonomously, and had intersected mainly on engineering and technical matters. Moreover, most of the activity had occurred within the boundaries of Ottawa. In the early 1960s, however, Public Works determined to lease from private developers, rather than build its own government office accommodation. For the first time, in a major way, the development industry, particularly the Campeau Corporation, was allied to Public Works and through it to the federal cabinet. This collaboration created a sharp conflict with both the NCC (a federal agency thought not a department), and Ottawa city hall.

It reached an initial peak in quarrels over building heights in the core. Those calling for restraint — the NCC and some elements in the city — lost. Ottawa, within a few hundred feet of Parliament Hill, was covered with high-rise buildings.

Building heights from 1914 had been limited in the city centre to prevent commercial buildings from overshadowing Parliament Hill. Limitations were modified in 1965 to permit a dish-like configuration, with the heights of buildings permitted to increase the further the buildings were away from the Hill, up to a height of 150 feet.[33] The new regulation had been in place only a matter of months when the Campeau Corporation sought permission to build its massive Place de Ville, to heights double those in the bylaw. Council compromised on a 250-foot limit. Height limitations were broken almost as they had been put in place, though high-rise development in city cores was possibly an irresistible phenomenon of the sixties.

The genesis of Campeau's Place de Ville development is nonetheless somewhat unusual and somewhat murky.[34] It occurred in spite of the objections of the NCC, which saw high-rise development in the "Parliamentary Precinct" as running contrary to its efforts to create an outstanding national capital setting. The city, with its development-oriented council, succumbed more than it either agreed or objected. The signals coming from the federal authority were, after all, somewhat confusing. Despite the protests of the NCC, which traditionally had a strong link with the prime ministers, it was clear that a special relationship existed between Campeau, a known Liberal supporter, and the government of the day. More to the point, the prime tenant in the new Campeau development was

A bane of the growing city were the cross-town lines of the Canadian National Railways (originally John R. Booth's railway). Beginning in 1957, the right-of-way was converted to an automobile expressway, The Queensway, opened in 1965. Here, in 1963, construction is crossing Elgin Street, and about to cross the Rideau Canal. The Pretoria Bridge is at centre right.

The effect of capital beautification is at its most evident at Rideau Falls. The mills are gone. City Hall (1958) dominated the scene in this 1968 photo by Alex Onoszko.

The centre of the city becomes the centre of the capital, 1968. Dominating Confederation Square and Park are the War Memorial (centre) and the National Arts Centre (lower left). The old Union Station (right of the canal) is now a government conference centre. The Chateau Laurier Hotel is across the street.

to be government of Canada, under the new leasing policy of Public Works. In this sense, the federal government, through Public Works, had prevailed over a federal commission, the NCC, as well as the city, in directing the "private" development of the downtown. The whole process reached its zenith in 1969, when Campeau was permitted to construct a 342-foot building (Place de Ville, Phase II) in the core, in which government again was to be the chief tenant.

The determinant and direct influence of the federal government (as opposed to the NCC), on the fortunes of the city was felt again in 1969. In that year, it launched a policy to help Hull "catch up".[35] Plans were announced — for Place du Portage and subsequently Les Terrasses de la Chaudière — that would shift some 25,000 public servants to the Hull side of the river and effectively end Ottawa's long reign as the (nearly) exclusive site for headquarters personnel. This time, the NCC was more of a collaborator. It had assembled part of the site (purchased by the government from the Eddy company), and collaborated with the city of Hull in provision of new services for the complexes. It also built on its own hook (ignoring local municipalities) the Portage Bridge, linking the core of Hull with the core of Ottawa, and inevitably, their street systems. Once again, there was a somewhat unclear relationship of the federal Liberals with the Campeau Corporation, the major contractor in the Hull development.

As for the City of Ottawa (and the Regional Municipality of Ottawa-Carleton), it could only protest such unilateral action and, even then, not too loudly. Government, after all, did much good. Still, the city was not only faced with new municipal economic competition, and more complex inter-governmental regulations, but with the costs (especially for access roads) for up-graded, inter-provincial transportation facilities for public servants, now living and working in large numbers throughout the Ottawa and Hull regions.

The year 1969 in some ways marked the end of the era in which the NCC had not only a plan (Gréber's) agreeable to most, but a chestful of treasures it was prepared to bestow on the city, and which the city gratefully accepted. But by the end of the 1960s, it had become clear that the NCC would have to share federal planning jurisdiction, not only with federal departments, such as Public Works, over such matters as Place de Ville and Place du Portage, but with the city, too. In the 1960s, the city generated and approved its first comprehensive plan. It came at a time when the NCC had

largely completed the Gréber Plan. At the end of the sixties, it was a huge planning and technical agency with not much building left to do, and not much of a plan to do it from. It was an engine with much unused capacity, a situation pregnant with mischief.

The NCC, headed in 1969 by Douglas Fullerton (a non-engineer) as chairman, sought a new role and decided, among other things, to become involved directly in the creation of a "lively core" and in the drafting of a plan for the National Capital Region. Both, strictly speaking, were the jurisdiction of the city and regional governments, both of which had residual grievances with the NCC over its tendency to be rather high-handed. Perhaps more important, the NCC showed a striking insensitivity to the new imperatives of both regional and, more important, neighbourhood planning. It assumed that planners, especially its planners, knew best. Such premises were being completely turned over inside the city, where citizen planning was taking priority. Though the NCC was a partner in the late 1970s in the development of the massive Rideau Centre, to rehabilitate the heart of the city, it was ultimately only done in collaboration with the city, the federal government, and the private sector, and over the vigorous protests of nearby neighbourhoods. It also launched a number of "people" activities, and took over the Rideau canal rink (begun by the city) to create the longest skating surface in the world. But these activities, as much as they were welcomed, were insufficient to patch over more fundamental differences. One of the worst was at the regional level.

In the 1970s the NCC drew up a plan that proposed development of the region on an axis from the southeast corner of the Ottawa region (where a provincial-federal landbank had been established with little local participation), to the northwest corner of the Hull region, in the area of Lucerne and Aylmer. Regional planners on both sides of the river saw a contrary axis of development, from the south or southwest on the Ottawa side, to the northeast (or Gatineau area), on the Hull side. Though it was clearly a plan that favoured local land-developers, it was rooted in the various communities, which, however fragmented, were always vigorous and highly territorial.

The attack on local autonomy was carried further by Fullerton after his resignation in 1973 as NCC chairman, when appointed to study governance in the national capital region. His 1974 report, "The Capital of Canada: How Should it be Governed," started from the premise that the national capital was, among other things, a

Developer Robert Campeau, president of Campeau Corporation, in his Ottawa office, 1967.

Campeau Coporation's Place de Ville, the dark towers in the foreground, in 1967. This was the beginning of the high-rise core. The effect of the LeBreton Flats clearance (between the towers and the river) is evident. Wartime "temporaries" are flanked by the National Library and Public Archives (top) and the Justice Building (bottom). They face, across Wellington, the Memorial Buildings (1949-1958), the most distant of them situated where Nicholas Sparks originally had his home.

"jurisdictional swamp".[36] He proposed a "supra government", with a role for all levels of jurisdiction. The report, however, seemed more to show evidence of the federal inability to deal with local government, as well as an inability to cope with new planning perspectives and priorities. A decade before, the local governments had unanimously rejected a provincial report that recommended similar streamlining for the Ottawa region, though, of course, not as a politically independent capital region. Fullerton's report was redolent of the assumptions of Ordnance: the desire for symmetry and the inherent virtue of the representatives of the senior jurisdiction. It was not acted on.

As indicated, much had changed at the local level by the 1960s. In Ottawa, the city had developed a degree of maturity in its engineering, planning, and other civic departments and had undergone the shock of a major administrative survey. An improved and larger local bureaucracy, given political nerve, could now hold its own with federal operatives. And the political nerve began arriving in the late 1960s with the new breed of local politicians who were neighbourhood-based. The NCC, whether on matters of planning policy or technique, was no longer given the final word.

In any case, the city had two critical planning issues of its own to work out, and the NCC was not welcome to interfere in either. One focused on neighbourhoods, and the other on the region.

Much of the planning done by the city in the 1950s and 1960s was oriented to the demands of expansion and development, in particular the servicing demands of the suburban developments springing up in the empty lands of the 1950 annexation. By the 1960s, however, a reaction had set in from the neighbourhood level. Perhaps the first portents were the protests over the Lower Town East urban renewal proposal, launched in 1966 (after almost a decade of preliminary studies) without telling the affected residents.[37] The reaction, led by the church, derailed the project until 1968, when it proceeded in a revised format. Still, it was a response to a plan created by planners according to their premises.

The more significant reaction, over the long term, was the organization, in the late 1960s, of various Ottawa communities concerned with protecting their neighbourhoods from the worst effects of growth and bigness. In time, they came to feel that they, not planners, businessmen, or developers should set the agenda for their neighbourhoods, or perhaps even for the city. The feeling came to extend to federal agencies, as well.

Initial activity seems to have been galvanized by the Pretoria Bridge incident.[38] In 1968, DeLeuw, Cather, international planning consultants, recommended that the city (among other things) run a major east-west transportation corridor through Ottawa East and the Glebe, via the line of the Pretoria Bridge, a nineteenth-century stone drawbridge over the Rideau Canal (since restored as a heritage structure). Concerned individuals from central city neighbourhoods — Ottawa Centre and Sandy Hill, as well as Ottawa East and the Glebe — were drawn together in a protest movement that successfully stopped the proposed corridor. A number of the activists, including Lorry Greenberg, Michael Cassidy, and Joe Cassey, in time gained local office, and, with activists like Ralph Sutherland from the West End, formed the core of a reform movement. Others continued to develop opposition to threats to their own neighbourhoods. Apart from the evident politicization, the Pretoria Bridge incident showed that communities could beat city hall and unrestrained development. Like-minded citizens from various neighbourhoods also got to know each other, and in May, 1970, the Federation of Citizens Committees of Ottawa-Carleton was organized as an umbrella group from, initially, thirty-eight community organizations.

But three, essentially middle-class organizations, starting from rather self-interested concerns for their neighbourhoods, ultimately forced significant changes in planning and politics at city hall.

In October, 1970, city council approved a 420-unit public housing proposal for the west end of the city, despite protests of the two local aldermen, and the proven failure of such projects. The proposal politicized one west-end community association, whose leader, lawyer David Hill, subsequently became chairman of the Pinecrest Queensway Citizens Committee. It became the steering body for a neighbourhood plan, and with Centre Town and Sandy Hill associations, changed the direction of city planning, particularly with regard to the notion that the neighbourhoods, not planners, should establish the planning premises and objectives. Sandy Hill and Centre Town however, had different motives from Pinecrest. As two of the oldest and most central communities, both by the 1960s were under severe pressure from commercial building moving outwards from the core, and commuter and other traffic moving in from the suburbs. The fine old homes and neighbourhoods of the turn-of-the-century middle-class seemed doomed to destruction or

Skaters on the world's longest rink, the Rideau Canal. The National Arts Centre is at the left.

To the left are the spires of the Chateau Laurier, to centre left, the Daly Building, one of the few original commercial buildings in the ceremonial core. To the right is the Westin Hotel, part of the "Rideau Centre," a recently completed complex combining stores, a hotel, and convention centre.

downgrading, as both areas started becoming zones of transition.

But they remained attractive. Both had large stocks of fine homes, and both areas were flanked by major projects of capital beautification. They were both, courtesy of the NCC, equipped with attractive amenities. Both were close to the jobs and the more vibrant night-life of downtown Ottawa, which until the late 1960s, was characterized as much by its dullness as by its crudity.

In Sandy Hill, the chief concern was probably traffic and the destruction of low-rise residences. In Centre Town, it was these factors and the flight of families, threatening the closure of schools and consequent destruction of a framework of residential life, that triggered activity. Both areas were eventually designated as subjects for neighbourhood plans. These actions in the early 1970s paved the way for re-gentrification of each neighbourhood. Throughout the decade, and into the 1980s they became the chief focus of the "white painters" of the new middle-classes of the public service. Both neighbourhoods also sent a full complement of reform politicians to city hall, many of them, like those from the west end, women.

The emergence of neighbourhood action — at the micro level — coincided with imperatives in the region — at the macro level. Indeed, neighbourhood activity heavily influenced regional planning, charged with the movement of traffic in and out of the core, and also provided models of community activity for urban fringe communities that fought, unsuccessfully, through the 1970s a regional plan in which the focus of expansion was southward along the Rideau River corridor.[39]

Regional government of course had its own peculiar evolution, with, again, much heightened activity at the end of the 1960s and into the early 1970s. Wartime Ottawa had been a small city, both in terms of its area and its population, but already during the war years, the population had begun to spill into the surrounding townships, for the most part without urban services.[40] The initial effort to control this growth was by the Ottawa Planning Area Board, established in 1947, under provincial legislation, and the almost concurrent efforts by the FDC to convince the county municipalities to establish a greenbelt, by means of zoning and other restrictions. But the planning instrument, in the face of development-minded county and township governments, was too fragile an instrument to control growth; and the tax bases were too shallow (chiefly agricultural), to properly service massive residen-

tial development. On all three fronts — the city's need for residential expansion, the Department of Public Works' need for office accommodation "at Ottawa", and FDC desire for a greenbelt — indicated a more direct confrontation. The first solution was simple and crude. In 1950, the city annexed huge areas of Gloucester and Nepean townships, almost to the inner edge of the proposed greenbelt, more than quadrupling its area, and embracing most of the populated areas that had developed in the county. Nubs of the old townships remained within the greenbelt. The FDC, for its part, determined in 1958 to create the greenbelt by purchase, and, if necessary, by expropriation. Regional planning was made redundant.

In the early 1950s, then, actions had been taken that would, it was believed, ensure controlled development of the capital — Ottawa — for the foreseeable future. It thus became the chief preoccupation of the city in the 1950s and 1960s to service and develop its much expanded jurisdiction.

The city, it seemed at the time, had the necessary technical capacity and financial capacity to do so. It had also purchased, in the late 1940s, the private traction and power companies — though the former, especially, was completely worn out — and had the means to provide a coherent system of transportation as well as other services, like water and sewer, throughout an expanded jurisdiction. With help from the NCC it had managed to do so by the 1960s.

Growth, however, exceeded all expectations, and the massive annexation of 1950 proved insufficient. By the 1960s, residential development was again proceeding rapidly in some of the nearby townships, both inside and outside the greenbelt. And it was also becoming clear by the end of the 1960s that the federal government had every intention of developing facilities on the Québec side of the river. There was little the city could do about the latter. And not much it could do about the former.

The only instrument of control — or really coordination — was the old Ottawa Planning Area Board, which was provided most of its technical expertise by the city. As early as 1962, it was clear that it was "Coming Apart At The Seams".[41] Nepean, Gloucester, and Eastview had established their own planning staffs, and were clearly going to pursue their own interests. They had also become sufficiently self-conscious that they were prepared to fight tooth and nail any suggestion of annexation or amalgamation. In March, 1962, the Ottawa Board of Control asked the provincial Minister of

Municipal Affairs to assign some of his staff to study the problems between Ottawa and the surrounding municipalities.[42] A similar pattern had developed on the Hull side of the river, and its mayor had made a similar request of the Québec government. But if nothing else, all the local governments were dead set against a Federal District, like that of Washington, D.C. There was a powerful sense, for whatever the reason, sentiment or profit, to maintain local independence.

In her letter of transmittal, Ottawa's mayor, Charlotte Whitton, sought some form other than the Federal District, or a super government like Toronto's metro. She was looking for "... some other basis for co-operation other than zoning and land use and at the same time retain our individual autonomy." She noted that studies with respect to regional sewer and water had been carried out prior to the 1950 annexation, but no comparable projections had been done in other areas. The mayor said there was a need "... to estimate and allocate the responsibility in respect to area service for our educational institutions..., hospitals..., fire, police, traffic, transportation and law enforcement, and magisterial and judicial functions ...."[43] In October of 1962 the province said it would direct a full-scale study, if asked, but only by 1964 was one under way, headed by Murray V. Jones. Jones reported May 31, 1965, and recommended a "multi-community government". Old communities would be dissolved, and new communities of equal size, operating within the framework of a regional government, were proposed. Though it was a solution to the knotty problem of "federal" government at the local level, almost no-one in the region was prepared to accept it. It solved the problem of competing local identities by submerging them. For Ottawa, especially, any solution that wiped away its unique status as the "National Capital" was intolerable.

The various regional municipalities had their own peculiar solutions. A metro-type government had a large following. Ottawa's Board of Control proposed a "twin-city" plan: a new, expanded Ottawa, and a sprawling rural metropolis of Carleton, in effect the solution of 1950. This time, the city would expand to the greenbelt and pick up Eastview (now Cité Vanier) and Rockcliffe Park Village in the process. The former, French, and the latter rich and influential, were unenthusiastic, as were Nepean and Gloucester, once again to be reduced to rural townships.

In the event, the Ontario government created a regional district, which came to be known as the Regional Municipality of Ottawa-Carleton (RMOC). It was to be run by a thirty-member council, selected from the elected representatives of the member municipalities. No municipal boundaries were to be changed, Ottawa would have an absolute majority (sixteen members) on the council (it now has only a plurality), and the chairman for the first years would be appointed by the province. A review (ultimately the Mayo Report), was to be carried out within the first decade of operation. RMOC went into operation 1 January 1969, with a former reeve of Rockcliffe, Dennis Coolican, appointed as chairman.

There was grudging agreement by the member municipalities. After twenty years of debate and deadlock, no-one had come up with a more satisfactory solution. The new region was responsible chiefly for infrastructure, like sewer and water, and had a number of shared jurisdictions, like roads, with member municipalities. In time, it took over a number of other functions, notably public transit and social service. But its chief strength was probably its mandate to plan, and to create a regional scheme to which the municipalities would be obliged to conform, in general terms, while retaining a parallel planning function within their own administrations. Inevitably there was conflict between the regional and the local plans, but perhaps more important, between the regional plans of both RMOC and those of the new Outaouais Regional Government in Québec, and the plans of the NCC for the national capital. All areas of jurisdiction, federal, regional, local, and neighbourhood, had plans by the 1970s, not to mention those of developers and, especially in the Rideau River Valley, of the conservationists.

At the outset, Ottawa dominated the region, not only because of its size (296,248 versus 100,000), and voting and taxing power, but because of its technical expertise. It wanted big urban services and was prepared to pay for them. To some degree, this was true of Eastview, Rockcliffe, and parts of Nepean and Gloucester. But other areas in the region, mostly rural, preferred minimal services and low taxes. Though there was tension at the outset between "urban" and "rural", it did admit of resolution.

What became more of a problem by the end of the 1970s, was the growing power of some of the regional townships, notably Nepean, Gloucester, and March-Kanata, in relation to Ottawa. All were concerned with expansion and "extensive" development. All had overflowing schools. Ottawa, preoccupied with these concerns

10 Federal land ownership in the core: By the 1980s, Government had come to dominate the centre of the city. It moved out from Parliament Hill and Major's Hill to embrace Confederation Square and Park, as well as both sides of Wellington and Sussex streets. It reclaimed much of what Ordnance relinquished in the 1840s.

11 Regional municipalities, etc: Superimposed on the old cities of Ottawa and Hull are the two regional governments, and on them, the National Capital Region. The last exerts its influence through its ownership of land, including the greenbelt, in the absence of constitutional authority.

through the 1950s and 1960s, had come to a sudden stop in growth, and was more interested in intensive, quality-of-life matters. Its council — and its representatives to the region — reflected the change by the end of the 1970s. They were more concerned with neighbourhood, rather than development politics.

By the end of the 1970s, a series of *détentes* appeared to have been reached, in which Ottawa City proper recognized formally, and was prepared to ensure, the continued safety of the self-conscious neighbourhood communities of which it was comprised. At the same time, it had accustomed itself to a less than pre-eminent role in the region, while asserting, and sometimes achieving a near-equal role with federal agencies, chiefly the NCC and Public Works, which themselves, with capital building mostly completed and public service growth slowed, were to become rather muted.

POLITICS AND COMMUNITY LIFE

Politics and community life in Ottawa after the war period was subjected to a series of shocks unparalleled in the history of the city. Ottawa, by the mid-seventies, was still the biggest kid on the block, but not by much. It had become a one-dimensional, well-paid, civil service town. The city also had to respond to a federal corporation, actively engaged in urban development. It was planning and building vast clusters of offices for its employees. And through its agencies, notably the Federal District Commission, and its successor, the National Capital Commission, it was literally creating a "National Capital" as an act of symbolic nationalism, variously mixed up with federal government patronage. That meant, at the least, a bilingual city.

Apart from the problems peculiar to Ottawa, the city was also caught up in the changes common to many Canadian cities in the period. Typical of these, was a major interventionist thrust in the areas of education, welfare, and planning, all of which involved increasing provincial oversight of both funding and programs. It meant both a more sophisticated administration and a more sensitive appreciation of provincial government moods. More so than most, "The role of Ottawa-Hull as federal capital ensured fragmented, multilevelled competition between intervening governments." "Local politics become intergovernmental relations."[44]

Two-year terms were introduced for the city council of 1940 and,

under the leadership of Mayor Stanley Lewis, entrenched even further the dominance of the small merchant and businessman from the central part of the city. The structural peeling away of contending interests — from industrialists to labour — the distractions of the war emergency, and the "economist" regimen established in the mid-30s, became a Lewis trademark until his retirement from politics in 1947, and also informed post-war politics. Lewis was followed in office by E.A. Bourque, another small businessman, and the first French Canadian to hold the mayoralty in a generation. Next to the small businessman, lawyers, and other professionals, often closely associated with the mercantile community, filled the positions for the eleven (two-man) wards, the Board of Control, and the mayor's chair. Of the forty-six people who won elective office, only one identifiable "labour" candidate sat on council in the entire decade of the forties, plus nine civil servants. Public service representation, by the 1950s, however, was more commensurate with its numbers. Labour disappeared.[45]

The council of the early 1940s ran a small city in a small way. Its main concern was to balance budgets in order to dissolve Depression debt, and, after 1945, to repair the urban plant run down by Depression and war. But, by the fifties, it was evident that rather different and rather larger problems would have to be attended to.

Development — both private and government — boomed, and the city councils of the post-war period responded enthusiastically to its needs, in particular in the provision of services. There was little control that could be asserted in any case. Ottawa had no development plan, or even comprehensive zoning. Regulation was chiefly by building bylaw. In any case, few politicians of the 1940s and 1950s would have dared raise their voice against development.

Development-minded politicians from the pre-1950 city, of course, received much support from a rapidly growing electorate in the areas annexed in 1950. Three new wards — Carleton, Westboro and Gloucester — were added in 1950 to the eleven that comprised the pre-annexation city. In a major redistribution in 1963, reflecting suburban growth, the annexed areas came to make up all or large parts of five of the ten new city wards. Lower Town, in particular, was much eclipsed, but francophone Ottawa, underwritten by federal bilingual programs, was beginning its upward climb in the city's society, and in the process its movement out of the traditional enclave in Lower Town to a place of more general influence in the urban community and its politics.

12 Ottawa Wards: 1950 (top) and 1980 (bottom): The huge annexation of 1950 produced three new wards (Gloucester, Westboro, and Carleton) in its wake. By 1980 they were covered by the automobile suburbs of the booming Government city. Nine wards were created out of the original three. The political strength of the suburbs almost equalled that of the entire pre-war city. Cité Vanier and Rockcliffe Park Village remain autonomous islands.

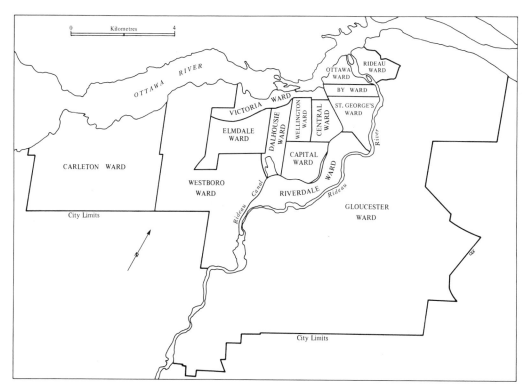

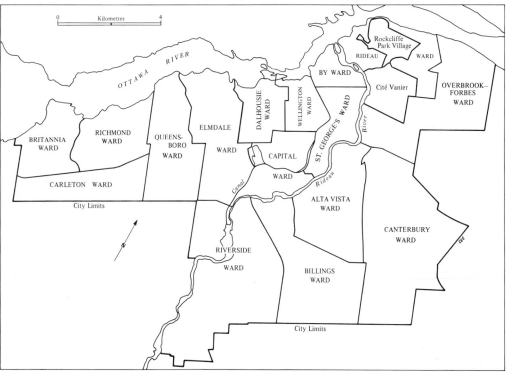

Stanley Lewis, mayor of Ottawa from 1936 to 1948, the longest-serving mayor in the city's history.

It was women, however, who made the most dramatic impact on the Ottawa scene. Notable women were a not uncommon fixture in the Ottawa community, whether in politics or the Civil Service, and their wartime role in Ottawa had been signal. They proved somewhat resistant to expectations that they would return after the war to traditional roles in the home and voluntary sector. The local council of women, in particular, urged political activity, and the challenge was (unexpectedly) picked up in 1948 by Marjorie Mann, a CCF stalwart, who sought, unsuccessfully, an aldermanic seat in Elmdale Ward. Two years later, Charlotte Whitton, a nationally prominent name in social work, successfully ended the male monopoly of Ottawa politics.

As the result of a newspaper challenge, Whitton in 1950 sought election to the Board of Control, in a campaign largely organized and run by women, their campaign badge a needle and thread. She not only won, but received the largest number of votes among the four controllers. She thus became, without previous political experience, the "senior" controller and deputy mayor. And, when the mayor-elect died seven months into his two-year term, tradition dictated that city council confirm the "senior" controller as mayor. Whitton was a newcomer, despite her experience and high profile in child-welfare work, and also something of an interloper. She, as was traditional, had not served time in the aldermanic vineyard before moving up to Board of Control. Nor had she spent much time on the Board before circumstance hoisted her to the top. There was some resistance from the men on the Board, as well as from the aldermen, to her confirmation as mayor. She was eventually confirmed, but the experience appears to have left her suspicious of and somewhat bitter towards her Board of Control executive. She was something of a loner, and a maverick by inclination, as well as an unrepentant Tory. As a politician, she more accurately falls into the category of the urban populist. Her support was intensely personal, and represented a channel for discontent that the populists of the early years found more often among the lower classes. In Whitton's case, the bulk of support seems to have come from women, and largely middle-class, Anglo-Protestant women, an under-class of sorts. Typical of the populist, she proved incapable of developing her personal support into an organized majority. Co-operation might have substituted for majority. But neither Whitton nor the Board of Control was so inclined. Her earliest experiences with her Board likewise provided a legacy of

Charlotte Whitton (1896-1975), controversial mayor of Ottawa from 1951-56 and 1961-64. She retired from politics in 1972.

Mayor Marion Dewar (1978-1985) headed a reform coalition that dominated local politics in the late 1970s and early '80s. It owed much to the influence of women.

resentment. The result was that, though dominating the headlines, she was largely ineffective at city hall. She won a second term in her own right for 1953-1954, again for 1955-1956, and temporarily retired from local politics to run (unsuccessfully) federally.

Whitton's energy and abrasive personality, apart from the clear resistance by the city "fathers", was almost a guarantee of volatile politics. But the rapid structural changes in the Ottawa community ensured they would be explosive. The emerging elements in the fifties and sixties were the suburbs and their creators, the development companies; the upwardly mobile Francophone community; and the direct and powerful intervention of the federal government in the city-building process. Whitton not only represented the old *élite* of the central city, but epitomized the old values of the valley Tories: a suspicion of bigness, a commitment to things British, and a distrust of government intervention. Elected on women's votes, and clearly a vehicle for women's aspirations, she, in fact, spent most of her energy in office battling bigness, the French, and government.

Whitton's return to politics in 1959, was perhaps more pointedly a challenge to development and growth. She won the mayor's chair for 1960-1962 by a narrow margin in a four-way race. As usual, the bulk of her support was in the central wards of the city. She was returned to office for 1962-1964 with a somewhat enlarged majority. As mayor, she had railed against uncontrolled subdivision in the 1950s, but it was subsequent councils, under Mayor George Nelms, that imposed effective subdivision controls, though they were generally pro-growth. In the 1960s, still as mayor, her concern for development was directed largely against Robert Campeau, the rags-to-riches wunderkind, who had become the largest developer in the city and, with the link to Ottawa Construction Association, a major political force in the city. He was, moreover, French, and came to enjoy a special relationship with the federal Liberals. Whitton termed him the "fifth controller", and the pair engaged repeatedly in the '60s in a campaign of white-hot vituperation that was the joy of the headline writers across the nation, and the despair of the editorial gurus of the Ottawa papers. Though Whitton generally won the verbal battles with Campeau and her council colleagues, she almost always lost the political decisions. Campeau, well-informed and omni-present, seemed to have more information than the mayor and greater influence. And he was riding the dominant currents of change. Whitton could be the

lightening-rod of protest, but once again could not make it effective.

The problem lay in the times, and in Whitton's personal philosophy. She opposed, as a traditional Conservative, bigness, in any form, whether in the private sector, like the Campeau Corporation, or in the public sector, in the form of government intervention. Opposed to big government as a means of controlling big development, she had few alternatives but to pare growing development down to an appropriate size. It was a strategy doomed to failure, especially given her propensity to believe that as mayor for all the people she had a mandate to proceed independently. She tended to forget that all the controllers had the same mandate, and that in law, the council, of which she was only one vote, was supreme. She tended to believe that she was responsible to all the people all the time, and to Board and Council on a lesser scale.[46] She tended to concentrate her administration in her office and delegate power (real or otherwise) to whom she chose.

> ...she chose her "cabinet" of advisors as she wished, without regard to whether its members had been elected to office.
> Her most trusted advisers were usually members of the city's technical staff; seldom were they elected members of city council or board of control.[47]
> Mayor Whitton stood or fall [sic] on the calibre of her personal administration.[48]

By 1964 she had proven as unable to control development as she was unwilling to give it free rein. Many were simply fed up. The *Citizen* argued before the 1964 municipal campaign that "...she ...vulgarized the office of Mayor with her lack of dignity, her inability to co-operate with her colleagues, and her dictatorial attitude toward city council."[49] She had also alienated the French community with her refusal to extend bilingual traffic signs, on the ground that provincial law did not require them "...yet insisted on introducing racist application forms for civic employment, even though the law clearly prohibited them."[50] In the 1964 campaign, in a straight two-way race, she was handily beaten by Controller Don Reid. She subsequently returned to city council as an alderman, devoted to the end "...to the British monarchy, the flags with Union Jacks, and the English language for the capital until the province of Ontario says otherwise."[51] It is perhaps appropriate to note that the Campeau-led development of high-rise core began in

1965, the year after Whitton's defeat.

Still, the real campaign for reform probably began in the 1966 elections when Reid was challenged by the NDP-supported Rev. Donald Stirling. Though the campaign was vituperative — Sterling alleging a conspiracy of control backed by Campeau money — the result was never in doubt, and Stirling was sunk without a trace. But in succeeding years, more plausible candidates, notably Ralph Sutherland from the West End and Lorry Greenberg and Michael Cassidy from Centre town, mobilized the latent anti-development support at the neighbourhood level, and translated it into election victory: for Greenberg a seat on the Board of Control and ultimately, the mayor's chair. Greenberg, as a result of visits to other cities, perceived a movement away from growth and toward quality-of-life issues, and determined that by the early 1970s, he could achieve high local office with "people power".[52] By the mid-1970s, again on the basis of neighbourhood organization, a number of other reform aldermen were on city council, notably Joe Cassey, Marion Dewar, and Brian Bournes. In 1978 Dewar became mayor, heading a relatively reform-oriented Board of Control and council, which voted the Board out of existence.[53] She was one of five women in top positions in the region, and had established a trend that, by 1982 elections, would put a near majority of women on city council.

The reform movement in the 1970s was moved along somewhat by the structural changes in the city and region. Development in the 1970s was concentrated less in the city and more in the region, and the priority concerns were at the neighbourhood level, and with quality-of-life issues. These, in turn, had provided an organizational focus and much of the organization was provided by women, no longer living vicariously through men. It was perhaps an inevitable step to move from neighbourhood organization to successful local politics. Whitton had been a curious path-finder.

The politics of neighbourhood by the 1970s thus muted those of race and religion, as well as those of labour. City politics remained uncommmitted to party, but as usual in Ottawa, it was fairly widely known where sentiments lay. The reformers who emerged in the 1970s and 1980s were generally NDP or left-leaning Liberal; their opponents were, at the core, Conservative, like Claude Bennett, who went on to become a provincial cabinet minister, Garry Guzzo, who became a family court judge, or Pierre Benoit, who became mayor and subsequently joined the Campeau Corporation.

The new political contention was at its most evident in the old central wards of the city. At various levels of government, they had elected representatives of all parties, as well as provided much of the strength for populist mayors like Whitton and Greenberg, and reformist councillors like Cassey, Bourns, and, ultimately, Mayor Marion Dewar. In this sense, it would appear, that a mixture of impulses by the 1970s was galvanizing the politics of the central area of the city, though almost all of them were middle-class. Of much muted centrality were the politics of race and religion.

Ottawa was a new city in its politics. They were governed by a kind of middle-class factionalism at the ward level. And at the level of the city, by neutral and brokerage practices that enabled it to swim in corporate shoals and the complex channels of inter-governmental relations.

CONCLUSION

A rapid transformation of Ottawa — particularly its re-creation as a new city — in the years after 1945, greatly altered many of the premises on which it was originally built and, for more than 100 years, operated. Most evident, of course, was the emergence to dominance of the federal government, and the activities, like tourism, that flowed from its pre-eminence. Other activities, notably those associated with lumbering, declined or disappeared. Likewise, division along racial and religious lines became less pronounced. Francophones, with greater educational and job opportunities, were integrated into the major economic engine, and increasingly taken out of the territorial ghettos. Religious cleavage became less pronounced as it, too, became less territorial. Yet the influence remains real, protected by roots deep in the educational system. Economic class patterns altered, too, as the working-man's town disappeared, and economic divisions came more to mirror hierarchies within government. On the urban landscape some communities, like LeBreton Flats, were wiped from the map. Others, like Lower Town and Upper Town, retained their physical form, but were refilled with the new culture of government people. Other alterations were made to the landscape in the cause of symbolic nationalism, or due to the demands for amenities of a stable, salaried middle-class. Ottawa became prettier and more orderly, and, at least in terms of imported culture, more interesting.

The new Canadian Museum of Civilization, designed by Douglas Cardinal. Scheduled to open in 1986, it is the first federal showcase to be located in Hull, and is a final element in a ring of federal parks and buildings that command the waterfront on both sides of the Ottawa River.

But much remains as it was. Fragmentation, marginality, and corporate oversight are still central. Though the main city is probably less divided than at any time in its history, a new sort of division, always latent, and situated at the regional level, has emerged strongly since the war. Large, territorially-based, self-conscious communities compete with Ottawa proper for both business and influence: Nepean, Gloucester, and Kanata, among others, on the Ontario side of the river; Hull, Gatineau and Aylmer, among others, on the Quebec side. Large regional governments contend with each other and within themselves. Metropolitan Ottawa is the second city in Ontario; metropolitan Hull the third in Quebec. Together, they rank in population among the largest in Canada. Yet the lack of influence is clear. There is a sense of population overweight, and probably the major reason is that there is still no common agenda, and still no community able to set one. It is a metropolis made up of undigested pieces, reluctant or unable to co-operate. The sense of an agglomeration of small communities persists.

Ottawa, too, remains a city on the margin: economically, politically, and culturally. The reasons are complex and ancient. Location on a provincial boundary is central. Ottawa and Hull are both distant from their respective capitals, and from the weight of their respective provincial populations, which is such a telling force in democracies, where representation is by the combination of people and territory. The city also falls within the economic shadow of Montreal, only 190 kilometres (or 120 miles) distant, and, more generally, within the shadow of a post-war corporate and branch-plant economy. Few corporate headquarters are in the Ottawa or Hull regions. Telling economic decisions are made elsewhere. Equally there is little autonomous, local capital to underwrite activities ranging from football teams to symphony orchestras. Small capital, divided among punctual and competing communities, with little real influence in provincial or federal politics, and little sense of their history limits the influence of what, in population terms, is a big place. Finally, the pool of economic, political, and cultural leadership is itself limited by the capital function. At best, what Ottawa gets is again "stuck on". Those in charge of government, whether politicians or the senior bureaucracy, are not available to provide leadership for the community. Their talents, their influence, and their access to money are effectively sidelined. The primary loyalties of the elected members are to constituencies scattered across the country, and those of the bureaucracy to a government corporation bound to act in the national interest, not a local one. Moreover, many in government are birds of passage, subject to electoral defeat, or to postings outside the "headquarters" community. Office clerks, no more than the prime minister, are available to represent the "city" at Queen's Park or in Parliament, to lobby for it in international money markets, or to lead the charge for a new concert hall or hockey rink. The very fact of being the national capital vitiates the influence of the city. And, in the present as in the past, Ottawa the "capital" will often take actions — whether the funding of railways or high-tech centres, or planning the national capital — that run counter to the needs, interests, and advice of Ottawa the "city".

Yet national government is only the latest in a long line of corporate-like bodies that have dominated the life of the city: Ordnance, the timber and lumber concerns, the power and traction monopolies, the railways. The central economic facts of the city have always been rather apart from it. All, nonetheless, have tended to usurp the collective legacy for their own purposes, perhaps most symbolically, in its very streets. Ordnance actually stopped its incorporation over control of the streets; the horse-car company built a double-tracked railway in them; and the railways blocked hundreds of them. The federal authority now owns most of the property abutting the main downtown streets, and asserts design control of structures along all its ceremonial routes. National ceremonies and processions take precedence over all other functions on the streets of the capital.

The city's corporate-like enterprises have given it much, but generally on their terms, and in their interest. It has been a matter, in the main, of *noblesse oblige*. And, perhaps, for Ottawans, it has become customary. In the end, the story of Ottawa, the city, is very much one of reconciling economic bigness with a mosaic of individual and community life on what is still, in effect, the frontier.

Appendix
Statistical Tables

<table>
<tr><td colspan="4" align="center">TABLE I
Population of Bytown and Area, 1824-1851</td></tr>
<tr><th>Year</th><th>Bytown</th><th>Nepean Township[1]</th><th>Bathurst and/ Dalhousie Districts[1]</th></tr>
<tr><td>1824</td><td></td><td></td><td>2,116</td></tr>
<tr><td>1825</td><td></td><td></td><td>2,381</td></tr>
<tr><td>1826</td><td></td><td></td><td>2,842</td></tr>
<tr><td>1827</td><td></td><td></td><td>3,327</td></tr>
<tr><td>1828</td><td>1,000[2]</td><td>2,758</td><td>5,617</td></tr>
<tr><td>1829</td><td></td><td>2,630</td><td>5,786</td></tr>
<tr><td>1830</td><td></td><td></td><td>6,346</td></tr>
<tr><td>1831</td><td></td><td></td><td>7,507</td></tr>
<tr><td>1832</td><td>940[3]</td><td>3,018</td><td>7,011</td></tr>
<tr><td>1833</td><td></td><td></td><td>8,342</td></tr>
<tr><td>1834</td><td></td><td>3,336</td><td>8,601</td></tr>
<tr><td>1835</td><td></td><td>3,186</td><td>8,877</td></tr>
<tr><td>1836</td><td>3,000[4]</td><td>3,352</td><td>9,471</td></tr>
<tr><td>1837</td><td>1,300[5]</td><td>3,411</td><td>10,101</td></tr>
<tr><td>1838</td><td></td><td>3,707</td><td>9,558</td></tr>
<tr><td>1839</td><td></td><td>3,995</td><td>10,232</td></tr>
<tr><td>1840</td><td>2,171[6]</td><td>3,716</td><td>10,128</td></tr>
<tr><td>1841</td><td>3,122[6]</td><td>5,722</td><td>12,337</td></tr>
<tr><td>1845-46</td><td>7,000[7]</td><td></td><td></td></tr>
<tr><td>1847</td><td>5,000[2]</td><td></td><td></td></tr>
<tr><td>1848</td><td>6,275[8]</td><td></td><td>19,245[9]</td></tr>
<tr><td>1849</td><td>6,284[10]</td><td></td><td></td></tr>
<tr><td>1850</td><td>6,259[11]</td><td></td><td></td></tr>
<tr><td>1851</td><td>7,760[12]</td><td></td><td>23,637[12]</td></tr>
</table>

<table>
<tr><td colspan="4" align="center">TABLE II
Population Growth in Ottawa, 1851-1981</td></tr>
<tr><th>Year</th><th>Population</th><th>Numerical Change</th><th>Percent Change</th></tr>
<tr><td>1851</td><td>7,760</td><td></td><td></td></tr>
<tr><td>1861</td><td>14,669</td><td>6,909</td><td>89.0</td></tr>
<tr><td>1871</td><td>21,545</td><td>6,876</td><td>46.9</td></tr>
<tr><td>1881</td><td>27,412</td><td>5,867</td><td>27.2</td></tr>
<tr><td>1891</td><td>37,269</td><td>9,857</td><td>36.0</td></tr>
<tr><td>1901</td><td>59,928</td><td>22,659</td><td>60.8</td></tr>
<tr><td>1911</td><td>87,062</td><td>27,134</td><td>45.3</td></tr>
<tr><td>1921</td><td>107,843</td><td>20,781</td><td>23.9</td></tr>
<tr><td>1931</td><td>126,872</td><td>14,029</td><td>17.7</td></tr>
<tr><td>1941</td><td>154,951</td><td>28,079</td><td>22.1</td></tr>
<tr><td>1951</td><td>202,045</td><td>47,094</td><td>30.4</td></tr>
<tr><td>1961</td><td>268,206</td><td>66,161</td><td>32.8</td></tr>
<tr><td>1971</td><td>302,341</td><td>34,135</td><td>12.7</td></tr>
<tr><td>1981</td><td>295,163</td><td>-7,178</td><td>-2.4</td></tr>
</table>

Source: *Census of Canada.* These figures correspond closely to those collected by the City Assessor, except for 1881 and 1891, which were 25,633 and 43,229 respectively. It is hard to account for the 1881 discrepancy, but in 1891 the census did NOT include recently annexed New Edinburgh in the Ottawa totals.

Sources:
[1] "District Population Returns," PAC RG5 B26, to 1841, inclusive. (Figures include Bytown).
[2] Estimate in City of Ottawa, Assessment Commissioner. *Report,* 1906, p. 89.
[3] Estimate. In 1832, Bouchette estimated there were just under 150 houses in Bytown. In 1848, the census calculated a density of 6.2 people per inhabited dwelling. (See 1848 *Census,* Table I, in Vol. IV of the 1871 *Census,* pp 26-27.) Using this multiplier, a figure of 940 is obtained.
[4] Estimate given in a letter from Maria E. Burrow to Mary Blake, Bytown, 8 Feb. 1837, Keefer Collection, PAC MG24 I 106, Item 15. It appears high.
[5] A figure given by the attorney-general of Upper Canada in the adjudication of a dispute between the residents of Bytown and Nepean Township. See Harry and Olive Walker, *Carleton Saga* (Ottawa: the Runge Press, 1968), pp 95-96.
[6] Letterbook of the Corresponding Secretary, Bytown and Ottawa Emigration Society, "Secretary to Peter McGill," Bytown, 10 April 1841, PAC MG23 I 152. This was from impressionistic accounts a year of considerable increase.
[7] An estimate in Wm. H. Smith. *Smith's Canadian Gazetteer* (Toronto: H. and W. Rowsell, 1846), p. 24.
[8] 1848 *Census* in op. cit.
[9] This figure for Dalhousie District: others in column for Carleton County. Population of District/County from 1848 (inclusive) on, is calculated separately from that of Bytown/Ottawa. 1848 *Census* in op. cit.
[10] "Population of Electoral Divisions, 1849," in the *British Parliamentary Papers Relating to Canada and the Canadian Boundary* (Irish University Press, 1969), Vol. 18, 1849[1025].
[11] *The Packet,* Ottawa, 28 Sept. 1850.
[12] 1851 *Census* in Vol. IV of the 1871 *Census,* Table E, pp 32-33.

TABLE III
French and Irish Roman Catholics in Lower Town, Ottawa, 1859-1901

Year	French Roman Catholics Ottawa	French Roman Catholics Lower Town	Irish Roman Catholics Ottawa	Irish Roman Catholics Lower Town
1859	2,800	2,588*	2,875	1,641
1871	7,214	5,709	5,521	3,416
1881	9,384	6,998	6,517	2,972
1891	12,790	9,612	8,399	2,868
1901	19,027	12,103	11,498	2,710

* This may be high, but another census reported in the *Packet,* 28 September 1850, put 95 per cent of French Canadians east of the Rideau Canal, in effect Lower Town.

Sources: For 1859, "Report on the Roman Catholic Population," prepared by Rev. Father Dandurand, parish priest of the Cathedral, and published in the Ottawa *Tribune,* 14 January 1860. For other years, Canada *Census.* Some plausible assumptions are made to generate these figures. In the matter of Father Dandurand's figures, the assumption is that Lower Town was 100 per cent Catholic. For the census figures, since the census makes no distinction between Catholic and Protestant Irish, a matter of great significance in Ottawa, the assumption is that census figures embrace a tiny number of Catholics who were neither French nor Irish.

TABLE V
Ethnic Origins of Ottawa Population

Date		British Isles[1]	French	German	Jewish	Italian	Total
1871	no.	14,064	7,214	179	—	23	21,545
	(%)	(65)	(34)				
1901[2]	no.	36,051	19,027	1,248	398	305	57,640
	(%)	(63)	(33)	(2.2)	(0.7)	(0.5)	
1911	no.	52,734	26,732	2,379	1,776	643	87,062
	(%)	(60)	(31)	(2.7)	(2.0)	(0.7)	
1931	no.	78,512	37,465	2,735	3,316	1,369	126,872
	(%)	(61)	(30)	(2.2)	(2.6)	(1.1)	
1951[3]	no.	121,716	57,399	3,938	3,900	2,150	202,045
	(%)	(60)	(28)	(1.9)	(1.9)	(1.1)	
1971[3]	no.	166,800	75,160	10,570	5,555	12,355	302,435
	(%)	(55)	(25)	(3.5)	(1.8)	(4.1)	

[1] No distinction is made in the census between Protestant and Roman Catholic Irish in this category, though the two groups form distinctive communities in Ottawa. Roman Catholic Irish account for about 30 per cent of the British Isles category.

[2] Figures for 1891 origins not recorded in census; those for 1901 are substituted. 1901 census figures may be skewed by an apparent failure to include the entire Ottawa population. Total population, by origin, is given as 57,640. Total population, as given elsewhere, was 59,928. Percentages based on the lower total.

[3] The undentified by origin form one of the largest categories in 1951 and 1971: "Other and Not Stated" (1951), 3,253; and "Other and Unknown" (1971), 11,685.

[4] Changes in categories in the 1981 census make comparisons with other years untenable. It enumerates large numbers of those with mixed origins. Those of "British" (not British Isles) origin numbered 138,040 and of "French" origin 60,810. "British and French" numbered 13,265; "British and Other" 10,360; "French and Other" 2,145; "British, French and Other" 2,175; and "European and Other" 2,320. Chinese became a major group at 5,075, as did Asian Arab at 4,475. German was 7,165, Jewish 4,955, and Italian 11,195.

Source: *Census of Canada.*

TABLE IV
Ottawa, Occupational Groups, 1851-1871

	City Population		Agriculture	Commercial	Domestic	Industrial	Prof.	N/C	Total
1851	7,760	no.	47	271	479	747	72	624	2,240
		%	2.1	12.1	21.4	33.3	3.2	27.9	100.0
1861	14,669	no.	48	382	361	1,383	149	587	2,910
		%	1.6	13.1	12.4	47.5	5.1	20.2	99.9
1871	21,545	no.	38	1,102	1,319	2,744	762	1,404	7,369
		%	0.5	15.0	17.9	37.2	10.3	19.1	100.0

Source: *Census of Canada.*

TABLE VI
Origins of the Population of Ottawa, by Wards, 1871 and 1901

	1871 Number	1871 Percent	1901 Number	1901 Percent
Lower Town Wards (By and Ottawa)				
English	1,102	10.1	988	5.9
French	5,709	52.5	12,085	71.5
Irish	3,416	31.1	2,591	15.3
Scotch	538	5.0	412	2.4
Others	111	1.0	826	4.9
	10,876		16,902	
Centre Town Wards (Wellington, Capital, and Central)				
English	1,100	27.2	6,636	30.1
French	154	3.8	1,444	6.6
Irish	1,929	47.8	8,524	38.7
Scotch	784	19.4	4,462	20.2
Others	72	1.8	975	4.4
	4,039		22,041	
St. George's Ward				
English	908	26.1	1,865	21.2
French	379	10.9	2,187	24.8
Irish	1,502	43.2	3,180	36.1
Scotch	622	17.9	954	10.8
Others	63	1.8	621	7.1
	3,474		8,807	
Chaudière/LeBreton Wards (Victoria and Dalhousie)				
English	611	19.4	2,134	21.4
French	972	30.8	3,293	33.0
Irish	1,174	37.2	3,189	32.0
Scotch	341	10.8	1,013	10.2
Others	58	1.8	341	3.4
	3,156		9,970	

Source: *Census of Canada.*

TABLE VII
Mortality by Ward, Nationality, and Religion: Ottawa, 1885

	Deaths as Percentage of Total for Year ending 31 October, 1885	Population as Percentage of Total for Census of 1881
Wards		
By	37.9	18.1
Ottawa	28.5	24.0
St. Georges	12.1	16.5
Wellington	18.5	30.6
Victoria	3.0	10.8
Nationalities		
French	43.0	34.2
Irish	28.9	35.0
English	20.6	17.9
Scotch	6.1	10.7
Religions		
Roman Catholic	75.2	58.0
Protestant	24.8	42.0

Soucres: Mortuary Returns of the federal Department of Agriculture, as printed in the Annual Report of the Medical Health Officer, Ottawa. And, *Census of Canada, 1881.*

TABLE VIII
"Headquarters" Civil Service, 1901-1981*

Year	Total	Permanent	Temporary
1901	895[1] (1,219)[2]		
1911	4,179[3] (3,219)[2]		
1921	10,035[3] (8,434)[2] (12,118)[5]	(7,588)[5]	(4,530)[5]
1925	10,091[4]	6,478	3,613
1931	11,766[4]	8,009	3,757
1939	11,848[4]	7,564	4,284
1941	19,593[4] (17,546)[3]	7,419	12,174
1945	34,740[4]	6,777	27,963
1951	30,069[4] (31,424)[6]	10,799	19,270
1961	36,945[6]		
1971	43,225[6]		
1981	42,215[6]		

* Statistics on the Civil Service were not collected routinely before the mid-1920s, and, even after, numbers are problematic. They were derived from reports submitted by departments, which were variously conscientious. After 1951, Statistics Canada made its counts on the basis of payroll statistics, which do not correspond to the earlier procedures. Some important distinctions should be noted: Ottawa embraced both "inside" or headquarters employees and "outside" ones. For example, the Post Office Department was "inside", but local post offices were "outside". Distinctions must also be made between permanent and temporary employees (who may be full- or part-time), and full-time and part-time employees (who may be permanent or temporary). Census figures are by "industry" and effectively reflect jobs of those living in Ottawa as a "place of residence". Ottawa as a "place of work" in 1981 embraced 143,500 employees in "federal administration". Obviously, many people working in Ottawa lived in surrounding municipalities, including those in Quebec. Especially after 1971, numbers working in Hull increased significantly with the completion of federal buildings in that city. Overall, distinctions among place of residence and place of work have in recent years become very pronounced.

Sources:
[1] "The Civil Service List of Canada, 1901," House of Commons, *Sessional Papers,* #30, 1902. Numbers were counted by the author.
[2] Calculated from *Civil Service Employees* (King's Printer: Ottawa, 1923) and located in PAC, RG 14 D2, Vol. 102, File 121.
[3] *Census of Canada,* 1921, 1931, and 1941. Figures for 1921 and 1931 embrace provincial government employees, but their numbers seem small, amounting to only 75 in 1941.
[4] DBS, *Statistics of Civil Service of Canada* for years cited. The returns for the end of March were used for the various years.
[5] *Canada Year Book.* Figures as at December 31, 1921. All other figures for permanent and temporary employees from *Statistics of Civil Service,* op. cit.
[6] *Census of Canada,* for the respective years. Only federal employees are included, and among these "defence".

TABLE IX
Ottawa's Labour Force by Industry, 1951-1981

	1951 Male	1951 Female	1961 Male	1961 Female	1971 Male	1971 Female	1981 Male	1981 Female
Total	57,884	29,727	71,086	40,038	83,855	57,655	88,790	76,260
Manufacturing	7,597	2,093	7,203	1,945	6,225	2,160	6,180	2,630
Construction	4,614	108	6,124	208	6,030	445	5,200	655
Transportation, Communication, Utilities	5,170[1]	1,183[1]	6,001	1,563	6,505	2,050	7,170	3,510
Trade[2]	8,561	3,768	9,769	4,915	9,985	6,755	12,050	9,250
Finance, Insurance, Real Estate	1,836	2,313	2,723	2,768	3,030	3,550	4,270	5,330
Service[3]	6,343[4]	8,868[4]	9,705	14,569	16,390	20,520	26,285	33,225
Public Administration						6,225		
Total	22,350[5]	11,041[5]	27,151	12,933	29,830	17,130	26,025	20,430
Federal, Incl. Defence	20,777	10,647	24,603	12,342	26,930	16,290	23,325	18,890

[1] Combines categories of "Transportation, Storage, Communications" with "Electricity, Gas, Water". [2] "Commerce" in 1951 and 1961.
[3] "Community, Business and Personal Service" in 1971. [4] "Service" less "Government" sub-category. [5] "Government" sub-category.
Source: *Census of Canada.*

TABLE X
Ottawa's Population by Birthplace, 1851-1981

Year	Quebec	Canada Ontario	Other	British Isles England	Ireland	Scotland	U.S.	Germany	Italy
1851	2,056[1]	2,420[2]	21	320	2,486	307	100	1	—
1861	3,644[3]	5,541[4]	81	959	3,249	666	402	34	11[5]
1871	6,154	9,980	168	1,488	2,548	549	444	60	8
1881	7,172	14,689	415	1,458	2,388	540	457	104	8
1891	9,170	21,120	548	1,947	2,336	614	787	278	76
1901	12,295	36,521	931	2,447	2,021	727	1,369	369	189
1911	13,620	56,894	1,525	6,057	1,756	1,671	1,920	602	348
1921	15,865	70,832	3,123	7,922	1,519	2,530	2,206	382	441
1931	18,370	86,188	3,173	8,147	1,378	2,873	2,367	356	435
1941	22,139	106,583	6,808	8,196	1,173	2,811	2,737	268	417
1951	25,949	138,150	14,057	10,005	692[6]	3,092	3,042	425	625
1961	30,786	170,598	25,068	12,527	781[6]	3,517	3,378	3,166	4,976
1971[10]	—	186,235[7]	67,000[8]		16,154[9]		4,255	3,120	6,920
1981[11]		169,980[7]			13,120[9]		4,435		

[1] Given as "Ontario, French Origin."   [2] Given as "Ontario, not of French Origin."   [3] Given as "Canada, French Origin."
[4] Given as "Canada, not of French Origin."   [5] Given as "Italy, Greece."   [6] Northern Ireland only.
[7] Given as "Canada, Province of Residence."   [8] Given as "Canada, Other Provinces."
[9] "United Kingdom", includes Northern Ireland.
[10] This census included 18,745 in the "Other" category, including, it would seem, many from the eastern Mediterranean and Orient.
[11] German and Italian embraced in European.
nb. Throughout, "Canada, Other" includes Newfoundland.
Source: *Census of Canada.*

TABLE XI
Ottawa's Major Religion Affiliations, 1851-1981

Year	Roman Catholic	Anglican[1]	Methodist/United[2]	Presbyterian
1851	4,798	952	544	828
1861	8,267	3,351	1,008	1,761
1871	12,735	4,274	1,520	2,298
1881	15,901	4,825	2,173	3,059
1891	21,189	6,702	3,260	4,173
1901	30,525	9,645	5,706	7,576
1911	43,245	15,076	7,668	12,825
1921	51,097	19,784	9,188	17,564
1931	61,198	22,650	21,749	9,145
1941	76,607	27,281	26,903	9,981
1951	94,992	37,448	39,758	11,126
1961[3]	127,407	46,689	51,242	13,231
1971[4]	148,685	46,595	47,685	12,640
1981[5]	142,570	38,120	40,095	not given

[1] "Church of England", 1851-1891, incl.: "Anglican", 1901-1941, incl.; "Church of England in Canada," 1951; "Anglican Church of Canada," 1961-1981.
[2] "Methodist" from 1851 to 1921, incl., "United" from 1931 to 1981.
[3] This census listed 5,718 as "Others", the fifth largest category.
[4] This census listed 14,985 as "No Regligion".
[5] This census listed 26,115 as "No Religious Preference".
Source: *Census of Canada.*

TABLE XII
Ottawa Population by Age and Sex: 1851-1971

Year	Total[1]		Under 20		20-50		Over 50	
	Male	Female	Male	Female	Male	Female	Male	Female
1851	3,862	3,898	2,028	2,045	1,551	1,607	250	211
1861	7,258	7,411	3,671	3,906	3,101	3,051	472	433
1871[2]	10,351	11,194	5,595	5,826	3,879	4,593	877	773
1881	12,968	14,444	6,360	6,556	5,125	6,333	1,482	1,553
1891	17,602	19,667	7,940	8,434	7,531	8,982	2,109	2,227
1901	27,442	30,198	11,680	12,354	12,273	14,115	3,429	3,673
1911				no data				
1921	50,245	57,598	20,160	21,210	22,765	28,079	7,093	8,076
1931[3]	59,183	67,689	22,822	23,681	25,743	31,534	10,599	12,445
1941	72,600	82,351	23,641	24,388	34,377	40,733	14,582	17,230
1951	94,629	107,416	32,360	32,310	42,563	50,153	19,706	24,953
1961	129,035	139,171	51,297	50,055	54,112	57,568	23,626	31,548
1971	145,315	157,030	52,880	51,185	62,125	64,155	30,305	41,685
1981[4]	137,865	153,985						

[1] Small numbers, in total, of age "Not Given" to 1931, inclusive.
[2] Categories available only as "to 21", "21-51," and "51 and over".
[3] Categories available only as "20-49" and "50 and over" for last two columns.
[4] Detailed data not available at time of compilation.
Source: *Census of Canada.*

TABLE XIII
Regional Municipality of Ottawa-Carleton, Population, 1901-1981

	1901	1911	1921	1931	1941	1951	1961	1971	1981
TOTAL	46,904	119,384	152,868	174,056	206,367	246,298	358,410	471,931	546,849
Cities									
Ottawa	64,226[1]	87,062[2]	107,843	126,872	154,951	202,045[3]	268,206	302,341	295,163
Vanier	—	3,169	5,324	6,686	7,966	13,799	24,555	22,477[4]	18,792
Nepean[5]	5,840	5,170	10,867	11,142	13,859	3,744[3]	19,753	64,606	84,361
Gloucester[5]	7,778	7,075	8,397	8,412	9,871	6,473[3]	18,301	37,145	72,859
Kanata[6]									19,728
March Township	1,184	967	894	822	829	710	968	5,822	
Villages									
Rockcliffe Park	—	—	—	951	1,480	1,595	2,084	2,138	1,869
Townships									
Cumberland[7]	4,198	4,033	4,163	4,016	3,847	4,051	5,478	9,294	16,177
Osgoode	4,818	4,598	4,686	4,271	4,095	4,141	5,786	7,757	9,360
Rideau[8]									9,052
North Gower	2,235	1,923	1,847	1,820	1,777	1,942	2,694	3,726	
Marlborough	1,584	1,339	1,087	944	886	807	953	1,167	
West Carleton[9]									9,929
Fitzroy	2,767	2,488	2,494	3,308	2,225	2,203	2,310	2,357	
Torbolton	1,002	842	739	725	719	711	757	1,366	
Goulborn[10]	2,765	2,358	2,201	1,982	1,893	2,054	2,146	5,341	9,559
Stittsville[11]	—	—	—	—	—	—	1,508	1,994	
Richmond[11]	469	428	413	405	457	610	1,215	2,122	

[1] Including Hintonburg (2,798) and Ottawa East (1,500) annexed in 1907.
[2] Including parts of Nepean Township, known as Ottawa South and Rideauville, annexed in 1907.
[3] Heavily populated portions of Nepean Township, annexed to Ottawa in 1946 and 1950, and portions of Gloucester Township, 1950.
[4] Before 1971, Town of Eastview.
[5] Nepean City created from Township 24 November 1978; Gloucester City created from Township 1 January 1981.
[6] Created Hazeldean-March, 23 June 1978, and renamed City of Kanata 22 November 1978. Consisted of March Township and parts of Nepean and Goulbourn Townships.
[7] Formerly part of Russell County. All other jurisdictions part of Carleton County.
[8] Created 1 January 1974 from North Gower and Marlborough Townships.
[9] Created 1 January 1974 from Fitzroy and Torbolton Townships.
[10] Created 1 January 1974 from Goulborn Township and the Villages of Stittsville and Richmond.
[11] Villages prior to 1974.
Source: *Census of Canada.*

TABLE XIV
Building Permits and Taxable Assessment, Ottawa, 1867-1970

TABLE XIV (continued)

Year	Building Permits Issued[1]	Taxable Assessment
1867		5,011,840
1871		5,970,159
1881		10,393,275
1891		17,638,110
1901	397	1,000,000	25,067,205
1902	472	797,150	27,420,740
1903	372	1,003,800	29,362,495
1904	237	1,126,400	32,321,925
1905	315	1,534,000	33,002,540
1906	362	1,728,975	37,973,180
1907	355	2,364,950	41,318,150
1908	507	1,794,075	44,880,080
1909	683	4,527,590	50,508,205
1910	671	3,022,650	55,175,811
1911	657	2,997,610	63,287,155
1912	627	3,621,850	76,169,219
1913	545	3,991,380	95,720,676
1914	469	4,396,920	100,158,087
1915	323	1,605,160	105,107,168
1916	264	1,530,400	111,028,756
1917	196	1,041,017	109,695,713
1918	257	2,635,612	111,322,235
1919	550	3,232,322	114,392,261
1920	559	3,358,977	120,463,606
1921	700	2,716,409	129,630,150
1922	1,021	5,021,872	135,673,359
1923	838	3,521,817	137,059,227
1924	671	2,540,670	140,152,378
1925	744	4,911,685	141,634,075
1926	621	3,101,748	142,155,312
1927	722	6,446,045	144,725,982
1928	750	5,420,900	145,838,403
1929	677	3,403,323	149,323,059
1930	730	6,213,900	154,324,513
1931	615	3,162,460	158,419,864
1932	530	1,549,515	159,631,543
1933	475	916,065	159,527,851
1934	526	1,257,000	157,380,486
1935	536	4,097,240	156,480,054
1936	531	1,781,855	152,010,016
1937	586	2,325,445	152,518,791
1938	616	5,137,509	153,275,685
1939	574	2,050,656	156,140,517
1940	563	2,799,675	154,416,958
1941	752	4,860,615	155,145,174
1942	620	7,291,388	158,754,450
1943	831	3,618,060	162,554,395
1944	881	2,942,647	164,025,936
1945	1,038	3,004,561	165,711,463
1946	1,217	7,049,495	166,631,900

Year	Building Permits Issued[1]	Taxable Assessment
1947	1,140	8,426,135	171,457,614
1948	1,313	8,503,790	177,814,589
1949	1,364	10,235,354	184,902,065
1950	2,826	36,101,962	189,259,457
1951	2,360	30,427,313	225,415,299
1952	2,484	23,609,590	237,880,510
1953	2,945	36,372,135	247,893,118
1954	3,314	50,539,480	328,741,835
1955	3,831	57,016,115	375,481,247
1956	3,678	57,527,215	396,798,877
1957	3,767	74,445,465	416,821,377
1958	4,598	88,850,475	437,389,648
1959	3,975	73,752,037	462,675,681
1960	3,785	55,706,477	489,334,625
1961	3,860	78,756,772	492,486,971
1962	3,272	66,323,776	546,999,670
1963	3,137	105,436,921	568,514,374
1964	2,714	106,662,935	588,260,712
1965	2,671	107,246,126	613,272,211
1966	2,171	127,435,060	673,622,014
1967	2,024	100,534,554	698,272,239
1968	2,237	105,080,351	723,746,374
1969	2,129	111,816,595	743,163,514
1970	1,916	205,671,654	772,366,599

Sources:

[1] Source to 1951, City of Ottawa, Building Inspector, *Annual Report*. It appears that the city engineer was empowered to issue building permits under the Building Bylaw of 1890 (#1079), but this was not done until 1901. The Building Bylaw of 1910 (#3064) required a permit. It is also unclear at what point the federal government agreed to take out permits for its building activities, as it is not bound by local bylaws. Source after 1951, *Ottawa Directory*.

[2] Source to 1951, City of Ottawa, Assessment Commissioner, *Annual Report*; after 1951, *Ottawa Directory*. Assessment figures in Ottawa are badly skewed since federal property is exempt. In 1951, for example, exemptions totalled $145,359,175, of which $84,094,129 was "Dominion Government" property, and $5,475,802 property of the Federal District Commission.

TABLE XV
Bytown Mayors, 1847-1854

John Scott . . . . 1847 and 1850[1]
John Bower Lewis 1848
Robert Hervey 1849
Charles Sparrow 1851
R. W. Scott 1852
J. B. Turgeon 1853
Henry J. Friel 1854

City of Ottawa Mayors, 1855-1985

John Bower Lewis . . . . 1855, 1856 and 1857
Edward McGillivray . . . . 1858 and 1859
Alexander Workman . . . . 1860, 1861 and 1862[2]
Henry J. Friel . . . . 1863, 1868 and 1869
M. K. Dickinson . . . . 1864, 1865 and 1866
Robert Lyon 1867
John Rochester . . . . 1870 and 1871
E. Martineau . . . . 1872 and 1875
T.P. Featherston . . . . 1874 and 1875
C. B. L. Fellows 1876
W. H. Waller 1877
C. W. Bang 1878
Charles H. Mackintosh . . . . 1879, 1880 and 1881[3]
Pierre St. Jean, M.D. . . . . 1882 and 1883
C. T. Bate 1884
Francis McDougal . . . . 1885 and 1886
McLeod Stewart . . . . 1887 and 1888[4]
Jacob Erratt . . . . 1889 and 1890
Thomas Birkett 1891
Olivier Durocher . . . . 1892 and 1893
George Cox 1894
William Borthwick . . . . 1895 and 1896
Samuel Bingham . . . . 1897 and 1898
Thomas Payment . . . . 1899 and 1900
W. D. Morris . . . . Part of 1901
James Davidson . . . . Part of 1901
Fred Cook . . . . 1902 and 1903
James A. Ellis . . . . 1904, 1905 and part of 1906 and 1913
Robert Hastey . . . . Part of 1906
D'Arcy Scott . . . . 1907 and part of 1908
Napoleon Champagne . . . . Part of 1908, part of 1909
Charles Hopewell . . . . 1909, 1910, 1911 and 1912
Edward R. Hinchey . . . . President of Council, part of 1912
Taylor McVeity 1914
Nelson D. Porter . . . . 1915 and 1916
Harold Fisher . . . . 1917, 1918, 1919 and 1920
Frank H. Plant . . . . 1921, 1922, 1923 and 1930
Henry Watters . . . . Part of 1924
John P. Balharrie . . . . 1925, 1926 and 1927
Arthur Ellis . . . . 1928 and 1929
John J. Allen 1931, 1932, 1933
Patrick Nolan . . . . 1934 and 1935

TABLE XV *(continued)*
Bytown Mayors, 1847-1854

J. E. S. Lewis 1936, 1937, 1938, 1939, 1940, 1941,
1942, 1943, 1944, 1945, 1946, 1947, 1948
E. A. Bourque . . . . 1949 and 1950
Grenville Goodwin . . . . Part of 1951
George H. Nelms . . . . 1957, 1958, 1959 and 1960
Charlotte Whitton . . . . Part of 1951, 1952, 1953, 1954, 1955,
1956, 1961, 1962, 1963 and 1964
Donald B. Reid . . . . 1965, 1966, 1967, 1968 and 1969
Kenneth H. Fogarty, Q.C. . . . . 1970, 1971 and part of 1972
Pierre Benoit . . . . Part of 1972, 1973, 1974
Lorry Greenberg . . . . 1975, 1976, 1977 and Part of 1978
Marion Dewar . . . . Part of 1978, 1979-1985
Jim Durrell . . . . 1985—

[1] Resigned 28 October 1850 and replaced by Charles Sparrow. Acting mayor during much of Scott's term, prior to his resignation, was H.J. Friel.
[2] Election of Workman as mayor for 1862 was set aside by Court of Queen's Bench, April 1862. Ald. Lees was selected by City Council as its chairman.
[3] Resigned 4 July, 1881. Office declared vacant.
[4] Election of 1888 voided by courts in a decision brought down in January of 1889. There was, in a legal sense, no mayor in 1888, though Stewart acted as *de facto* mayor until June, 1888, when he was replaced by Jacob Erratt as "acting" mayor.

Source: City of Ottawa Archives.

Notes

INTRODUCTION

1 Various names seem to have been applied to river, sometimes two or three simultaneously. Champlain called it the River of the Algonquins. In the middle of the seventeenth century, as a result of a French—Iroquois detente, the river was opened to the Outaouais, an Algonquian tribe, and thereafter the French tended to prefer "rivière de l'Outaouais", though "Grande Rivière" was also used. Some writers argue that "Grand River" originated with English travellers and was francized to "Grande Rivière". Then, it seems, some English anglicized it back to "Great River" or adopted in English, "River Ottawaes", "River of the Ottawa", or "Ottawa River". The word "Ottawa" appears to derive from the proto-Algonquian "ata: we: we", he trades, sells, cf. George F. Aubin, *A Proto-Algonquian Dictionary* (Ottawa, 1975). My thanks to Prof. William Cowan, Linguistics, Carleton University, for guidance in this latter.

2 As cited in H.A. Innis, *The Fur Trade in Canada* (Toronto, 1964), p. 207.

3 H.P. Biggar, ed., *The Works of Samuel de Champlain* (Toronto, 1922), vol. II, p. 268.

4 Bruce S. Elliott, "'The Famous Township of Hull': Image and Aspirations of a Pioneer Quebec Community," *Social History/Historie Sociale*, XII, p. 24 (1979).

5 *British Parliamentary Papers* (Dublin, 1969), Vol. VI, p. 375, Henry Goulbourn to George Harrison, 23 March 1819, re: dispatch from Richmond, 14 January, 1819.

6 Ibid., p. 376, Lt.-General Cockburn, "Report on the Military Settlement in the Neighbourhood of the Rideau," 26 November, 1818.

7 M.S. Cross, "The Age of Gentility: The Formation of an Aristocracy in the Ottawa Valley," Canadian Historical Association, *Historical Papers*, 1967, p. 107.

8 Cockburn, op cit.

9 *British Parliamentary Papers*, op. cit., p. 385, "Extract of a report to Wellington relative to BNA provinces by a commission of which Maj.-Gen. James C. Smyth was president," 9 September 1825.

10 PAC, RG8, "C" Series, vol. 42, pp. 97-98, Dalhousie to By, 26 September, 1826.

11 The best descrpition of speculation in early Bytown is that by Michael Newton in National Capital Commission, *Lower Town Ottawa* (Ottawa, 1979), Vol I, ch. 6.

12 PAC, Hill Collection, MG24 I9, vol. II, pp. 317-328, Dr. Alex Christie to Billy Tyrconnell, nd. (probably 1828).

13 Ibid.

14 PAC, RG8, "G" Series, vol. C61 (micro C2620). Entrance Valley 275 acres, plus 20 acres of Sparks's land for canal right-of-way, plus 84 acres of Sparks's land as the Barracks Hill Bulge.

15 PAC, Hill Collection, MG24 I9, vol. 18, pp. 4,462-4,464, By to Capt. Airey, nd. (probably 1829)

16 Ibid.

17 For an excellent appreciation of the difficulties Dalhousie and By would create by their unusual appropriation of land for the Ottawa townsite, see PAC, RG1 E1, vol. 61, pp. 278-398, R. B. Sullivan, "Report Relating to lands under the control of the Respective Officers of Ordnance . . .," Minutes of the Executive Council, Kingston, 5 March, 1842.

CHAPTER ONE

1 J. Wilson to Rev. William Bell, as cited in Edward F. Bush, *The Building of the Rideau Canal, 1826-1832* (Parks Canada, Manuscript Report Series #185, Ottawa, 1976), p. 33.

2 PAC, Hill Collection, MG24 I9, vol. 5, pp. 1392-1393. S. Derbishire to A. Christie, 9 April, 1842.

3 *British Parliamentary Papers*, op. cit., vol. 1, Simon McGillvray, as cited in "Minutes of Evidence before the Select Committee on the Civil Government of Canada," 3 June, 1828.

4 PAC, Hill Collection, MG24, I9, p. 1140, Christie to Derbishire, 25 April, 1841.

5 Ibid., p. 615, "Agricola", Letter 3, 6 February, 1833.

6 Marsha Hay Snyder, *Nineteenth Century Industrial Development in the Rideau Corridor: A Preliminary Report* (Parks Canada, Manuscript Report Series #215, Ottawa, 1977).

7 "Aggregate Account of the Rateable Property in the Bathurst District, 1840," Province of Upper Canada, Assembly, *Journals*, 1841 app. U; and Province of Canada, Assembly, *Journals*, 1846, app. H.

8 "Agricola", op. cit.

9 *The Packet*, October, 1850.

10 Town of Bytown, *Minutes*, 26 March, 1849.

11 Ibid.

12 "Bytown in 1837," typescript in PAC, Hill Collection, MG24 I9, p. 4065.

13 Archives of Ontario, William Stewart Letterbooks, 1834-1846, Stewart to Messers. Campbell and Co., Glasgow, 10 December 1835.

14 There are a number of excellent studies on the period of the timber *trade*. Among the best are M.S. Cross, "The Dark Druidicial Groves: The Lumber Community and the Commercial Frontier in British North America" (Ph.D. Thesis, Toronto, 1968); and Sandra J. Gillis, *The Timber Trade and the Ottawa Valley, 1806-1854* (Parks Canada, Manuscript Report Series #153, Ottawa, 1975).

15 Stewart Letterbooks, op. cit., Stewart to Wood and Gray, Quebec City, 12 November, 1839.

16 Ibid., Stewart to Nagle [?], 5 April, 1842.

17 PAC, Hill Collection, MG24 I9, p. 1136, Christie to Derbishire, 25 April, 1841.

18 Ibid., pp. 1562-1563, Hamnet Pinhey to Christie, nd. (probably February, 1843).

19 Stewart Letterbooks, op. cit., Stewart to Ritchie, Montreal, 20 January, 1837.

20 Ibid., 26 April, 1837.

21 Ibid., 18 December, 1837.

22 Ibid., Stewart to McIntosh and Co., Montreal, 27 March, 1838.

23 Ibid., Stewart to John Kerr, Bytown, 9 September, 1839.

24 This important configuration noted by Cross, "The Dark Druidicial Groves," op. cit.

25 See, especially, the newspapers, and M.S. Cross, "The Shiners' War: Social Violence in the Ottawa Valley in the 1830s," *Canadian Historical Review*, LIV, 1 (1973): 1-26. The problem is that the censuses do not distinguish between the Protestant and Catholic Irish.

26 *The Packet*, 28 September 1850. This is a breakdown from an uncited source of the population of Bytown by ward. The main problem with the data is that the social character of about a fifth of the population of "Center Ward" was "Not Ascertained". According to the newspaper's figures, nearly 73 per cent of East Ward was Roman Catholic and some 64 per cent of the "ascertainable" population of Centre Ward was likewise. Some 53.5 per cent of the West Ward was Church of England, Church of Scotland or Methodist. Roman Catholics accounted for some 36 per cent of the population in the West Ward.

27 Michael Newton, "The Search for Heritage in Ottawa's Lower Town," *Urban History Review/Revue d'histoire urbaine*, IX, 2 (October, 1980).

28 Ordnance had to use such devices. *The Rideau Canal Act* gave it power to appropriate land only for "canal purposes", but not for purposes of defence or security.

29 PAC, Provincial Secretary's Office (PSO), Correspondence, RG5 C1, 1844-1845, vol. 148, no. 9756, James S. Elliott, Ordnance Commissioner, to Chas. Bagot, 31 March, 1842.

30 Ibid.

31 Bush, *The Builders of the Rideau Canal*, op. cit., p. 39.

32 John McTaggart, *Three Years in Canada* (London, 1839), vol. 2, p. 244.

33 Ibid., pp. 245-246.

34 Ibid., pp. 243-244.

35 Cross, "The Shiners' War," op. cit., p. 1.

36 Ibid.

37 The name "Shiner" has variously been attributed to: a corrpution of "Cheneur", French for oak; the shiny, grease-slicked hair favoured by the group; their shiny plug hats; and the shiny American half-dollars used by Ordnance to pay its contractors, and presumable passed on to the Irish in wages.

38 Cited in Cross, "Shiners' War," op. cit., p. 2.

39 PAC, Hill Collection, MG24, I9, pp. 1109-1110.

40 Except Lot (letter) O, near Rideau Falls, which Ordnance was ultimately able to control through a "permanent license of occupation". It could not have been too permanent, though, since most of Lot O fell into the hands of Thomas McKay.

41 PAC, RG8, "C" Series, vol. 42, p. 97, Dalhousie to By, 26 September, 1826.

42 PAC, Hill Collection, MG24, I9, p. 1059, Derbishire to Christie, 30 December, 1840.

43 Ibid., p. 1200, Derbishire to Christie, 14 July, 1984.

44 Ibid., p. 1154, Derbishire to Christie, 16 May, 1841.

45 Lucien Brault, *Ottawa, Old and New* (Ottawa, 1946), p. 81.

46 G.P. deT Glazebrook, "The Origins of Local Government," in F.H. Armstrong, et al, *Aspects of Nineteenth Century Ontario* (Toronto, 1974), pp. 36-47.

47 PAC, Hill Collection, MG24 I9, vol. 1, p. 44, manuscript of an editorial by "Viper" [Hamnett Pinhey], 184?.

48 Province of Canada, *Journals*, 30 May, 1846.

49 Ibid., 6 June, 1846.

50 *The Packet*, 13 November, 1849.

51 Ibid., 7 April, 1847.

52 Ibid.

53 Ibid.

54 Ibid.

55 Ibid.

56 A.R.M. Lower, *Great Britain's Woodyard: British America and the Timber Trade, 1763-1867* (Montreal and Kingston, 1973), p. 188.

57 PAC, PSO, Correspondence, RG5 C1, vol. 195, "Memorial of the Sheriff of the District of Dalhousie to the Governor General," Bytown, 23 December, 1845.

58 Ibid.

59 Ibid., "Report of a Committee of the Executive Council," 28 August, 1846.

60 "Bylaw #2", as printed in Edwin Welch, ed., *Bytown Council Minutes, 1847-1848* (Ottawa, 1978), p. 71. There is some confusion as to whether it is, in fact, Bylaw #3.

61 Ibid.

62 *The Packet*, 21 August, 1847.

63 Ibid., 18 September, 1847.

64 Ibid.

65 Bytown, *Minutes*, 18 September, 1847.

66 See John H. Taylor, "Introduction," *Urban History Review*, VIII, 1 (June, 1979), pp. 21-22. More detail on the cholera epidemic can be found in Geoffrey Bilson, *A Darkened House: Cholera in Nineteenth Century Canada* (Toronto, 1980), esp. pp. 78-82.

67 Description of the Stoney Monday riots can be found in M.S. Cross, "Stoney Monday, 1849: The Rebellion Losses Riots in Bytown," *Ontario History*, LXIII, 3 (1971), pp. 177-190; and in National Capital Commission, *Lower Town Ottawa (1826-1854)*, vol. I, op. cit., ch. XV.

68 As cited in *Lower Town Ottawa*, p. 282.

69 Ibid., p. 283.

70 *The Packet*, 6 October, 1849.

CHAPTER TWO

1 Charles P. Treadwell, *Arguments in Favor of the Ottawa and Georgian Bay Ship*

Canal (Ottawa, 1856), p. 37.

2 Ibid., p. 36.

3 *The Packet,* 29 March, 1851.

4 Gerald Tulchinsky, *the River Barons: Montreal Businessman and The Growth of Industry and Transportation, 1837-1853* (Toronto, 1977), esp. p. 174FF.

5 Note the problems upbound. Steamers carried cargo from Montreal to the Carillon Rapids, where it was trans-shipped to steamer for Ottawa. Then it was once again trans-shipped the seven miles to Aylmer, where it entered the "Upper Ottawa". Cargo was again trans-shipped at Chats Falls, and at several other points further up.

6 *Citizen,* 26 April, 1851, edit.

7 Town of Bytown, *Minutes,* 30 September 1850, 3 October, 1850, 14 October, 1850 and 10 May, 1852 for the stock. Also note that at the ratepayers' meeting of 19 October, 1850, the only vocal resistance in the form of a call for a poll, came from two members of the Upper Town community, viz., *The Packet,* 19 October, 1850. For the loan, see *Minutes,* 2 August, 1852, 25 July, 1853, and 1 August, 1853. As an indication of some resistance to the railway by this time, as well as the importance of national divisions in town, the *Citizen* chose to break down the ratepayers' vote by ethnicity, viz., the *Citizen,* 22 October, 1853.

	For	Against	
French Canadians	146	2	
Irish	134	99	(includes Orange and
Scotch	121	21	Green)
English,			
American, etc.	59	25	
	460	147	

8 The basic flaws appear to have been the drop in freight rates on the river, the deficiencies in construction of the line, which was of poor quality, and the St. Lawrence ferry crossing at Prescott, awkward at the best of times, and impossible when ice was on the river.

9 *Minutes,* 15 October, 1855.

10 See the *Citizen,* 16 May, 1863. The ringleaders, according to the newspaper, were McGillivray, a merchant and in 1858-1859 the mayor; Goodwin, sometime alderman and contractor; F. Clemow, ex-post office inspector and prominent member of Upper Town society; Sherwood the registrar of the county; Harris, the manager of the Ottawa branch of the Bank of Montreal; and Dr. Hunter, "a Yankee quack". Actually, a more respectable lot would be hard to find.

11 For example, a "Railway Tax" was imposed by the province for 1859, and city council refused to collect it. The city clerk was caught in the middle. The provincial government ordered him to collect it; city council ordered him not to. The province prevailed in the end.

12 *Minutes,* 1 December, 1862, "Report of the Finance Committee." This was the nadir.

13 *Citizen,* 3 January, 1863.

14 Ibid., for the membership of the MRAO.

15 PAC, The Bronson Papers, MG28 II 37, vol. 91, p. 99, Bronson and Weston to L. Barnes, 10 April, 1860.

16 *The Packet,* 29 April, 1848.

17 Ibid., 15 December, 1849.

18 R.W. Scott, *Recollection of Bytown: Some Incidents in the History of Ottawa* (Ottawa, 1911), p. 21.

19 *Citizen,* 22 October, 1853.

20 PAC, RG1 E1, vol. 37, "Proceedings in Council," 30 June, 1852.

21 *The Packet,* 22 October, 1853.

23 The Bronson Papers, vol. 93, p. 302, is a copy of a settlement with the Union Forwarding Co. for 1868 for "Freight Supply and Passage". The Chaudière lumberers, plus Hamilton, of Hawkesbury, and only the large lumberers, at that, co-operated in this way. Freight was moved up-river co-operatively, and then the cost was split according to cut. Eventually, six large Chaudière firms, plus Hamilton, in 1868 formed the Upper Ottawa Improvement Co. (ICO) to manage the log drive downstream and to construct the necessary improvements (like booms) to facilitate it. The company still operates. See The Upper Ottawa Improvement Co., *Charter General Acts, Private Acts and Bylaws* (Ottawa, 1952), and the company *Minutes,* held in the Ottawa Public Library. Information on the first board of directors courtesy ICO. See, also, Robert Reid.

24 Among the lumberers, only J.J. Harris and E.B. Eddy were minor subscribers to the stock of the CCR.

25 See Canada, *Sessional Papers,* "Bank Returns". I checked for 1877 (Paper 15, 1878), 1881 (Paper 22, 1882), 1889 (Paper 4, 1890), and 1902.

26 Ibid.

27 "List of Members," corrected to 1 March, 1898. Courtesy The Rideau Club.

28 At least this seems to be true for the Bronsons.

29 Bronsons in the 1860s were using the Montreal firm of Sincennes and McNaughton, though they did negotiate with the Angers firm, also of Montreal, and sometimes used the Dickinson firm. Though Dickinson is identified with Ottawa, the headquarters of the firm was actually in Montreal, and most of the boats were registered in Kingston. Viz., Bronson Papers, vol. 91.

A.R.M. Lower, in *The North American Assault on the Canadian Forest* (Toronto, 1958), p. 96, n. 16, citing Defebaugh, argues for the American "tramper" as the main form of transportation. That may have been true in the 1850s or for other valley firms, but the Chaudière group seems to have used a number of Montreal firms, which organized about 1860. Booth for a time had his own fleet.

30 Bronson Papers, vol. 91, various "Trial Balances". Practically every member of City Council seems to have done business with the firm, but amounts were rarely more than $200.

31 Bronson Papers, vol. 93, p. 279, "Memorial to the Commissioner of Public Works," May, 1867.

32 Ibid., vol. 91, p. 14, Harris, Bronson and Coleman and A.H. Baldwin to Downing and Sons, Concord, New Hampshire, 1857.

33 E.M. Roper, "The Industrial Development of Ottawa and Hull," Women's Canadian Historical Society of Ottawa, *Transactions,* vol. III, 1910, p. 16.

[34] PAC, Hill Collection, MG24 I9, p. 1058, Derbishire to Christie, 30 December, 1840.

[35] Ibid., p. 1649, Derbishire to Christie, 25 October, 1843.

[36] Ibid., p. 1648.

[37] "Memorial" of the City of Ottawa to the Queen, on the Seat of Government, 18 May, 1857, as cited in David B. Knight, *Choosing Canada's Capital* (Toronto, 1977), p. 159. On the subject of choosing Canada's capital, essential reading is this book of documents and its analytical companion: David B. Knight, *A Capital for Canada* (Chicago, 1977).

[38] *Documents Relating to the Construction of the Parliamentary and Departmental Buildings at Ottawa* (Quebec, 1862), p. 358.

[39] H.H. Killaly, "Report to the Commissioner of Public Works," dated 12 November, 1861, in ibid., p. 361.

[40] *Minutes*, 15 September, 1862.

[41] As cited in Robert Haig, *Ottawa, City of the Big Ears* (Ottawa, nd), p. 121.

[42] Estimate of John A. Macdonald, as reported in the *Citizen*, September, 1865.

[43] PAC, RG1 E1, vol. 90, p. 576, "Policy for Removal recommended by the Auditor of Public Accounts to the Executive Council," 8 September, 1865.

[44] *Ottawa, Union*, 1865.

[45] Ibid.

[46] Ibid.

[47] C.C.J. Bond, *City on the Ottawa* (Ottawa, 1961), p. 79.

[48] Minutes, 26 May, 1851.

[49] Ibid., 20 October, 1851.

[50] Board of Works, "Report #8", in *Minutes*, 3, June, 1872.

[51] Ottawa *Times*, 7 December, 1869.

[52] *Minutes*, 26 May, 1 June, 2 November, 1868.

[53] *The Packet*, 12 January, 1850.

[54] *The Gazette*, 6 April, 1848.

[55] As quoted in Shirley Woods, *Ottawa: The Capital of Canada* (Toronto, 1980), p. 128. It was the view of longtime clerk and sometimes poet and author, William Pittman Lett.

[56] *The Packet*, 11 January, 1851.

[57] Ottawa *Tribune*, 29 September, 1854, edit.

[58] Ottawa *Union*, 12 July, 1862.

[59] *Tribune*, 26 January, 1855, edit.

[60] *Minutes*, 15 January, 1855..

[61] Tribune, 26 January, 1855.

[62] Ibid.

[63] *The Gazette*, 21 May, 1857.

[64] Ibid.

[65] "Report of the Finance Committee," *Minutes*, 1 December, 1862.

[66] *Tribune*, 20 December, 1861.

CHAPTER THREE

[1] *Minutes*, 17 January, 1867.

[2] As quoted in Harry J. Walker, *The Ottawa Story Through 150 Years* (Ottawa, 1953), p. 29.

[3] Stanley T. Cope, "Impact and Response: The Dominion Government and Its Civil Service in Ottawa, 1867-1887" (Graduate Research Paper, Carleton, 1971), p. 39.

[4] *Citizen*, 22 September, 1869, as quoted in Cope, Ibid.

[5] Cope, op. cit., p. 5.

[6] Charlotte Whitton, *A Hundred Years A-Fellin'*, *1842-1942* (Ottawa, 1943).

[7] Robert Reid, op cit.

[8] As outlined in the *Urban History Review/Revue d'histoire urbaine*, VIII, 1 (June, 1979).

[9] Robert C. Douglas, "Confidential Report to the Hon. Sir Charles Tupper, Minister of Railways and Canals, on the Hydraulic Powers Situated on the St. Lawrence & Welland Canals" (Ottawa, 1882). Copy in the PAC Library. My thanks to Larry McNally for bringing this important document to my attention.

[10] Ald. Cox. Ottawa *Evening journal*, 2 January, 1892.

[11] Canada, *Statutes*, 1856, c. 112.

[12] Ottawa *Times*, 30 July, 1869.

[13] *Historical Sketch of the County of Carleton*, with a new introduction by C.C.J. Bond (Belleville, 1971), p. 88. Originally published as an *Illustrated Historical Atlas of the County of Carleton* (Toronto, 1879).

[14] *Citizen*, 2 and 3 June, 1875. Opposition seems to have come mainly from Lower Town.

[15] Ibid., 27 December, 1892.

[16] Ibid., 8 November, 1892.

[17] G.R. Stevens, *Canadian National Railways*, (Toronto, 1962), vol. II, p. 369.

[18] "Bank Returns," in Canada, *Sessional Papers*, were surveyed for 1877, 1881, and 1889. See No. 15 (1878), No.22 (1882), and No. 4 (1890)

[19] R. P. Gillis, "E.H. Bronson and Corporate Capitalism: A Study in Canadian Business Thought and Action, 1880-1910" (M.A. Thesis, Queen's, 1975), Abstract.

[20] Ibid., p. 156.

[21] K.P. Gillis, "Ottawa and Hull 1870-1930: A Description and Analysis of Their Industrial Structure," in Rolf Wesche and Marianne Kugler-Gagnon, eds., *Ottawa-Hull: Spatial Perspectives and Planning* (Ottawa, 1978), p. 19.

[22] Charles A. Bowman, *Ottawa Editor* (Victoria, 1966), p. 5.

[23] Estimates of the Irish population in the Lower Town wards (By and Ottawa) at mid-century had it almost on a par with the French. By 1871, the French population was 52.5 per cent of the Lower Town total, the Irish 31.1 per cent. By 1901, the French was 71.5 per cent; the Irish only 15.3.

[24] The census does not distinguish between Protestant and Catholic Irish, a matter of critical importance in Ottawa. About as close as one can estimate the Irish Catholic population is to take the entire Roman Catholic population, subtract those of French "race" and assume that most of the remainder were Irish.

[25] John F. Mcdonald, "An analysis of the location of Selected Occupations in Ottawa, 1870, 1902, 1945" (B.A. Thesis, Geography, Carleton, 1976), passim.

[26] Ibid., p. 57.

[27] Sheila Powell, "The Effects of the Introduction of Industry on Victoria

Ward, Ottawa, 1871" (Undergraduate research paper, History, Carleton, 1980), p. 8.

[28] John F. McDonald, "An Examination of the Forces Affecting the Location Decisions of Physicians in Ottawa: 1875-1915" (M.A. Thesis, Geography, Carleton, 1983), Abstract.

[29] John H. Taylor, Analysis of location of the Civil Service and Government in Ottawa in 1871 by race, religion, and income. Unpublished SYMAP analysis (Carleton, 1975).

[30] See Edward McKenna, "Unorganized Labour versus Management: The Strike at the Chaudiere Mills, 1891," *Social History/Historie Sociale*, V, 10 November, 1972), p. 190.

[31] Ibid.

[32] Eugene Forsey, *Trade Unions in Canada, 1812-1902* (Toronto, 1982), p. 157.

[33] McKenna, op. cit., p. 210.

[34] Forsey, op. cit., p. 84.

[35] Debi Wells, "'The Hardest Lines of the Sternest School': Working Class Ottawa in the Depression of the 1870s" (M.A. Thesis, Carleton, 1892) p. 26.

[36] Forsey, op. cit., p. 83.

[37] Ibid., pp. 117-119.

[38] Vic Parsons, "Daniel O'Donoghue: Independent Unionist or Political Partisan?" (Undergraduate research paper, History, Carleton, 1972), p. 14.

[39] Forsey, op. cit., p. 139.

[40] Ibid., pp. 144-145.

[41] *Journal*, 3 April, 1886.

[42] As cited in Wells, op. cit., p. 60.

[43] *Citizen*, 5 April, 1877, as cited in National Capital Commission, Lower Town Ottawa (Ottawa, 1981), vol. II, pp. 910-927.

[44] Ibid.

[45] Wells, op. cit., p. 62.

[46] Ibid., p. 63.

[47] See Diane R. Farmer, "Widowhood in the Parish of Notre Dame: An Examination of Death and Remarriage in Mid-Nineteenth Century Lower Town" (M.A. Research Essay, Institute of Canadian Studies, Carleton, 1981).

[48] *Minutes*, 29 September, 1859.

[49] Ibid.

[50] Ibid., 19 August, 1850.

[51] Ibid.

[52] Ibid., 12 January, 1852.

[53] Ibid., 28 March, 1852.

[54] Ibid., 11 April, 1853.

[55] Ibid., 18 October, 1858.

[56] Ibid., 21 November, 1859.

[57] Ibid., 18 December, 1876.

[58] Ibid., 26 February, 1855.

[59] Ibid., 4 February, 1856.

[60] Ibid., 25 January, 1875.

[61] Ibid., 7 February, 1881.

[62] Ibid., 18 February, 1878.

[63] Ibid., 1 November, 1875.

[64] Brault, op. cit., pp 226-227.

[65] Citizen, 7 April, 1877.

[66] Colleen McKernan, "Erskine Henry Bronson" (Undergraduate research paper, History, Carleton, 1982), p. 9.

[67] Ibid., p. 13.

[68] I am guided in the matter of Ottawa's architecture by the following: John Leaning and Lyette Fortin, *Our Architectural Ancestry* (Ottawa, 1983); C.J. Taylor, *Some Early Ottawa Buildings* (Ottawa, 1975); Harold Kalman and John Roaf, *Exploring Ottawa* (Toronto, 1983); C.C.J. Bond, *City on the Ottawa* (Ottawa, 1961); National Capital Commission, *Lower Town Ottawa* (Ottawa, 1979), vol. 1; and Parks Canada, architectural styles series: Christina Cameron and Janet Wright, *Second Empire Style in Canadian Architecture* (Ottawa, 1980), Mathilde Brousseau, *Gothic Revival in Canadian Architecture* (Ottawa, 1980), Nathalie Clerk, *Palladin Style in Canadian Architecture* (Ottawa, 1984), Leslie Maitland, *Neoclassical Architecture in Canada* (Ottawa, 1984), and Janet Wright, *Architecture of the Picturesque in Canada* (Ottawa, 1984).

[69] "Report of the Electric Light Committee," *Minutes*, 9 July, 1883.

[70] "Report of the City Engineer," dated 16 August, 1881, in *Minutes*, 19 September, 1881.

[71] "Mayor's Report on the Electric Light," dated 2 May, 1881, in *Minutes*, 2 May, 1881.

[72] *Minutes*, 15 January, 1886.

[73] "Report" of the Boston deputation, *Minutes*, 19 May, 1890.

[74] *Minutes*, 3 June, 1889.

[75] See "Report of City Engineer," Ottawa, *Annual Reports*, 1892, p. 24 ff; and "1st Report of the Special Committee on Water Works," *Minutes*, 17 October, 1870.

[76] Minutes, 20 May, 1869.

[77] "First Annual Report of the Superintendent of the Fire Brigade," *Minutes*, 6 April, 1868.

[78] Ibid.

[79] Ibid.

[80] "Report of the Fire Committee," *Minutes*, 28 April, 1851.

[81] Minutes, 11 June, 1849.

[82] Ibid., 28 April, 1851.

[83] Ibid., 13 February, 1860.

[84] Ibid., 19 August, 1872.

[85] Ibid., 18 November, 1874.

[86] Ibid., 25 June, 1888.

[87] Medical Health Officer, "Annual Report for the Year Ending December 31, 1875," *Minutes*, 1875, Appendix No. 2, p. 15.

[88] Ibid., p. 14.

[89] Ibid.

[90] Ibid., p. 17.

[91] Medical Health Officer, "Report", *Minutes*, 10 August, 1876, Appendix No. 2.

[92] *Minutes*, 19 September, 1853.

[93] *Citizen,* 23 March, 1866.

[94] As reported in *ibid.,* 23 March, 1866.

[95] *Minutes,* 19 November, 1866.

[96] *Minutes,* 1872, pp. 196-197.

[97] Ibid., 1881, p. 344.

[98] Ibid., 21 December, 1886.

[99] Ottawa, *Annual Reports,* 1896, "Police".

[100] "The Mayor's Address," *Minutes,* 20 January, 1879, p. 5.

[101] *Times,* 19 December, 1865.

[102] McKenna, "Unorganized Labour," op. cit., p. 188.

[103] Richard Lamothe, "Business and Politics in Carleton County," (Graduate research paper, 1979), pp. 22-23.

[104] *Citizen,* 30 December, 1890.

[105] *Minutes,* 5 November, 1883.

[106] Ottawa *Free Press,* 4 January, 1879.

[107] *Citizen,* 3 January, 1899.

[108] Ibid., edit.

[109] *Journal,* 20 December, 1898.

[110] Ibid., 29 December, 1898.

[111] Ibid., 20 December, 1898.

[112] Ibid., 3 January, 1899, edit.

CHAPTER FOUR

[1] John H. Taylor, Analysis of location of the Civil Service and Government in Ottawa in 1871 by race, religion and income. Unpublished SYMAP analysis (Carleton, 1975).

[2] C. Beattie, J. Desy, and S. Longstaff, *Bureaucratic Careers* (Canada, Royal Commission on Bilingualism and Biculturealism, Study No. 11), p. 5.

[3] Canada, House of Commons, *Debates,* 16 July, 1946, p. 3520.

[4] Canada, House of Commons, *Sessional Papers, 1907-1908,* Report No. 29a, p. 250.

[5] Ibid., p. 455.

[6] Ibid., p. 454.

[7] Ibid., p. 642.

[8] Ibid., p. 454.

[9] Louis Rosenberg, *Canada's Jews* (Montreal, 1939), p. 2.

[10] Irene Marcovitz, "A Mobility Study of a Sample Group of the Jewish Community of Ottawa, from 1900 to 1940" (Undergraduate research paper, History, Carleton, 1972).

[11] Claire Miller "Factors in the Development of the Jewish Community of Ottawa, from 1891 to 1939" (Undergraduate research paper, History, Carleton, 1976).

[12] Ibid.

[13] Ibid., p. 19. The successful outcome of the case was reported in the *Citizen,* 9 October, 1935.

[14] Clarence Aasen, "Ethnicity, Politics and Urban Planning: Political Uses of French and Italian Ethnicity in Two Local Area Planning Processes (Ph.D. Thesis, Waterloo, 1979), p. 92.

[15] Ibid.

[16] Ibid., p. 81.

[17] Ibid., p. 80.

[18] This quotation and subsequent information from "Working in Ottawa, the 1920s & 30s," an oral history project of the City of Ottawa Archives, manuscript experts. Original tapes in the City of Ottawa Archives.

[19] Anson A. Gard, *The Hub and the Spokes or The Capital and Its Environs* (Ottawa and New York, 1904) p. 147.

[20] Ibid., p. 113.

[21] Ibid., p. 73.

[22] Woods, *Ottawa: The Capital of Canada* (Toronto and Garden City, New York, 1980), p. 249.

[23] Much of the material on Ottawa's sporting history can be found in S.F. Wise and Douglas Fisher, *Canada's Sporting Heroes* (Don Mills, 1974).

[24] A brief survey can be found in *History of the Central Canada Exhibition* (Ottawa, 1976). See also *Minutes,* 1 April, 1889, for a summary of the early financial history of the exhibition. Probably the earliest exhibition in the city was the Bytown Industrial Exhibition of 1853, sponsored by the newly-organized Mechanics' Institute.

[25] This is evident from, among other evidence, the lists of officers and members of the various cultural societies. It is also clear from these lists that the OLSS was dominated by public servants, and that this was true to only a lesser degree of the Arts and Letters Club. It is notable that the subscription lists of periodicals purchased for the OLSS reading room contain only English material.

[26] Ottawa Literary and Scientific Society, *Transactions,* No. 4, 1906-1907, p. 3: Ottawa Room, Ottawa Public Library, manuscript collection.

[27] See D. John Fisher, "Elkanah Billings: A Most Victorian Scientist" (Undergraduate research paper, History, Carleton, 1984).

[28] Sandra Gwyn, *The Private Capital: Ambition and Love in the Age of Macdonald and Laurier* (Toronto, 1984). The activities of the society of the capital, headed by the vice-regal figures, is described in some detail here, and some indication is given of their impact on the society of the city.

[29] See Carl Betke, "Sports Promotion in the Western Canadian City: The Example of Early Education," *Urban History Review,* XII, 2 (October, 1983), pp. 47-56.

[30] Similarly, Morris Mott, "One Solution to the Urban Crisis: Manly Sports and Winnmipeggers, 1900-1914," Ibid., pp. 57-70.

[31] Material on Ottawa's symphony orchestras from David Gardner, *Twenty-one Seasons of the Ottawa Symphony Orchestra: A Celebration* (Ottawa, 1986). I am indebted to Prof. Gardner, who made his manuscript available to me prior to publication.

[32] Arts and Letters Club, "Scrapbook", contains the clipping from the *Citizen,* March, 1916, letter to the editor. Ottawa Room, Ottawa Public Library, manuscript collection.

[33] Ottawa Literary and Scientific Society, "Historical Sketch," in the OLSS Collection, op. cit., p. 12. See also Nancy Meggs, "Women in Transition: Madge Macbeth and the Role of Women in the Interwar Years" (Undergraduate research paper, History, Carleton, 1985).

[34] Brault, *Ottawa,* op. cit., p. 291.

[35] Ibid., p. 292.

[36] "Ottawa," in the *Encyclopedia of Canadian Music* (Toronto, 1984).

[37] Haig, *Ottawa,* op. cit., p. 135.

[38] Hilary Russell, *All That Glitters: A Memorial to Ottawa's Capitol Theatre and Its Predecessors* (Ottawa, 1975), p. 20.

[39] Ibid., p. 15.

[40] Anita Rush, "The Establishment of Ottawa's Public Library, 1895-1906" (Undergraduate research paper, History, Carleton 1981). To this paper I own my knowledge of the evolution of the OPL.

[41] Ibid., p. 2.

[42] Ibid., pp. 4-5.

[43] Ibid., passim.

[44] Ibid., p. 13.

[45] Ibid., p. 14.

[46] Ibid., p. 16.

[47] Ibid., p. 19.

[48] R. MacGregor Dawson, *W.L. Mackenzie King, A Political Biography 1874-1923* (Toronto, 1958), vol. 1, p. 98.

[49] Noulan Cauchon, "The New Federal District Commission for Ottawa," typescript of a speech delivered to the Town Planning Institute of Canada, Vancouver, May, 1927, in PAC, The Cauchon Papers, MG 30 C 105, vol. 2, p. 2.

[50] Sir Herbert Holt, chairman, *Federal Plan Commission on a General Plan for the Cities of Ottawa and Hull* (Ottawa, 1915), p. 125.

[51] M.J. Purdy, "An Inquiry into the Functions of a Ribbon Road, a Case Study of Bank Street, Ottawa, Ontario, 1891-1972" (M.A. Thesis, Geography, Carleton, 1974), p. 32.

[52] Ibid., Fig. 2.9.

[53] W. Watson, "A Study of Residential Evolution in Centre Town Ottawa" (B.A. Honours Thesis, Geography, Carleton, 1975), p. 41.

[54] *Citizen,* 24 November, 1923, as quoted in Carol Hilger, "The Coming of the Automobile to Ottawa" (Undergraduate research paper, History, Carleton, 1973), p. 11.

[55] Background on city planning in Ottawa and on Cauchon may be found in Sara Elizabeth Coutts, "The Failure of Town Planning in Ottawa, 1900-1927" (Graduate research paper, History, Carleton, 1981); and in her "Science and Sentiment: The Planning career of Noulan Cauchon" (Graduate Research Essay, Institute of Canadian Studies, Carleton, 1982).

[56] *Citizen,* 4 April, 1912.

[57] *Free Press,* 26 June, 1912.

[58] *Citizen,* 5 February, 1912.

[59] *Citizen,* 10 April, 1912.

[60] *Citizen,* 29 June, 1912.

[61] Ottawa Town Planning Commission, "Report #6", *Minutes,* 20 November, 1922, p. 587.

[62] Draft Zoning Plan submitted to City Council, 17 August, 1922, in Ottawa Town Planning Commission, "Report #7", *Minutes,* 5 September, 1922, p. 471.

[63] As cited in David St. Charles, "The Ottawa Town Planning Commission" (Undergraduate research paper, History, Carleton, 1971), p. 38.

[64] Mayor Harold Fisher, *The Dominion Government and the Municipality of Ottawa* (Ottawa, 1918), p. 1.

[65] Ibid., p. 2.

[66] Wilfred Eggleston, *The Queen's Choice: A Story of Canada's Capital* (Ottawa, 1961), passim.

[67] PAC, King Papers, micro C2294, p. 119579, Ahearn to King, 3 January, 1927.

[68] Other major sources for this section include: John H. Taylor, "City Planning and the Planning of the Capital" (Unpublished MS presented to the Canadian Historical Association, Annual Meeting, Ottawa, 1982); Coutts, op. cit.: Roger Turcotte, "Commissions as Policy-Making Instruments: Toward Making Ottawa a National Capital" (Graduate Research Paper, History, Carleton, 1974); National Capital Commission, *Parliamentary Precinct: Previous Studies* (Ottawa, nd); Joint Committee of the Senate and House of Commons, "Report on the Federal District Commission," 1 August, 1944, in PAC, RG34, vol. 298, file 253(1); National Capital Commission, *Report to the Joint Parliamentary Committee,* June 1975, in Doc. NCC 17/1975(c).

[69] Brault, *Ottawa,* op. cit., pp. 251-252, 256.

[70] *The Packet,* 31 March, 1849.

[71] Ibid.

[72] Ibid., 19 May, 1849.

[73] Cox to E. Ryerson, as cited in the *Tribune,* 24 August, 1855. I owe this quotation and much of the analysis of the period to J.A. Bishop, "The Establishment of Separate Schools in Ottawa: Local Conflict Against a Provincial Background" (Graduate research paper, History, Carleton, 1976), p. 24.

[74] Robert Choquette, *Language and Religion: A History of English-French Conflict in Ontario* (Ottawa, 1975).

[75] Ibid.

[76] M.R. Lupul, "Educational Crises in the New Dominion to 1917," in J. Donald Wilson, Robert M. Stamp and L.-P. Audet, eds., *Canadian Education: A History* (Scarborough, 1970), p. 284.

[77] Ibid., p. 285.

[78] For a history of the system, see Janet Keith, *The Collegiate Institute Board of Ottawa: A Short History: 1843-1969* (np, nd).

[79] Carleton College, *First Annual Calendar, 1942-1943,* pp. 3-4.

[80] A review of the development of St. Patrick's College may be found in H.A. MacDougall, *St. Patrick's College (Ottawa), 1929-1979: Ethnicity and the Liberal Arts in Catholic Education* (Carleton University, Ottawa, 1982).

[81] For a detailed look at the epidemics and the related crises over pure water, see Sheila Lloyd, "The Ottawa Typhoid Epidemics of 1911 and 1912: A Case Study of Disease as a Catalyst for Urban Reform," and Chris Warfe, "The Search for Pure Water in Ottawa, 1910-1915," both in a special issue of the *Urban History Review,* VIII, 1 (June, 1979).

[82] J.A. Pinard, chairman, to the members of the Board Health, "A 'retrospect' of Operations During 1911," *Minutes,* 1912, pp. 35-39.

[83] "Estimates", Minutes, 1913.

[84] Medical Health Officer, "Annual Report for the Year Ending December 31, 1939," Ottawa, *Annual Reports,* p. 64.

[85] Dr. C. Laidlaw, "Report of the Chairman of the Board of Health," dated 1 January, 1919, Ottawa, *Annual Reports,* pp. 97-98.

[86] Sharon Cook, "Class, Gender, Social Reform and the Aged: The Protestant Home for the Aged and the Refuge Branch of the Protestant Orphans' Home of Ottawa" (Graduate Research paper, History, Carleton, 1985); and Lyneita Swanson, Peggy Sykes, Shannon McSheffrey, Jill St. Germain and Barb Verbaas, "Coming of Age: A Social History of the Glebe Centre Incorporated, 1886-1980" (Department of History Collaborative, Carleton, 1985).

[87] For my knowledge of the YWCA, I owe a debt to Diana Pederson, Doctoral Candidate, History, Carleton.

[88] Nola Abrams, "Ottawa and its Initial Response to Tuberculosis, 1880-1910" (Graduate research paper, Carleton, 1983), p. 5.

[89] Beverley Hastings McBride, "Tuberculosis Treatment in Ottawa 1905-1909" (Undergraduate research paper, History, Carleton, 1980).

[90] Judith C.M. Roberts-Moore, "Maximum Relief for Minimum Cost? Coping with Unemployment Relief in Ottawa During the Depression, 1929-1939" (M.A. Thesis, University of Ottawa, 1980), p. 13.

[91] Ibid., p. 24.

[92] As cited in ibid., p. 75.

[93] *Citizen,* 1 January, 1901.

[94] Ibid., 3 January, 1901, edit.

[95] Ibid., 1 January, 1901.

[96] Ibid., 3 January, 1901.

[97] Ibid., 5 January, 1904.

[98] Ibid., 1 November, 1898.

[99] Ottawa, Board of Control, *Minutes,* 10 January, 1908.

[100] Ibid.

[101] Ibid., 15 January, 1908.

[102] Ibid., 4 February, 1908.

[103] Much of the statistical material on the Ottawa political scene, I owe to Charles Henderson, "The Nature of Urban Politicians in Ottawa, 1920-1970" (Undergraduate research paper, Carleton, 1972).

[104] See G.-Raymond Laliberté, Une société secrète: l'Ordre de Jacques Carties (Montreal, 1983).

CHAPTER FIVE

[1] *Citizen,* 26 June 1946.

[2] R. Keith, "A Geographic Investigation of Ottawa's Trade Area" (Honours Thesis, Geography, Carleton, 1970), p. 16.

[3] See Ibid.

[4] *Citizen,* 28 July, 1981.

[5] Ibid., 15 October, 1981.

[6] M. A. Hoey, "Ottawa-Carleton's High Technology Industries: A Locational Factor Study" (Honours Thesis, Geography, Carleton, 1981), table 4.5.

[7] Ibid., table 4.4.

[8] S. Vander Meulen, "The Recent Emergence of a High Technology Industrial Sector in Ottawa-Carleton" (Honours Thesis, Geography, Carleton, 1980), p. 26.

[9] W.J. Cowie, "The Location of Manufacturing Activity in Ottawa, 1951-1971: Its Relation to Theoretical Geography" (Honours Thesis, Geography, Carleton, 1971), p. 27.

[10] *Citizen,* 16 May, 1969.

[11] L. Dorken, "Population Density Changes in Ottawa from 1941 to 1976" (Honours Thesis, Geography, Carleton, 1978), p. ii.

[12] *Citizen,* 5 July, 1956.

[13] Ibid., 18 January, 1962.

[14] Ibid., 20 August, 1963.

[15] Ibid., 12 December, 1963.

[16] Ibid., 6 December, 1967.

[17] Ibid., 6 August, 1975.

[18] Ibid., 15 October, 1970.

[19] Ibid., 22 August, 1972.

[20] J.H. Francis, "Special Patterns of Ottawa, 1961-1971" (Honours Thesis, Geography, Carleton, 1975), p. 64.

[21] B.A. Jamieson, "Classification of Urban Sub-Areas: the Factorial Ecology of Ottawa, 1961" (Honours Thesis, Geography, Carleton, 1973), p. 23.

[22] *Citizen,* 21 October, 1955.

[23] Ibid., 18 March, 1962.

[24] Ibid., 14 July, 1975.

[25] See Wilfred Eggleston, *The Queen's Choice: A Story of Ottawa's Capital* (Ottawa, 1961).

[26] Ibid., p. 185.

[27] Joint Committee of the Senate and House of Commons on Relations between the Federal Government and the City of Ottawa, "Second and Final Report," in Senate, *Journals,* 8 George VI, pp. 336-340.

[28] *Citizen,* 27 September, 1945.

[29] The Joint Committee of the Senate and House of Commons appointed to Review and Report upon the Progress and Programs of the Federal District Commission, "Second and Final Report," in PAC, RG34, vol. 298, file 253(1), 1956, p. 4.

[30] Ibid.

[31] Project d'aménagement de la Capitale Nationale, *Rapport Général* (Ottawa, 1950).

[32] Robert Haig, *Ottawa: City of the Big Ears* (np, nd), p. 260. Charlotte Whitton was not invited to the opening. See *Citizen,* 2 June, 1969.

[33] City of Ottawa, Bylaw AZ-64. See *Citizen,* 17 June 1965.

[34] Helen Deachman and Joy Woolfrey, "High Rises and Super Profits: The Marriage of State and Capital," in Dimitri Roussopoulos, ed., *The City and Radical Social Change* (Montreal, 1982).

[35] *Citizen,* 16 May 1969.

[36] Douglas H. Fullerton, "The Capital of Canada: How It Should Be Governed," special supplement of the *Citizen,* 1974, p. 4.

[37] P.J. Franklin, "Urban Renewal: A Case Study: Lower Town East, Ottawa, Ontario" (Honours Thesis, Geography, Carleton, 1972), p. 33.

[38] I owe much to Beth Moore-Milroy and Caroline Andrew for providing

me with a preview of their findings in a current study of the development of community organizations in Ottawa and its relationship to the planning process.

[39] The group had successfully lobbied the region to alter its original plan with a thrust southward down the Rideau River corridor. The altered plan was confirmed by the Ontario Municipal Board, but was overturned by the Minister of Municipal Affairs, Claude Bennett, who, in effect, put the original plan, one favoured by the development industry, back in place.

[40] The best discussion of the expansion of the city on suburban communities is in Eva Taylor and James Kennedy, *Ottawa's Britannia* (Ottawa, 1983).

[41] *Citizen,* 21 April, 1962.

[42] Ibid., 16 March, 1962.

[43] Ibid.

[44] Caroline Andrew, "Ottawa-Hull," in Warren Magnusson and Andrew Sancton, *City Politics in Canada* (Toornto, 1983), p. 141.

[45] Henderson, "The Nature of Urban Politicians," op cit.

[46] *Citizen,* 1 February, 1965.

[47] Ibid.

[48] Ibid.

[49] Ibid., 28 November, 1964.

[50] Ibid.

[51] Ibid., 2 December, 1964.

[52] Interview with former mayor, Lorry Greenberg, Ottawa, 29 March, 1983.

[53] *Citizen,* 3 February, 1978.

Suggestions for Further Reading and Research

Ottawa has received much popular attention, but much of the best scholarly work remains in the "informal domain" of the thesis and the research paper. Coverage is very uneven. As a general rule, the interested reader will find greater value in this material and in primary sources than in much of the secondary literature.

Bibliographic and Research Materials

General finding aids to most published and much unpublished material on Ottawa are Alan Artibise and Gilbert Stelter, *Canada's Urban Past, A Bibliography to 1980 and Guide to Canadian Urban Studies* (Vancouver, 1981), which should be supplemented by the annual bibliography, prepared by Elizabeth Bloomfield, in the *Urban History Review/Revue d'histoire urbaine;* the Public Archives of Canada, *Union list of Manuscripts in Canadian Respositories,* 2 vols. (Ottawa, 1975, with supplements, 1976, 1979); Olga Bishop, *Bibliography of Ontario History, 1867-1976,* 2 vols. (Toronto, 1980); and the extensive National Capital Commission, *A Bibliography of History and Heritage of the National Capital Region* (Ottawa, revised edition, 1978). The chief guide to newspaper holdings is National Library of Canada, *Union List of Canadian Newspapers Held by Canadian Libraries* (Ottawa, 1977).

Collections of books, reports, pamphlets, and similar printed material on Ottawa, often not listed in standard bibliographies, can be found in the catalogues of the two university libraries, the Ottawa Room of the Ottawa Public Library, the Public Archives of Canada Library, the National Library, the Historical Society of Ottawa, the City of Ottawa Archives, the library of the National Capital Commission, various departmental libraries of the federal government, and the *Centre de Recherche en Civilsation Canadian Française* at the University of Ottawa. The "Ottawa" entry in the subject index of the Canadian Institute for Historical Microreproduction, which is microfilming pre-1900 publications with a Canadian involvement, should be consulted.

The major primary sources — manuscript and record groups, maps, photographs, and pictures and prints — are held at the Public Archives of Canada and the City of Ottawa Archives. Important collections at the former include the Bronson Papers (MG28 II 37) and the Hill Collection (MG24 I9). The city archives, of recent vintage, holds essential civic documents, like Council and Board of Control *Minutes.* and harbours a growing manuscript collection of local figures and institutions. Many collections, however, remain outside the various public archives, most especially the diocesan and other archives of the Roman Catholic church. The Public Archives of Ontario contains important material, notably the Stewart Papers, and the official correspondence between the province and the city, which has particular significance, since much city correspondence was destroyed in the City Hall fire of 1931.

The bulk of thesis material is to be found at the University of Ottawa and Carleton University. Doctoral and masters theses are generally deposited in university libraries, but these, and the more numerous graduate and honours research essays, are generally held by individual departments. Many are identified in the footnotes of this volume. Federal departments, with their keen interest in Ottawa, have also produced much outstanding material, little of it widely known. Most notable are the publications of Parks Canada, in History, Architecture, and Archaeology, available through the Canadian Government Publishing Centre, Ottawa, and its unpublished Manuscript Report Series, which includes valuable studies on the Rideau Canal and many government and heritage buildings in Ottawa; and more general studies like, Sandra Gillis, *the Timber Trade and the Ottawa Valley, 1806-1854* (Report #153, Ottawa, 1975). Much valuable work has also been done by the National Capital Commission, notably the two-volume study of Michael Newton, *Lower Town Ottawa,* vol. 1, 1826-1854 (Manuscript Report 104, Ottawa, 1979), and vol. 2, 1854-1900 (Manuscript Report 106, Ottawa, 1981). Likewise, both the city hall and the regional government, often in their planning departments, have extensive libraries of reports and studies, especially covering the last generation.

Much of interest can be found in royal commissions, and their related studies, notably the Royal Commission on Bilingualism and Biculturalism, and the Royal Commission on the Status of Women. The *Dictionary of Canadian Biography* can be consulted for individuals.

Published works

Among the essentially chronological or narrative works, the older ones are generally better, notably Lucien Brault, *Ottawa: Capitale du Canada, de son origine à nos jours* (Ottawa, 1942), or in English as *Ottawa, Old and New* (Ottawa, 1946); Courtney Bond, *City on the Ottawa* (Ottawa, 1965 and rev. ed. 1971), and *The Ottawa Country* (Ottawa, 1968); Wilfred Eggleston, *The Queen's Choice* (Ottawa, 1961); Robert Leggett, *Rideau Waterway* (Toronto, 1955, second ed., 1986); *Ottawa Waterway: Gateway to Continent* (Toronto, 1962, rev. ed., 1975); and Harry and Olive Walker, *Carleton Saga* (Ottawa, 1968). Robert Haig, *Ottawa: City of the Big Ears* (np, nd) is a useful chronology, with no pretence to narrative. Shirley E. Woods, *(Ottawa: The Capital of Canada* (Toronto, 1980) and Bond, *Where Rivers Meet* (np, 1984) are more recent recapitulations. The best of recent works on Ottawa, though really official Ottawa, is Sandra Gwyn, *The Private Capital* (Toronto, 1985). More than any of the other books noted, it documents sources. Her bibliography can be usefully consulted. Guides to the city's architecture include Harold Kalman and John Roaf, *Exploring Ottawa* (Toronto, 1983) and John Leaning and Lyette Fortin, *Our Architectural Ancestry* (Ottawa, 1983). But these, like most of the general histories of the city, are notorious for a lack of documentation. For the serious student, at any rate, any further study means re-doing the research.

In this sense, the reportorial or contemporary histories are a more useful guide, such as (and almost alone for the French) Alexis de Barbezieux, *Histoire de la province Ecclésiastique d'Ottawa et de la Colonisation dans la vallée de l'Ottawa*, 4 vols. (Ottawa, 1897); *Illustrated Historical Atlas of the County of Carleton* (Toronto, 1879), reissued in facsimile as *Historical Sketch of the County of Carleton*, intro. by C.C.J. Bond, (Belleville, 1971); Anson A. Gard, *The Hub and the Spokes or The Capital and Its Environs* (Ottawa and New York, 1904); William Pittman Lett, *Recollections of Old Bytown* (Ottawa, 1874); R.W. Scott, *Recollections of Bytown* (Ottawa, 1910?); John McTaggart, *Three Years in Canada* (London, 1839), and numerous others.

Analytical history on Ottawa can be said to begin with Arthur R.M. Lower, *Settlement and the Forest Frontier in Canada* (Toronto, 1936); *The North American Assault on the Canadian Forest* (Toronto, 1938); and *Great Britain's Woodyard* (Montreal, 1973). More specific to the valley is M.S. Cross, "Dark Druidicial Groves: The Lumber Community and the Commercial Frontier in British North America to 1854," (PhD Thesis, Toronto, 1968), and his articles: "The Lumber community of Upper Canada, 1815-1867, " *Ontario History*, 52 (1960); "The Age of Gentility: The Creation of an Aristocracy in the Ottawa Valley," Canadian Historical Association, *Historical Papers* (1967); "Stony Monday, 1849: The Rebellion Losses Riots in Bytown," *Ontario History* 63 (1971); and "The Shiners' War: Social Violence in the Ottawa Valley in the 1830s," *Canadian Historical Review* 54 (1973). Courtney Bond and J.W. Hughson, *Hurling Down the Pine* (Old Chelsea, 1964) is an important study of local lumberers.

Scholarly works for the pre-Confederation period include: W.E. Greening, "The Lumber Industry in the Ottawa Valley and the American Market in the 19th Century," *Ontario History* 62 (1970); G.C. Lucas, "Presbyterians in Carleton County to 1867," (MAThesis, Carleton, 1973); Francis J. Audet, *"Les députés de la vallée de l'Ottawa, 1792-1867,"* *Canadian Historical Review*, 16 (1935); and David B. Knight, *A Capital for Canada: Conflict and Compromise in the Nineteenth Century* (Chicago, 1977), and *Choosing Canada's Capital: Jealousy and Friction in the the 19th Century* (Toronto, 1977).

Important material for the post-Confederation city includes: articles by Peter Gillis and David Knight in Rolf Wesche and Marianne Kugler-Gagnon (eds.), *Ottawa-Hull, Spatial Persepectives and Planning/ Perspectives spatiales et aménagement* (Ottawa, 1978). Other articles in this volume are important for the contemporary city. Questions of fire, disease, and water are covered in a special issue of the *Urban History Review/Revue d'histoire urbaine* 8 (1979) that includes articles by John Taylor, Jon Fear, Sheila Lloyd, and Chris Warfe. The work of Peter Gillis, apart from that noted above, is critical: "E.H. Bronson and Corporate Capitalism: A Study in Canadian Business Thought and Action, 1880-1910" (MA Thesis, Queen's, 1975); "The Ottawa Lumber Barons and the Conservation Movement, 1880-1914, *Journal of Canadian Studies* (1974); and "Big Business and the Origins of the Conservatice Reform Movement in Ottawa, 1890-1912," ibid. (1980) Other key references are James Trotman, "Ottawa in 1878; Land Use Patterns in a Canadian City." (MA, Geography, Carleton); Clarence Aasen, "Ethnicity, Politics and Urban Planning: Political Uses of French and Italian Ethnicity in Two Local Planning Processes" (PhD, Waterloo, 1979);and David Gardner, *Twenty-one Seasons of the Ottawa Symphony Orchestra: A Celebration* (Ottawa, 1986).

Studies of the more contemporary city include Caroline Andrew, "Ottawa-Hull," in Warren Magnusson and Andrew Sancton, eds., *City Politics in Canada* (Toronto, 1983); the student papers in two volumes edited by Donald C. Rowat, *Urban Politics in Ottawa-Carleton: Research Essays* (Ottawa, 1974, second edition, 1983), and *Recent Politics in Ottawa-Carleton* (Ottawa, 1985); as well as Rowat's "Ottawa", in Rowat, ed., *The Government of Federal Capitals* (Toronto, 1973); Bernard a Léveillé and G. Lord, *Profile: Ottawa-Hull. The Political and Administrative Structures of the Metropolitan Region of Ottawa* (Ottawa, 1974); Jaap Shouten, "Public Land Policy and Metropolitan Development: The Case of Canada's Capital," *Contact* 9 (1977); the studies of Charlotte Whitton by P.T. Rooke and R.L. Schnell, including the recent "An Idiot's Flowerbed — A Study of Charlotte Whitton's Feminist Thought, 1941-1950," in Veronica Strong-Boag and Anita Clair Fellman, eds., *Rethinking Canada* (Toronto, 1986); and William DeGrace, "Canada's Capital 1900-1950: Five Town-Planning Visions," *Environments* 17 (1985).

Index